Final Report of the Thirty-sixth Antarctic Treaty Consultative Meeting

ANTARCTIC TREATY
CONSULTATIVE MEETING

Final Report
of the Thirty-sixth
Antarctic Treaty
Consultative Meeting

Brussels, Belgium
20–29 May 2013

Volume I

Secretariat of the Antarctic Treaty
Buenos Aires
2013

Published by:

Secretariat of the Antarctic Treaty
Secrétariat du Traité sur l' Antarctique
Секретариат Договора об Антарктике
Secretaría del Tratado Antártico

Maipú 757, Piso 4
C1006ACI Ciudad Autónoma
Buenos Aires - Argentina
Tel: +54 11 4320 4260
Fax: +54 11 4320 4253

This book is also available from: *www.ats.aq* (digital version)
and online-purchased copies.

ISSN 2346-9897

Contents

VOLUME II

PART II. MEASURES, DECISIONS AND RESOLUTIONS (Cont.)

PART III. OPENING AND CLOSING ADDRESSES AND REPORTS

1. Reports by Depositaries and Observers
Report of the USA as Depositary Government of the Antarctic Treaty and its Protocol
Report of Australia as Depositary Government of CCAMLR
Report of the UK as Depositary Government of CCAS
Report of Australia as Depositary Government of ACAP
Report by the CCAMLR Observer
Report of SCAR
Report of COMNAP

2. Reports by Experts
Report of ASOC
Report of IHO
Report of IAATO

PART IV. ADDITIONAL DOCUMENTS FROM ATCM XXXVI

1. Additional Documents
Abstract of SCAR Lecture

2. List of Documents
Working Papers
Information Papers
Secretariat Papers
Background Papers

3. List of Participants
Consultative Parties
Non-Consultative Parties
Observers, Experts and Guests
Host Country Secretariat
Antarctic Treaty Secretariat

Acronyms and Abbreviations

ACAP	Agreement on the Conservation of Albatrosses and Petrels
ASOC	Antarctic and Southern Ocean Coalition
ASMA	Antarctic Specially Managed Area
ASPA	Antarctic Specially Protected Area
ATS	Antarctic Treaty System or Antarctic Treaty Secretariat
ATCM	Antarctic Treaty Consultative Meeting
ATCP	Antarctic Treaty Consultative Party
CAML	Census of Antarctic Marine Life
CCAMLR	Convention on the Conservation of Antarctic Marine Living Resources and/or Commission for the Conservation of Antarctic Marine Living Resourcess
CCAS	Convention for the Conservation of Antarctic Seals
CEE	Comprehensive Environmental Evaluation
CEP	Committee for Environmental Protection
COMNAP	Council of Managers of National Antarctic Programmes
EIA	Environmental Impact Assessment
HCA	Hydrographic Committee on Antarctica
HSM	Historic Site and Monument
IAATO	International Association of Antarctica Tour Operators
ICG	Intersessional Contact Group
ICSU	International Council for Science
IEE	Initial Environmental Evaluation
IHO	International Hydrographic Organization
IMO	International Maritime Organization
IOC	Intergovernmental Oceanographic Commission
IP	Information Paper
IPCC	Intergovernmental Panel on Climate Change
IPY	International Polar Year
IPY-IPO	IPY Programme Office
IUCN	International Union for Conservation of Nature and Natural Resources
RFMO	Regional Fishery Management Organization
SATCM	Special Antarctic Treaty Consultative Meeting
SCAR	Scientific Committee on Antarctic Research

SCALOP	Standing Committee for Antarctic Logistics and Operations
SC-CAMLR	Scientific Committee of CCAMLR
SP	Secretariat Paper
SPA	Specially Protected Area
UNEP	United Nations Environment Programme
UNFCCC	United Nations Framework Convention on Climate Change
WG	Working Group
WMO	World Meteorological Organization
WP	Working Paper
WTO	World Tourism Organization

PART I
Final Report

1. Final Report

Final Report of the Thirty-sixth Antarctic Treaty Consultative Meeting

Brussels, 20–29 May 2013

(1)   Pursuant to Article IX of the Antarctic Treaty, Representatives of the Consultative Parties (Argentina, Australia, Belgium, Brazil, Bulgaria, Chile, China, Ecuador, Finland, France, Germany, India, Italy, Japan, the Republic of Korea, the Netherlands, New Zealand, Norway, Peru, Poland, the Russian Federation, South Africa, Spain, Sweden, Ukraine, the United Kingdom of Great Britain and Northern Ireland, the United States of America, and Uruguay) met in Brussels from 20 to 29 May 2013, for the purpose of exchanging information, holding consultations and considering and recommending to their Governments measures in furtherance of the principles and objectives of the Treaty.

(2)   The Meeting was also attended by delegations from the following Contracting Parties to the Antarctic Treaty which are not Consultative Parties: Austria, Belarus, Canada, Colombia, Cuba, Czech Republic, Greece, Hungary, Malaysia, Monaco, Portugal, Romania, Slovak Republic, Switzerland, Turkey and Venezuela.

(3)   In accordance with Rules 2 and 31 of the Rules of Procedure, Observers from the Commission for the Conservation of Antarctic Marine Living Resources (CCAMLR), the Council of Managers of National Antarctic Programs (COMNAP) and the Scientific Committee on Antarctic Research (SCAR) attended the Meeting.

(4)   In accordance with Rule 39 of the Rules of Procedure, Experts from the following international organisations and non-governmental organisations attended the Meeting: the Antarctic and Southern Ocean Coalition (ASOC), the International Association of Antarctica Tour Operators (IAATO), the International Hydrographic Organization (IHO), International Union for the Conservation of Nature (IUCN) and the World Meteorological Organisation (WMO).

(5)   The Host Country Belgium fulfilled its information requirements towards the Contracting Parties, Observers and Experts through the Secretariat Circulars, letters and a dedicated website.

Item 1: Opening of the Meeting

(6)   The Meeting was officially opened on 22 May 2013. On behalf of the Host Government, in accordance with Rules 5 and 6 of the Rules of Procedure, the Executive Secretary of the Host Government Secretariat Mr Luc Marsia called the Meeting to order and proposed the candidacy of the distinguished diplomat Ambassador Mark Otte as Chair of ATCM XXXVI. The proposal was accepted.

(7)   The Chair warmly welcomed all Parties, Observers and Experts to Brussels. Delegates observed a minute of silence in honour of the passing of Ambassador José Manuel Ovalle Bravo, who served as the Head of Delegation of Chile to the Special Antarctic Treaty Consultative Meeting held in The Hague, Netherlands, in September 2000, the fatal accident during the construction of Jang Bogo Station and the tragic loss of three Canadian crew members whose aircraft crashed en route from Amundsen-Scott South Pole Station to Mario Zucchelli station at Terra Nova Bay on 26 January 2013.

(8)   His Serene Highness Prince Albert II of Monaco addressed the Meeting, by praising the history of cooperation between Antarctic Treaty Consultative Parties, and encouraging Parties to build on the example of the two out of 80 Antarctic research stations that were operated as multi-national stations. Reinforcing the importance of international scientific cooperation, which he believed was necessary to address issues such as climate change and sustainable fishing in Antarctica, he encouraged Parties to extend to adjacent marine areas the principles they had achieved in the adoption of the Antarctic Treaty and its Environmental Protocol.

(9)   The Hon. Didier Reynders, Deputy Prime Minister and Minister of Foreign Affairs of Belgium, welcomed Parties to Belgium for the third time in the history of the ATCM, and recalled Belgium's long history of Antarctic exploration. He highlighted matters requiring close attention and swift action by Parties, including the cumulative impacts of climate change, bioprospecting, tourism, and Marine Protected Areas (MPA), and expressed Belgium's support for the development of a multi-year strategic work plan. Finally, he reminded the Parties of their responsibility for ensuring that

science had an influence on policies, which in turn would have repercussions for the global community.

(10) The Hon. Melchior Wathelet, State Secretary for Environment, Energy and Mobility, Belgium, reminded delegates that Belgium was an original signatory to the Antarctic Treaty and one of the first Parties to support the development of the Environmental Protocol. He encouraged Parties to remain faithful to the spirit of these instruments, by promptly addressing the issues of climate change, bioprospecting and tourism in Antarctica.

(11) The Hon. Philippe Courard, Secretary of State for Science Policy in Belgium, said that Belgium's Antarctic engagement, which began with the 1897 Belgian Antarctic Expedition led by Adrien de Gerlache, continued in the present day through the work of 10 to 15 scientists each year at Belgium's Princess Elisabeth Station. He also pointed to some key areas of research including climatology, and noted that an 18 kilogram meteorite recently discovered by Belgian and Japanese scientists was housed in the National History Museum in Brussels.

(12) The Hon. Michel Rocard, former Prime Minister of France and Ambassador for the Poles, appealed to the Parties to increase their level of international scientific cooperation. Ambassador Rocard announced his joint initiative with Australia's former Prime Minister the Hon. Robert Hawke and H.S.H. Prince Albert II to foster an improved level of cooperation between national Antarctic programmes, including through the sharing of transport and station logistics. He further commented on the importance of striking a balance between national interests and the resources at their disposal, and expressed a view that multi-national efforts would enhance and harmonise international science.

(13) The Chair thanked His Serene Highness and the Ministers for their suggestions and advice which would be helpful in the forthcoming discussions at the meeting.

Item 2: Election of Officers and Creation of Working Groups

(14) Minister Fábio Vaz Pitaluga, Representative of Brazil (Host Country of ATCM XXXVII), was elected Vice-chair. In accordance with Rule 7 of the Rules of Procedure, Dr Manfred Reinke, Executive Secretary of the Antarctic Treaty Secretariat, acted as Secretary to the Meeting. Mr Luc Marsia, head of the Host Country Secretariat, acted as Deputy Secretary. Dr Yves Frenot of France continued as Chair of the Committee for Environmental Protection.

(15) Four Working Groups were established:

- Working Group on Legal and Institutional Affairs;
- Working Group on Tourism and Non-governmental Activities;
- Working Group on Operational Matters;
- Special Working Group on Search and Rescue.

(16) The following Chairs of the Working Groups were elected:

- Legal and Institutional Affairs: Professor René Lefeber of the Netherlands;
- Tourism and Non-governmental Activities: Ambassador Donald Mackay of New Zealand;
- Operational Matters: Dr José Retamales of Chile;
- Special Working Group on Search and Rescue: Ambassador David Balton of the United States.

Item 3: Adoption of the Agenda and Allocation of Items

(17) The following Agenda was adopted:

1. Opening of the Meeting
2. Election of Officers and Creation of Working Groups
3. Adoption of the Agenda and Allocation of Items
4. Operation of the Antarctic Treaty System: Reports by Parties, Observers and Experts
5. Operation of the Antarctic Treaty System:
   (a) General Matters
   (b) Czech Republic's request to become a Consultative Party
6. Operation of the Antarctic Treaty System: Review of the Secretariat's Situation
7. Development of a Multi-year Strategic Work Plan
8. Report of the Committee for Environmental Protection
9. Liability: Implementation of Decision 4 (2010)
10. Safety and Operations in Antarctica, including Search and Rescue
11. Tourism and Non-Governmental Activities in the Antarctic Treaty Area

12.Inspections under the Antarctic Treaty and the Environment Protocol

13.Science Issues, Scientific Cooperation and Facilitation

14. Implications of Climate Change for Management of the Antarctic Treaty Area

15. Education Issues

16.Exchange of Information

17.Biological Prospecting in Antarctica

18.Preparation of the 37th Meeting

19.Any Other Business

20.Adoption of the Final Report

(18) The Meeting adopted the following allocation of agenda items:

- Plenary: Items 1, 2, 3, 4, 5b, 8, 18, 19, 20, 21
- Legal and Institutional Working Group: Items 5a, 6, 7, 9, 17
- Tourism Working Group: Item 11
- Operational Matters Working Group: Items 10, 12, 13, 14, 15, 16
- Search and Rescue Special Working Group: Item 10.

(19) The Meeting agreed that Item 5b would be addressed solely by the Consultative Parties.

(20) The Meeting also decided to allocate draft instruments arising out of the work of the Committee for Environmental Protection and the Working Groups to a legal drafting group for consideration of their legal and institutional aspects.

Item 4: Operation of the Antarctic Treaty System: Reports by Parties, Observers and Experts

(21) Pursuant to Recommendation XIII-2, the Meeting received reports from depositary governments and secretariats.

(22) The United States, in its capacity as Depositary Government of the Antarctic Treaty and its Environmental Protocol, reported on their status (IP 72). In the past year, there had been no accessions to the Antarctic Treaty or the Protocol. There were 50 Parties to the Treaty and 35 Parties to the Protocol. Subsequent to the submission of IP 72, the United States confirmed that it had received confirmation from the United Kingdom that it had ratified Measures 1 (2005), 15 (2009), and 16 (2009). One application for Consultative

Party status had been received, from the Czech Republic, and circulated to Consultative Parties by diplomatic channels and via the Secretariat. The United States, supported by others, urged Consultative Parties to actively pursue approval of outstanding Measures.

(23) Australia, in its capacity as Depositary for the Convention for the Conservation of Antarctic Marine Living Resources (CCAMLR), reported that there had been one new accession to the Convention since ATCM XXXV: Panama acceded to the Convention on 20 March 2013, and the Convention entered into force for Panama on 19 April 2013 (IP 41). There were 36 Parties to the Convention.

(24) The United Kingdom, in its capacity as Depositary of the Convention for the Conservation of Antarctic Seals (CCAS), reported that there had been one accession to the Convention since ATCM XXXV: Pakistan acceded to the Convention on 24 April 2013. The United Kingdom also reported that following a request from Spain, all CCAS Parties had confirmed that it could accede to the Convention, and that Spain was currently considering accession.

(25) Australia, in its capacity as Depositary for the Agreement on the Conservation of Albatrosses and Petrels (ACAP), reported that there had been no new accessions to the Agreement since ATCM XXXV, and that there were 13 Parties to the Agreement (IP 40).

(26) The Executive Secretary of CCAMLR reported on the outcomes of CCAMLR XXXI, which was held in Hobart, Australia in October 2012 (IP 1). He reported that the Commission approved a Non-Contracting Party-IUU Vessel List, noting that at least seven vessels were considered to have engaged in Illegal, Unregulated and Unreported (IUU) fishing activities in the Convention Area in 2011/12. A number of these vessels had persistently engaged in IUU fishing activates in the CCAMLR Area. He noted that in 2011/12 five members harvested 161,143 tonnes of krill, compared to a total reported catch of 180,992 tonnes in 2010/11. In 2011/12, the reported total catch of toothfish was 11,329 tonnes by 11 members, compared to 14,669 tonnes in 2010/11. The reported total catch of icefish was 1012 tonnes by two members. The Commission noted possible signs of recovery for populations of icefish and marbled rock cod near the South Shetland Islands, but agreed that this fishery would remain closed. An increasing number of vessels notified for exploratory fisheries and the Commission requested that further consideration be given to limiting capacity in exploratory fisheries. On seabirds, the total extrapolated mortalities in the Convention Area were

estimated to be 225. Twelve vulnerable marine ecosystems were registered in 2012, and the Commission endorsed advice on the implementation of measures to avoid and mitigate significant adverse impacts on such ecosystems. The Commission also welcomed the Scientific Committee's progress towards establishing a representative system of marine protected areas arising from three technical workshops held during 2012. The Commission also scheduled special meetings in Bremerhaven, Germany, in July 2013 to further consider proposals for the establishment of MPAs in the Ross Sea region and East Antarctica . The Commission endorsed the advice of the Scientific Committee in respect of ATCM management plans for Antarctic Specially Protected Areas and Antarctic Specially Managed Areas. The Commission agreed to a new conservation measure (91-02) highlighting the values of ASPAs and ASMAs and requesting members to ensure that their vessels are aware of the locations of ASMAs and ASPAs which include marine areas and their associated management plans. This responded to a concern over krill fishing that had occurred in 2010 in ASMA 1 and ASPA 153 and again in 2012 in ASPA 153.

(27) The President of the Scientific Committee on Antarctic Research (SCAR) presented the SCAR Annual Report (IP 4), and referred to BP 20, which highlighted a selection of recent key science papers published since ATCM XXXV. In July 2012, SCAR approved five new Scientific Research Programmes: on (i) the State of the Antarctic Ecosystem, (ii) Antarctic Thresholds – Ecosystem Resilience and Adaptation, (iii) Antarctic Climate Change in the 21st Century, (iv) Past Antarctic Ice Sheet Dynamics, and (v) Solid Earth Response and Cryosphere Evolution. SCAR remained committed to supporting Treaty Parties by progressing scientific knowledge of the Antarctic. On climate change, SCAR has published a major update to the key points of the Antarctic Climate Change and the Environment (ACCE) report, concerning impacts on Antarctic and Southern Ocean marine and terrestrial biota. To improve the quality of the data available to understand the key role of the Southern Ocean in the climate and ecosystem functioning of the planet, a new Southern Ocean Observing System portal had been established. Further, the first SCAR Antarctic and Southern Ocean Science Horizon Scan was underway, to assemble experts to identify the most important scientific questions to be researched over the next two decades. SCAR invited experts from all Parties to contribute via *www.scar.org*.

(28) The Executive Secretary of the Council of Managers of National Antarctic Programs presented the COMNAP Annual Report (IP 3). She noted that COMNAP would celebrate its 25th anniversary this year. For this meeting

COMNAP noted that it had collaborated with others to prepare two working papers, including a review of ATCM recommendations relating to operations (WP 1), and an update on actions arising from COMNAP workshops on Search and Rescue coordination and response (WP 17). COMNAP and SCAR were planning two joint workshops for the year, on the Southern Ocean Observing System, and on Antarctic conservation challenges.

(29) Colombia presented IP 104 *Colombia in Antarctica* and announced its intention to establish a national research programme with an expedition to Antarctica in 2014/2015, and to ratify the Environmental Protocol and CCAMLR. Colombia looked forward to collaborating with other Parties in protecting the Antarctic continent. In response to a query from the United Kingdom, Colombia clarified that it intended to ratify the Environmental Protocol and CCAMLR before the expedition took place.

(30) The representative of the Antarctic and Southern Ocean Coalition (ASOC) presented IP 106 *Report of the Antarctic and Southern Ocean Coalition,* which described ASOC's recent work and outlined main issues of concern. ASOC had submitted 12 papers to the meeting, which addressed key environmental issues and aimed at helping the ATCM and CEP achieve more effective environmental protection and conservation of Antarctica. ASOC congratulated Norway and the United Kingdom for ratifying Annex VI (Liability) of the Environmental Protocol, and encouraged other Parties to do the same. In light of the many pressures Antarctica was facing, from global climate change and human activities, ASOC looked forward to concrete actions taken from ATCM XXXVI.

(31) The representative of the World Meteorological Organization (WMO) reported on its recent activities. The WMO had contributed to WP 1 and to intersessional discussions on information exchange on Antarctic tourism, increased cooperation, and search and rescue. WMO, through its Executive Council Panel of Experts on Polar Observations, Research and Services (EC-PORS) was active in four main areas: observations, research, services, and engagement. Under observations, EC-PORS was exploring opportunities to expand its Antarctic Observing Network (AntON) and implement the observing component (CRYONET) of the Global Cryosphere Watch. In research, EC-PORS advocated for the Global Integated Polar Prediction System (GIPPS) covering forecasts, predictions and projections on hours/seasonal/decadal timescales thus addressing increasing needs for more accurate weather forecast and projections in Polar Regions and was seeking support for its international coordination office in Bremerhaven, Germany.

The EC-PORS Task Team on Services continued to map service requirements for target regions and propose pilot projects, while also exploring the potential for a Polar Regional Climate Centre and Outlook Forums. The Inter-agency Steering Group on the Long-Term Cooperative Polar Initiative is developing a concept paper for possible International Polar Initiative (IPI). IPI represents a novel attempt to efficiently respond to the existing challenges of polar observations, research and environmental services and may have a potential to help develop more sustained observing systems and environmental information services for the Polar Regions. Parties were encouraged to visit the WMO website under its "Polar Activities" link.

(32)   The International Hydrographic Organization (IHO) Observer presented IP 2 *Report by the International Hydrographic Organization*, which described the state of hydrographic surveying and nautical charting of Antarctica. Over 90 per cent of Antarctic waters remained unsurveyed, which posed serious risks for maritime incidents and impeded the conduct of maritime activities. While the level of human activity was dramatically increasing, the IHO was concerned that resources for surveying activities were diminishing. In order to prevent disasters, the IHO recommended that the ATCM: consider the serious shortfalls in hydrography and charting in Antarctica and its impact on activities; consider encouraging Parties to increase their support for surveying and charting of Antarctica; encourage States to allocate appropriate resources to accelerate the production of paper charts and Electronic Navigation Charts of Antarctica; and adopt the proposed ATCM Recommendation on hydrography and nautical charting developed by the IHO Hydrographic Commission on Antarctica.

(33)   The representative of the International Association of Antarctica Tour Operators (IAATO) presented IP 99 *Report of the International Association of Antarctic Tour Operators 2012-13*. IAATO explained that last year, for the first time in five years, visitor numbers had risen, and had reached over 34,000, although this level was unlikely to be sustained in the coming season. IAATO had adopted a new five-year Strategic Plan, which outlined the vision and values of the organisation. Consistent with its "disclose and discuss" policy, IAATO highlighted some tourism incidents that occurred in 2012/13. IAATO further stressed that its operators and their passengers had contributed more than USD 440,000 to scientific and conservation organisations active in Antarctica and the sub-Antarctic. IAATO also expressed its gratitude for the cooperation it had received from Parties, COMNAP, SCAR, CCAMLR, IHO/HCA, ASOC and others in the interest of the long-term protection of Antarctica.

Item 5a: Operation of the Antarctic Treaty System: General Matters

(34) COMNAP introduced WP 1 *Review of ATCM Recommendations on Operational Matters*, submitted jointly with IAATO, IHO, SCAR, WMO, which proposed revisions to twenty-eight recommendations in four categories relating to operational matters. This paper was intended to provide further expert advice, and suggested amendments were presented in three attachments to this paper. Attachment A contains the suggestions for the twelve recommendations which required updating; Attachment B contains the suggestions for the two recommendations which required further advice from COMNAP and SCAR; and Attachment C contains the suggestions for the eight recommendations related to meteorology from WMO.

(35) The Meeting thanked COMNAP and other expert bodies for the excellent additions made on reviewing recommendations on operational matters that require reconsideration, exemplifying the ATCMs progressive review of the appropriateness of measures.

(36) Several Parties were supportive of the recommendations provided and suggested Parties could conduct further intersessional discussions on this large and complex body of work.

(37) It was noted that Recommendation XV-20 (1989) on Air Safety in Antarctica should be updated as soon as possible, preferably at this meeting.

(38) The Meeting adopted Resolution 1 (2013) *Air Safety in Antarctica.*

(39) The Meeting agreed to establish an intersessional contact group (ICG) on the review of ATCM Recommendations on Operational Matters which would allow for the participation of both lawyers and experts with the aim of:

   • Updating relevant ATCM Recommendations and Measures annexed to WP 1 referred to above with the exception of Recommendation XV-20 (1989) on Air Safety in Antarctica.

(40) It was further agreed that:

   • Observers and Experts participating in the ATCM would be invited to provide input;
   • The Executive Secretary would open the ATCM forum for the ICG and provide assistance to the ICG; and
   • The United States would act as convener and report to the next ATCM on the progress made in the ICG.

(41) France introduced WP 44 *The exercise of jurisdiction in the Antarctic Treaty Area,* which reported on the work of the Intersessional Contact Group (ICG) chaired by France. The exchanges focused on some of the questions likely to generate difficulties in the enforcement of domestic law in the Antarctic Treaty area presented by France at ATCM XXXV (WP 28). They were based on fictional cases of damages to the environment and of an assault against a person.

(42) The Meeting agreed that the issue of the exercise of jurisdiction was very important and thanked France for coordinating work that provided valuable information to the ATCM.

(43) A number of Parties raised concerns regarding the establishment of a database, particularly with personal information of their nationals, or the inclusion of the fictitious case studies. Some of these Parties preferred to continue with the exchange of information only, which would be helpful for taking better decisions on the issue without the establishment of a database, while others were supportive of continuing discussions on the establishment of a database without the inclusion of fictitious cases. Australia noted the large number of proposals before ATCM XXXVI regarding information exchange and expressed support for a systematic and comprehensive review of the information exchanged by Parties.

(44) The Meeting noted the concern that it could be confusing to incorporate fictitious cases in the database next to real cases intended to be a future reference. France agreed that fictitious cases should not be included in an exchange of information, and that this could be written into the Terms of Reference for continued intersessional discussion.

(45) France reassured the Meeting it had no intention of incorporating private/personal information within the information exchange, and that it would be limited to already publically available information on cases and laws which have relevance to the Antarctic, including how the powers given to station commanders and ship and aircraft captains differ between states, and whether these persons have any powers with respect to infractions committed in the Antarctica Treaty area.

(46) France noted that two real cases and two fictitious cases had been proposed in the ICG but the real cases had been withdrawn after some Parties had expressed their concern. Two fictitious cases were used in the ICG discussions without any concerns being raised.

(47) The Meeting agreed to continue to consider exercise of jurisdiction in the Antarctic Treaty area and to extend the mandate of the ICG established at ATCM XXXV *mutatis mutandis* (Final Report ATCM XXXV, paragraphs 47-49).

(48) Chile introduced WP 66 *Intersessional Contact Group Report on Cooperation in Antarctica*, which reported on the results of discussions on cooperation since the last Meeting and contained a summary of contributions by participants. The paper presented the principal discussion areas: information exchange, cooperation in educational matters, cooperation on logistical issues and joint research. The paper recommended that the Electronic Information Exchange System (EIES) be improved; cooperation in education and dissemination be enhanced; further education of scientists in Antarctic science be encouraged; cooperation in logistical and operational matters be strengthened; better communication between different national Antarctic programmes be facilitated; and the joint use of existing bases be promoted. Chile suggested the forum support the work carried out in the ICG on jurisdiction and to further collaboration in the area of Search and Rescue (SAR). For addressing these recommendations, Chile suggested renewing the mandate of the ICG.

(49) Many Parties congratulated Chile and the ICG's work on cooperation and expressed support for the recommendations, noting that several of them were mentioned as priorities for the multi-year strategic work plan. On cooperation for educational matters, COMNAP indicated that it already had a database compiling training courses of national programmes.

(50) The Meeting agreed to continue to consider improving cooperation in Antarctica and to extend the mandate of the ICG established for this purpose at ATCM XXXV *mutatis mutandis* (ATCM XXXV Final Report, paragraphs 51-54).

(51) The Russian Federation presented IP 43 *Implementation of the new Russian legislature "On regulation of activity of the Russian citizens and the Russian legal entities in the Antarctic"*, which reported that a new Russian law had created a legal basis for its government's ratification of Measure 4 (2004) on insurance and contingency planning, Measure 1 (2005) on Annex VI on liability, and Measure 15 (2009) on landing of persons from passenger vessels. These measures were approved by the Government in March 2013. In July 2012 the Government endorsed a plan to develop further related legislation. The Government of the Russian Federation had also adopted provisions in November 2012: to designate the Russian Federal Agency for Hydrometeorology (Roshydromet) as the agency to appoint observers, monitor compliance and organise inspections and research; and to make the

Russian Arctic and Antarctic Research Institute responsible for ensuring that Russian research in the Antarctic meets international standards and obligations. The Russian Federation intended to adopt additional laws necessary to complete its legal framework by early 2014.

(52) France introduced IP 79 *Strengthening Support for the Protocol on Environmental Protection to the Antarctic Treaty*, jointly prepared with Australia and Spain. This paper contained a report on representations conducted in accordance with Resolution 1 (2012) to encourage the 15 States that are Antarctic Treaty Parties but are not yet Party to the Environmental Protocol to ratify it. France reported that Denmark, Portugal, Austria and Malaysia had begun the necessary processes and expected to ratify by the end of 2013. Eight other Parties were taking a longer-term approach, necessitated by internal difficulties and financial consequences. France had provided information to several Parties to assist in their efforts at ratification.

(53) Australia thanked France for introducing IP 79 and other Consultative Parties for joining in the representations which had been organised by Australia, France and Spain. Australia confirmed that the overall response to the representations was positive and a clear recognition of the enduring importance of the Environmental Protocol. Spain agreed that the Protocol was the ATCM's most important tool in protecting the Antarctic environment. Australia and Spain supported continuing with representations in the intersessional period.

(54) The Meeting commended Parties that had participated in demarches for their work on this matter and confirmed that the issue was of importance to all Parties. Noting that some specific questions had been raised, particularly in relation to the financial and administrative implications of acceding to the Protocol, the Meeting agreed that the intersessional work should continue and welcomed the offer by Australia, France and Spain to continue to coordinate this intersessional work and to report to ATCM XXXVII on the outcomes of follow-up representations in the 2013/14 intersessional period.

(55) Parties considered and agreed an indicative template for ICGs (as shown below), in accordance with paragraph 62 of the ATCM XXXV Final Report.

The Meeting agreed to establish an intersessional contact group (ICG) on [topic] with the aim of:

- *[objective];*
- *[any further objectives];*

It was further agreed that:

- *Observers and Experts participating in the ATCM would be invited to provide input;*
- *The Executive Secretary would open the ATCM forum for the ICG and provide assistance to the ICG; and*
- *[Parties] would act as convener and report to the next ATCM on the progress made in the ICG.*

Item 5b: Operation of the Antarctic Treaty System: Czech Republic's request to become a Consultative Party

(56) The Hon. Vladimír Galuška, Deputy Minister of Foreign Affairs for the Czech Republic, informed the Meeting that the Czech Republic had formally submitted a request for Consultative Party status to the depositary government on 18 April 2013. The Czech Republic had been a non-Consultative Party since 1962, and actively conducted substantive scientific research in the Antarctic since 1994. It has operated its own Johann Gregor Mendel Antarctic station since 2006, which houses 25 scientists and supports a diverse range of scientific activities in geosciences, climatology, biology, and the production of a topographical and geological map of the northern part of James Ross Island. The Czech Republic welcomed the collaboration of other Parties at its station.

(57) The Czech Republic further noted that it had approved all Environmental Protocol Annexes that are in force, and pursuant to Decision 4 (2005) declared its intent to approve all Recommendations and Measures subsequently approved by all Consultative Parties. The Czech Republic would also consider the approval of other Recommendations and Measures, noted that its 2003 Act on Antarctica implemented international obligations into domestic law, and advised that it had established the Commission for Antarctica, all of which supported its application for Consultative Party status.

(58) The Consultative Parties thanked the Czech Republic for its presentation and commitment to approve Recommendations and Measures. A number of Parties highlighted the Czech Republic's efforts to meet the necessary requirements, including its active scientific research programme. Belgium and Argentina further highlighted positive experiences of close collaboration with the Czech Republic on the Antarctic Peninsula.

(59)   The Consultative Parties agreed that the Czech Republic had adequately fulfilled the necessary requirements, and was therefore accepted as a Consultative Party by consensus. The Consultative Parties invited the Czech Republic to report further information on its progress towards implementing ATCM instruments to ATCM XXXVII in 2014.

(60)   The Meeting adopted Decision 1 (2013) *Recognition of the Czech Republic as a Consultative Party*.

Item 6: Operation of the Antarctic Treaty System: Review of the Secretariat's Situation

(61)   The Meeting reviewed SP 2 *Secretariat Report 2012/13*; SP 3 rev.1 *Secretariat Programme 2013/14*; SP 4 *Five year forward budget profile 2013-2017*.

(62)   Following informal discussions on the budget, the Executive Secretary had submitted a revised work programme and budget in SP 3 rev.1. The revised version was agreed by the Meeting, which then adopted Decision 4 (2013) *Secretariat Report, Programme and Budget*; Decision 2 (2013) *Re-appointment of the Executive Secretary*; and Decision 3 (2013) *Renewal of the Contract of the Secretariat's External Auditor*.

(63)   Reporting on the activities of the Secretariat, the Executive Secretary noted its support to three kinds of activities: ATCM and CEP Meetings; intersessional activities; and Information Exchange.

(64)   With regard to intersessional activities, the Executive Secretary highlighted the significant improvement of the ATS website which now offers several new functionalities making use of modern technologies so as to increase accessibility. He also referred amongst others to the improvement of the Electronic Information Exchange System (EIES) and the updating of three major databases, namely the Environmental Impact Assessments (EIA) Database; the Protected Areas Database which now includes a set of high resolution outlines usable for electronic Geographic Information System (GIS); and the Antarctic Treaty Database. The Secretariat reported on cooperation with the Scott Polar Research Institute (SPRI, Cambridge) which holds a vast collection of meeting documents to complement its archive database.

(65)   The Executive Secretary also outlined several personnel matters. In particular, he reminded Parties that in accordance with Staff Regulation 6.2,

the Executive Secretary appoints his Assistant Executive Secretary, whose current contract expires on 31 December 2014: he will be consulting with Parties to the Treaty on this appointment.

(66) The Meeting requested that the Executive Secretary make a presentation at ATCM XXXVII on the process for selecting the Assistant Executive Secretary, consistent with section 5 of Annex 3 to Decision 4 (2013).

(67) With respect to the workshop on the Multi-Year Strategic Work Plan, the Meeting expressed its gratitude to Norway, the United States, Australia and the Netherlands for their contributions to the special fund, which fully covered the costs of interpretation for the workshop.

(68) The Executive Secretary presented the audited financial report for 2011/12. The conclusion of the auditor was that the financial statements presented fairly, in all material respects, the financial position of the Antarctic Treaty Secretariat as of 31 March 2012, as well as confirming that its financial performance for this period was in accordance with International Accounting Standards and the rules agreed by the ATCM. The Executive Secretary drew attention of Parties to the expiration of the current auditor's contract by 1 October 2013 and proposed to renew it given that the work was considered satisfactory.

(69) Following the presentation of the provisional financial report 2012/13, the Executive Secretary reported a saving to the forecast budget due to reduced translation and interpretation costs. The Executive Secretary advised that the International Translation Agency (ITA) situated in Malta was selected in December 2012 as new contractor for translation and interpretation.

(70) In outlining the anticipated activities of the Secretariat in 2013/14, the Executive Secretary highlighted the support that would be provided to Brazil as the Host Country for ATCM XXXVII and CEP XVII. Additionally, the Secretariat will continue to develop further the EIES, and expand the databases, including for protected areas (GIS). The Secretariat also intends to continue cooperation with the Scott Polar Research Institute in identifying all missing ATCM documentation and integrating it into the ATS database.

(71) The Executive Secretary noted three specific features of the budget 2013/14. No increase of salaries is requested this year. Given the European tax law, no Belgian value added tax (VAT) is levied on services provided by ITA during ATCM XXXVI.

(72) Finally, the Executive Secretary pointed out the rise of expenses forecast in the coming budgets. However, no increase in contributions would be

expected for the next five years thanks to the surplus generated over the past years.

(73) Several Parties expressed their appreciation for the work undertaken by the Executive Secretary over the past years, particularly the efforts to use advanced technology resulting in lower costs.

(74) The Meeting congratulated the Executive Secretary on his reappointment and looked forward to continuing to work with him.

(75) The Executive Secretary reiterated his appreciation to the government of Argentina for its excellent support for the activities of the Secretariat and warmly thanked all Parties for his reappointment for a new four-year term, which was approved in the course of the Heads of Delegation meeting.

(76) In response to an invitation of the Executive Secretary, several Parties informed that their contribution to the budget 2012/13 was in the process of payment.

(77) The Meeting agreed that the open-ended Intersessional Contact Group on financial issues established by Decision 2 (2012) would continue to operate and its coordination would be the responsibility of the host country for each ATCM.

(78) France introduced WP 40 *Glossary of terms and expressions used by the ATCM*, jointly prepared with Belgium and Uruguay, which proposed that the ATCM adopt a comprehensive glossary of its terminology in the four official languages. Such a document would facilitate the work of the translators and would help avoid mistakes, inconsistencies and multiple translations of sentences and identical terms in different ways. France proposed a first contribution to such a glossary in French and English for the consideration of the Parties and suggested that interested Parties provide voluntary contributions in the four working languages in an ICG France would convene.

(79) Russia indicated its willingness to assist in a compiling a Russian version and drew the attention of the Meeting to IP 74 *On creating a four-language glossary of the main terms and definitions used in the Antarctic Treaty documentation* submitted by Russia in 1999, proposing a similar glossary. Russia is already undertaking work to provide a glossary in Russian for individuals working at its Antarctic stations. Several Spanish-speaking Parties agreed to assist in developing a Spanish glossary.

(80) The Meeting generally agreed on the usefulness of a glossary as a means to facilitate the work of translation and interpretation and assist the informal work of Parties. Some Parties raised concerns regarding the specific use and

cost of the glossary. Argentina stated that the incorporation of terms in the glossary and their translation should be on a consensus basis.

(81) Some delegates expressed concern that interpreting the terms of legally-binding instruments would require a lengthy, formal process, and further the concern that a glossary might be mistaken as an authoritative interpretation without an appropriate disclaimer.

(82) Some concern was expressed that the glossary might increase the costs to, and workload of, the Secretariat. It was stated that there should be no significant financial costs in developing and using the glossary. The Executive Secretary noted the importance of assuring the accuracy of the Final Reports of the ATCM and CEP and cited the availability, at no cost, of a thesaurus software developed by the European Union. The Secretariat is willing to organise the use of the software for translations.

(83) The Meeting agreed to the use of an ICG to further develop the glossary and reiterated that a resolution was not necessary to continue this work: that further development should result in no costs to the Secretariat and no effort other than uploading the glossary to its website; and that any glossary would include the following: "this glossary is intended to aid translation and interpretation and does not constitute an authoritative interpretation of the Antarctic Treaty and associated legal instruments".

(84) The Meeting agreed to establish an ICG on the further development of a glossary with the aim of:

- Aiding translation and interpretation; and
- Avoiding multiple translation of sentences and identical terms in different ways.

(85) It was further agreed that:

- Observers and Experts participating in the ATCM would be invited to provide input;
- The Executive Secretary would open the ATCM forum for the ICG and provide assistance to the ICG; and
- France would act as convener and report to the next ATCM on the progress made in the ICG.

(86) France introduced WP 45 *Budgetary issues: proposal to ensure that the Secretariat of the Antarctic Treaty benefits from the expertise of the*

"Coordination Regime", which followed the discussions held at ATCM XXXV on budgetary issues and proposed that the Secretariat become an "Associate" organisation to the "Coordination" regime so that it may benefit from the expertise and tools of the International Service for Remunerations and Pensions (ISRP) on ways to improve its salary adjustment method.

(87) Several Parties expressed their interest in this proposal and were of the view that it could result in an easier administrative and financial control for Parties and would ease the work of the ATCM. It could also result in savings. Several Parties stated that the contribution the Secretariat would pay should not exceed the possible savings. Several Parties questioned the applicability and suitability of the ISRP in the Antarctic Treaty Secretariat context and further doubts were expressed about potential benefits given the ISRP's location in Europe.

(88) The Meeting agreed to task the Secretariat to engage in discussion with the Coordination Regime and other appropriate entities to gather information on:

- Salary adjustment methods adapted to the Secretariat's situation, in order to improve the current method by basing it on clearer criterion that Parties would be able to control more effectively; and

- The potential contribution the Secretariat would have to pay.

(89) It was further agreed that the Secretariat would report to ATCM XXXVII on the results of these demarches.

Item 7: Development of a Multi-Year Strategic Work Plan

(90) The co-chairs (Australia and Belgium) introduced WP 67 *Co-chairs' Report of the Workshop on the Development of a Multi-Year Strategic Work Plan for the ATCM, Brussels, Belgium, 20-21 May 2013*, which described the background, the conduct of the Workshop, the outcomes and further steps. There was extensive discussion on whether all priorities and related actions should be scheduled over a five-year period or only those priorities to be considered at ATCM XXXVII. Most Parties acknowledged the importance of pursuing all priorities in a multi-year approach and agreed to take a step-by-step approach focusing initially on the priorities to be considered at ATCM XXXVII and related actions.

(91) It was agreed that the priorities to be given a particular focus at ATCM XXXVII should be:

Cooperation on:

- *conducting a comprehensive review of existing requirements for information exchange and the functioning of the Electronic Information Exchange System and the identification of any additional requirements;*
- *strengthening cooperation among Parties on current Antarctic-specific air and marine operations and safety practices, identifying any issues that may be brought forward to IMO and ICAO, as appropriate; and*
- *reviewing and assessing the need for additional actions regarding area management and permanent infrastructure related to tourism, as well as issues related to land-based and adventure tourism, and addressing the recommendations of the CEP tourism study.*

(92) It was also agreed that the Parties, Experts and Observers be invited to consult among themselves in the ICG on Antarctic Cooperation on the elaboration of priorities in the Plan.

(93) The Meeting adopted Decision 5 (2013) *Multi-Year Strategic Work Plan for the Antarctic Treaty Consultative Meeting.*

(94) ASOC presented IP 61 *Human impacts in the Arctic and Antarctic: Key findings relevant to the ATCM and CEP*, which stated that existing environmental management practices and governance systems were insufficient to meet the obligations of the Environmental Protocol. The paper suggested strategic and specific actions available to the Antarctic Treaty Parties, including wider use of existing environmental management tools, fuller compliance with the Protocol and its Annexes, proactive engagement on contentious and strategic issues, placing shared long-term visions and collective strategies at the heart of decision-making, and enhanced coordination and collaboration.

Item 8: Report of the Committee for Environmental Protection

(95) Dr Yves Frenot, Chair of the Committee for Environmental Protection (CEP), introduced the report of CEP XVI. The CEP had considered 46 Working Papers, 57 Information Papers, 5 Secretariat Papers and 7 Background Papers.

Strategic Discussions on the Future of the CEP (CEP Agenda Item 3)

(96) The Chair of the CEP advised that the Committee had welcomed the progress to develop an Antarctic Environments Portal, and had encouraged further development of this initiative, which aims to facilitate the link between Antarctic science and the CEP by providing ready access to independent, science-based information on priority issues.

(97) The Committee had noted that the Portal is an independent project and is not intended as a decision-making or political tool. In welcoming the initiative, the CEP had noted that issues such as governance, decision-making, the composition of the Portal's editorial board, geographic and linguistic representation, assurance that data would be independent and apolitical, the status of information published on the Portal, and long-term funding may need to be considered in its further development. Currently, it is an initiative of some individual Parties, including New Zealand, with support from Australia, Belgium, Norway and SCAR.

(98) The ATCM welcomed the progress on an Antarctic Environments Portal. The United States, Norway and Australia thanked New Zealand for the initiative, and for allocating resources to support the Portal. The United States also expressed its appreciation of SCAR's involvement.

(99) The Chair of the CEP advised that the Committee had discussed human impacts on the Antarctic environment. ASOC had reported on two international collaborative projects launched at the International Polar Year Oslo Science Conference, 2010, exploring human impacts and future scenarios for the Antarctic environment. The majority of the reports had concluded that existing environmental management practices and the current system of governance are insufficient today and in the future to meet environmental challenges and the obligations of the Environmental Protocol. The Committee had noted that such elements may be relevant to inform future discussions.

(100) The Chair of the CEP advised that the Committee had revised and updated its Five-Year Work Plan. The Committee had decided to elevate to priority 2 the topic of "Education and Outreach".

Cooperation with Other Organisations (CEP Agenda Item 5)

(101) The Chair of the CEP informed that the Committee had received reports from other organisations with common interests in the operation of the CEP. SCAR had presented its five new scientific research projects: a) State of the

Antarctic Ecosystem; b) Antarctic Thresholds – Ecosystem Resilience and Adaptation; c) Antarctic Climate Change in the 21st Century; d) Past Antarctic Ice Sheet Dynamics; and e) Solid Earth Response and Cryosphere Evolution. The SC-CAMLR Observer had presented the five issues of common interest with the CEP: a) Climate change and the Antarctic marine environment; b) Biodiversity and non-native species in the Antarctic marine environment; c) Antarctic species requiring special protection; d) Spatial marine management and protected areas; and e) Ecosystem and environmental monitoring.

(102) The Chair of the CEP advised that the Committee had noted the work towards the establishment of a representative system of Marine Protected Areas in CCAMLR and that the Committee had welcomed CCAMLR's ongoing work on MPAs.

(103) The United States expressed concern with the report of the observer from the Scientific Committee of CCAMLR, with regard to the issue of recent krill fishing in ASPA 153 and ASMA 1 at Admiralty Bay. The United States was pleased by the action taken by CCAMLR in adopting Conservation 91-02 (2012) which requires Contracting Parties to ensure that their vessels authorized to fish in the CCAMLR Convention area are aware of the locations and management plans of all designated ASPAs and ASMAs. As CCAMLR noted in adopting Conservation Measure 91-02, harvesting of marine living resources in ASPAs and ASMAs could jeopardize the high scientific value of the long-term ecosystem studies being carried out in these areas, undermining the goals established in the management plans of these areas. In the view of the United States, Consultative Parties, particularly those who are also Members of CCAMLR, should continue to give attention to this issue and, if further such instances occur, support appropriate action to address it.

(104) ASOC regretted that the proposed resolution supporting CCAMLR efforts on MPAs had not been agreed but welcomed the CEP's interest in the establishment of a representative system of marine protected areas. Referring to the Antarctic Oceans Alliance report summarised in BP 17 *Antarctic Ocean Legacy Update 1 – Securing Enduring Protection for the Ross Sea Region*, ASOC hoped that CCAMLR would adopt the two MPA proposals currently under discussion.

Repair and remediation of environmental damage (CEP Agenda Item 6)

(105) The Chair of the CEP advised that the Committee had considered the request from ATCM XXXIII, in Decision 4 (2010), for advice on environmental

issues related to the practicality of repair and remediation of environmental damage. New Zealand had reported on the work of a CEP intersessional contact group established in 2012 which listed a series of issues that would need to be taken into account when presented with repair and remediation activities.

(106) The ATCM welcomed the advice of the CEP on the issues that would need to be taken into account when presented with repair and remediation activities, and confirmed that the advice would be addressed in detail in the Legal and Institutional Working Group in 2014. The ATCM also noted that the CEP was ready to respond to any further requests.

(107) Some Parties highlighted the broader need to improve the dialogue between the ATCM and the CEP, and suggested that this could be addressed via the multi-year strategic work plan, and by closer attention by the ATCM to the recommendations arising from the work of the CEP.

(108) The Chair informed that the Committee had endorsed an Antarctic Clean-Up Manual proposed by Australia and the United Kingdom. The Committee had also encouraged Members and Observers to develop practical guidelines and supporting resources for inclusion in the manual in the future.

(109) Accepting the CEP's advice, the ATCM approved the Antarctic Clean-Up Manual by adopting Resolution 2 (2013) *Antarctic Clean-up Manual*. New Zealand encouraged Parties to use the Manual and invited them to contribute to its on-going development.

(110) The Chair advised that the Committee had discussed the decommissioning of Antarctic stations. France and Italy had presented a theoretical estimate of the costs of deconstructing Concordia Station, and Brazil had presented the results of its plan for the disassembling of Comandante Ferraz station, which was destroyed by a fire in 2012. The Committee had discussed the possibilities of sharing stations and reopening closed stations rather than building new ones. The Committee had suggested that the potential to decommission a station should be given serious consideration in the design phase, and had agreed to consider the issue of decommissioning in any future review of CEP's *Guidelines for Environmental Impact Assessment in Antarctica.*

(111) In response to a suggestion by the United Kingdom that the ATCM ask the CEP for advice on whether the EIA requirement in the Environmental Protocol was in line with current best practice, the CEP Chair clarified that regular updates of the guidelines was a high priority in the CEP Five-Year Work Plan.

Climate Change Impact for the Environment (CEP Agenda Item 7)

(112) The Chair informed that the Committee had received an update from SCAR of its Antarctic Climate Change and the Environment (ACCE) Report, which summarised advances in knowledge concerning how the climates of the Antarctic and Southern Ocean had changed, how they might change in the future, and the associated impacts on marine and terrestrial biota. In endorsing SCAR's recommendations, the Committee had decided to:

- Encourage SCAR and Treaty Parties to engage with the United Nations Framework Convention on Climate Change (UNFCCC) and the Intergovernmental Panel on Climate Change (IPCC) to ensure that climate change issues in the Antarctic and Southern Ocean are fully considered and that both bodies are made aware of the outcomes of the ACCE report and associated updates;

- Focus efforts on implementing the recommendations outlined by the Antarctic Treaty Meeting of Experts (ATME) on climate change and implications for Antarctic management and governance (2010); and

- Convey the key points of the ACCE updated report more broadly to ensure awareness of the critical role of Antarctica and the Southern Ocean in the climate system and the importance of associated impacts on the region.

(113) In response to SCAR's major ACCE update report, the Committee had established an ICG on effects of climate change to be jointly coordinated by the United Kingdom and Norway, in order to make progress on the environmental recommendations from the 2010 ATME on climate change.

(114) The Chair advised that in response to presentations from ASOC on recent findings of climate change research and actions that Parties could undertake to mitigate their impacts, on the potential importance to global warming of black carbon and other short-lived climate pollutants, and the acceleration of the mass loss of Antarctic ice sheets, widespread glacier retreat, and changes to West Antarctic Ice Sheets related to anthropogenic climate change, the Committee had noted the issue of short-lived climate pollutants and noted that these issues could be considered by the ICG on climate change.

(115) The Committee had also received a report from IAATO on the progress of its Climate Change Working Group, including additional efforts to raise

awareness of climate change in Antarctica, and a report from COMNAP on its analysis of cost/energy of national Antarctic programme transportation, and a survey on best practices for energy management.

(116) The ATCM highlighted the importance of the CEP's work on the effects of climate change and welcomed the establishment by the Committee of an intersessional working group. Australia further thanked the United Kingdom and Norway for volunteering to lead this work.

(117) Uruguay and Argentina emphasised the importance of ensuring that these discussions focused on the effects of climate change specifically on Antarctica.

Environmental Impact Assessment (CEP Agenda Item 8)

Draft Comprehensive Environmental Evaluations

(118) The Chair informed that no draft Comprehensive Environmental Evaluations (CEEs) had been submitted to CEP XVI.

Other EIA Matters

(119) The Chair advised that the Russian Federation had presented several documents related to the techniques and challenges when drilling into the subglacial lake beneath Vostok Station, and the discovery of an unknown group of bacteria in the first small sample of Lake Vostok water to be laboratory tested.

(120) China had presented its Initial Environmental Evaluation for the construction of an inland summer camp at Princess Elisabeth Land, which will provide logistics support, emergency rescue protection, and support local observation. China had stated that the camp construction would have no more than minor or transitory environmental impact. In response to questions from Members on the environmental impacts, size and planned duration of activity at the camp, China had indicated its willingness to exchange opinions, and to present further information on the camp construction progress at CEP XVII.

(121) The Republic of Korea had presented information on the progress of the Jang Bogo Station during the first construction season 2012/13. The Committee had noted the Republic of Korea's focus on environmental aspects of the construction and its efforts to address a fuel spill which had occurred. The Committee had also expressed its sincere condolences regarding the fatal accident during the station's construction.

(122) The Committee had also received information regarding: the legal requirements and permits granted by the Russian Federation for declared activities; an update on Brazilian efforts to rebuild its station; and an Initial Environmental Evaluation for establishment of the ground station for Earth observation satellites at India's Bharati Station at Larsemann Hills.

Italy had presented information and first evaluation on environmental issues concerning its proposal of building a gravel runway near Mario Zucchelli Station.

(123) Members and ASOC had raised several general issues in response to these papers, including: the assessment of cumulative impacts; the lack of common agreement on the criteria to determine whether an IEE or CEE was necessary for a particular activity; the prospect of operating joint scientific facilities; the need to assess gaps in knowledge; assessing impacts on wilderness; and the possibility that facilities established for science could later be used for other activities, for example tourism.

Area Protection and Management Plans (CEP Agenda Item 9)

Management Plans for Protected and Managed Areas

(124) The Chair informed that the Committee had had before it revised management plans for 16 Antarctic Specially Protected Areas (ASPAs) or Antarctic Specially Managed Area (ASMAs), two proposals to designate new ASPAs, and one proposal to designate a new ASMA. Three of these had been subject to review by the Subsidiary Group on Management Plans (SGMP) and the others had been submitted directly to CEP XVI.

(125) Accepting the CEP's advice, the Meeting adopted the following Measures on Protected Areas:

- Measure 1 (2013) *Antarctic Specially Protected Area No 108 (Green Island, Berthelot Islands, Antarctic Peninsula): Revised Management Plan.*

- Measure 2 (2013) *Antarctic Specially Protected Area No 117 (Avian Island, Marguerite Bay, Antarctic Peninsula): Revised Management Plan.*

- Measure 3 (2013) *Antarctic Specially Protected Area No 123 (Barwick and Balham Valleys, Southern Victoria Land): Revised Management Plan.*

- Measure 4 (2013) *Antarctic Specially Protected Area No 132 (Potter Peninsula, King George Island (Isla 25 de Mayo), South Shetland Islands): Revised Management Plan.*

- Measure 5 (2013) *Antarctic Specially Protected Area No 134 (Cierva Point and offshore islands, Danco Coast, Antarctic Peninsula): Revised Management Plan.*

- Measure 6 (2013) *Antarctic Specially Protected Area No 135 (North-east Bailey Peninsula, Budd Coast, Wilkes Land): Revised Management Plan.*

- Measure 7 (2013) *Antarctic Specially Protected Area No 137 (Northwest White Island, McMurdo Sound): Revised Management Plan.*

- Measure 8 (2013) *Antarctic Specially Protected Area No 138 (Linnaeus Terrace, Asgard Range, Victoria Land): Revised Management Plan.*

- Measure 9 (2013) *Antarctic Specially Protected Area No 143 (Marine Plain, Mule Peninsula, Vestfold Hills, Princess Elizabeth Land): Revised Management Plan.*

- Measure 10 (2013) *Antarctic Specially Protected Area No 147 (Ablation Valley and Ganymede Heights, Alexander Island): Revised Management Plan.*

- Measure 11 (2013) *Antarctic Specially Protected Area No 151 (Lions Rump, King George Island (isla 25 de Mayo), South Shetland Islands): Revised Management Plan.*

- Measure 12 (2013) *Antarctic Specially Protected Area No 154 (Botany Bay, Cape Geology, Victoria Land): Revised Management Plan.*

- Measure 13 (2013) *Antarctic Specially Protected Area No 156 (Lewis Bay, Mount Erebus, Ross Island): Revised Management Plan.*

- Measure 14 (2013) *Antarctic Specially Protected Area No 160 (Frazier Islands, Windmill Islands, Wilkes Land, East Antarctica): Revised Management Plan.*

- Measure 15 (2013) *Antarctic Specially Protected Area No 161 (Terra Nova Bay, Ross Sea): Revised Management Plan.*

- Measure 16 (2013) *Antarctic Specially Protected Area No 170 (Marion Nunataks, Charcot Island, Antarctic Peninsula): Revised Management Plan.*

- Measure 17 (2013) *Antarctic Specially Protected Area No 173 (Cape Washington and Silverfish Bay, Terra Nova Bay, Ross Sea): Management Plan.*

(126) In addition, the Committee had decided to refer the following revised management plan and proposal for a new ASPA to the SGMP for intersessional review:

- ASMA 1 (Admiralty Bay, King George Island, South Shetland Islands (Brazil, Ecuador, Peru, Poland));
- ASPA 141 (Yukidori Valley, Langhovde, Lützow-Holm Bay (Japan)).

    Proposed new ASPA at Stornes, Larsemann Hills, Princess Elizabeth Land (Australia, China, India, Russian Federation).

(127) China had also introduced a draft management plan for a new ASMA in the Dome A area, which aimed to enhance the protection of the site's scientific, environmental and logistical values. China had stated that its proposal was based not on the premise that more than one Party would necessarily be using the site but on a precautionary approach to likely future activities and interest in the region, and on the values to be protected. While congratulating China for the comprehensive report, several Members had questioned the justification for designating a new ASMA, and suggested that it might be premature. The Committee had accepted China's offer to lead further discussions on the proposed ASMA during the intersessional period.

Other Matters Related to Management Plans for Protected and Managed Areas

(128) The Chair informed that the Committee had noted the timeliness of reconsidering the whole process of designating ASPAs and ASMAs, and would return to this topic in the near future.

(129) The Committee had adopted the work plan for the SGMP's activities during the 2013/14 intersessional period.

(130) The Committee had also received reports from the management groups for ASMA 4 (Deception Island) and another report on activities in ASPA 171 Narebski Point.

Historic Sites and Monuments

(131) The Chair informed that the Committee had had before it proposals for four new Historic Sites and Monuments.

(132) Accepting the CEP's advice, the Meeting adopted the following Measures on Historic Sites and Monuments:

- Measure 18 (2013) *Antarctic Historic Sites and Monuments: Location of the first permanently occupied German Antarctic research station "Georg Forster" at the Schirmacher Oasis, Dronning Maud Land.*
- Measure 19 (2013) *Antarctic Historic Sites and Monuments: Professor Kudryashov's Drilling Complex Building, Vostok Station.*
- Measure 20 (2013) *Antarctic Historic Sites and Monuments: Upper "Summit Camp", Mount Erebus.*
- Measure 21 (2013) *Antarctic Historic Sites and Monuments: Lower "Camp E", Mount Erebus.*

(133) The Chair advised that the Committee had agreed to consider a review of the procedure for designating Historic Sites and Monuments in its Five-Year Work Plan. This would address a concern that, since many constructions in Antarctica might be considered to have historical value, this could lead to the designation of a large number of historic sites, which might be seen to contradict the Environmental Protocol's provision regarding clean-up of past activities in Antarctica.

(134) New Zealand had commended the high quality of the management plans for protected and managed areas, and urged the adoption of appropriate guidelines, to ensure that a historic site and monument designation would not be used by Parties to avoid cleaning up disused sites. Similarly, ASOC had noted the considerable effort and resources required of Parties to maintain historic sites, urged Parties to look carefully at alternatives to proposed historic site designations and noted that many were for quite recent items. Argentina had endorsed the continuation of previous discussions on historic sites and monuments.

Site Guidelines

(135) The United Kingdom, jointly with Australia, Argentina and United States, had reported on their on-site review of Site Guidelines carried out in conjunction with IAATO in January 2013. The review team had identified no significant

visitor impacts on the sites, other than those which had been the subject of previous discussion by the Committee. The Guidelines appeared to be successful in directing the way that most organised groups of visitors were using the sites, in order to avoid any adverse environmental impacts. At the same time, Site Guidelines remained only one of a range of potential tools to manage visitation.

(136) The Committee had endorsed several recommendations presented by the review team:

- Recommendation 1: That Parties continue to make efforts to ensure that all visitors to sites covered by ATCM Site Guidelines are aware and make use of the Guidelines. This should include recreational visits by National Antarctic Programme (NAP) personnel as well as visitors participating in private or non-commercial activity.

- Recommendation 3: That Parties continue to carry out on-site reviews of Site Guidelines, as determined by the individual requirements of the sites.

- Recommendation 7: That Parties should continue to seek input from IAATO and other non-governmental operators as appropriate, when revising or creating new Site Guidelines.

- Recommendation 8: That, where possible:
  - illustrated photo-maps should be used to assist in on-site interpretation of the provisions of the Site Guidelines;
  - a standardised map format should be developed for use across Site Guidelines;
  - that the Site Guidelines should include information on the date of their adoption and any subsequent revision; and
  - that the CEP considers the benefit of bringing all the Site Guidelines together with the similarly formatted General Guidelines as part of the practical package of information for visitors to Antarctica.

- Recommendation 9: That the CEP encourages the development, by IAATO and other non-governmental operators, of best-practice training assessment and/or accreditation schemes for Antarctic guides and expedition leaders, noting the CEP discussions in 2005 and 2006.

(137) The Committee had also considered several other recommendations, and noted that some coincide with recommendations of the CEP tourism study that the ATCM had requested the CEP to address. A specific task for answering this request was added to the CEP Five-Year Work Plan.

(138) The Committee had had before it proposals for the revision of 14 Site Guidelines and two new Site Guidelines. The Committee had endorsed the Site Guidelines for Yankee Harbour; Half Moon Island; Brown Bluff; Hannah Point; Cuverville Island; Danco Island; Neko Harbour; Pleneau Island; Petermann Island; Damoy Point; Jougla Point; Baily Head, Deception Island; Torgersen Island; Barrientos Island; Orne Harbour (new); and Orne Islands (new).

(139) The Meeting considered and approved 16 new Site Guidelines by adopting Resolution 3 (2013) *Site Guidelines for Visitors*.

(140) The ATCM expressed its appreciation of the CEP's work in reviewing the Site Guidelines. The United Kingdom reiterated that the list of revised guidelines should include both the original date of adoption and the date of any subsequent revision. New Zealand warmly welcomed the CEP's schedule of follow-up actions, particularly with respect to the recommendations on tourism.

(141) The Chair informed that the Committee had also received a report from IAATO on IAATO operators' use of Antarctic Peninsula landing sites and the ATCM's Visitor Site Guidelines in 2012/13. IAATO had noted that traditional ship-based tourism represented over 95 per cent of all landed activity, that the 20 most-visited sites represented 72 per cent of the total number of landings made, and that all but one of these most-visited sites – Portal Point – were covered by site specific management plans.

Human Footprint and Wilderness Values

(142) The Committee had considered a report from New Zealand on possible guidance material to assist Parties to take account of wilderness values when undertaking environmental impact assessments (EIAs). ASOC had also contributed information on mapping and modelling wilderness values in Antarctica, which summarised the recommendations of the Wildland Research Institute. The Committee had agreed to include the issue of wilderness in any future review of CEP's *Guidelines for Environmental Impact Assessment in Antarctica*.

Marine Spatial Protection and Management

(143) The Chair informed that no documents (except BP 17 *Antarctic Ocean Legacy Update 1 – Securing Enduring Protection for the Ross Sea Region*) had been submitted under this agenda item.

Other Annex V Matters

(144) In response to a presentation by the United Kingdom regarding the likely impact of climate change upon emperor penguin distribution range and breeding success, the Committee had endorsed the monitoring of emperor penguin colonies using remote sensing techniques to identify potential climate change refugia. The Committee also had noted that other techniques should be used to complement remote sensing, and had welcomed the offer of the United Kingdom to lead informal discussions on the issue during the intersessional period.

(145) The Committee also had thanked the Russian Federation for its work in outlining the value of monitoring programmes, particularly of Antarctic wildlife, in areas with existing or proposed management plans, in order to gather scientific evidence that would inform decisions about management plans. While the Committee had reiterated the importance of long-term monitoring of biological values both for the detection of long-term change and to confirm that the values to be protected are still relevant, it had not reached a consensus on the proposal of the Russian Federation regarding environmental monitoring related to protected areas. The Committee welcomed the Russian Federation's offer to lead informal intersessional discussions on this subject.

(146) The Committee had agreed that the work undertaken by the Russian Federation to generate classifications of major landscape types on the basis of environmental parameters provided useful data. The Committee also had noted that the work was complementary to the Environmental Domains Analysis adopted under Resolution 3 (2008), the Antarctic Conservation Biogeographic Regions adopted under Resolution 6 (2012), and previous work by Australia, New Zealand and SCAR.

(147) Belgium had highlighted potential threats to the conservation of terrestrial microbial ecosystems in Antarctica, and to future scientific research on these ecosystems through material prepared jointly with SCAR, South Africa and the United Kingdom. While some Members had noted the importance of work to protect microbial habitats, others had raised questions, including:

the difficulty of controlling the transportation of microbial organisms; the definition of "pristine area" as applied to micro-organisms in Antarctica; the possibility of establishing prohibited areas; and the current lack of decontamination methods.

(148) Belgium had reminded the ATCM that it was willing to lead an informal electronic discussion on the impacts of the human footprint in Antarctica and the long-term conservation and study of terrestrial and microbial habitats. Belgium had invited all interested Parties to participate in the discussion.

(149) The United Kingdom and Spain had presented information on Parties' information exchange practices associated with visits to ASPAs, which found that Parties had interpreted and implemented the protected area legislation in different ways. Spain and the UK had concluded that ASPA visitation data were likely to be of limited use for informing general and ASPA-specific environmental management practices without full and consistent disclosure by Parties. Several Members had expressed their concern and had recommended full and comprehensive information sharing to enable more coordinated and effective management of activities within ASPAs.

(150) Ecuador and Spain had reported on the recovery of moss communities on the tracks of Barrientos Island, and had indicated their intention to pursue additional monitoring on the central and coastal paths of the island.

Conservation of Antarctic Flora and Fauna (CEP Agenda Item 10)

Quarantine and non-native species

(151) The Chair advised that the Committee had endorsed the recommendations presented by Germany on the issue of biosecurity measures to prevent the transfer and introduction of non-native soil organisms. The Committee had agreed to take the work forward, under the leadership of Germany, via an open and informal working group, and had noted the readiness of SCAR, IAATO and ASOC to contribute to this work.

Other Annex II matters

(152) COMNAP had presented a review of the potential environmental impacts of hydroponics of the national Antarctic progammes of Australia, New Zealand and the United States, and the risk-based management measures in place.

Environmental Monitoring and Reporting (CEP Agenda Item 11)

(153) The Chair informed that Belgium and SCAR had presented the renewed international Antarctic Biodiversity Portal, *www.biodiversity.aq*, built on the legacy of the SCAR Marine Biodiversity Information Network and the Antarctic Biodiversity Information Facility. SCAR had demonstrated how the Portal provided access to both marine and terrestrial Antarctic biodiversity data.

(154) While the Committee had noted the initiative and acknowledged its great value, several members had raised questions related to: the interaction with the Antarctic Environmental portal; funding (both long-term and private); mapping; its relationship with other databases; and the Committee's involvement with the portal.

(155) New Zealand had congratulated Belgium and SCAR on the development of the biodiversity database. New Zealand had cited the work of the United Kingdom on emperor penguins as an example of the importance of the database, and had indicated New Zealand's willingness to work with Belgium to ensure complementarity with the Antarctic Environments Portal.

(156) SCAR had also presented its "Antarctic and Southern Ocean Science Horizon Scan" in order to identify the most important scientific questions that should be addressed by research in and from the southern polar region over the next two decades.

(157) The Republic of Korea and Germany had reported on a workshop about environmental monitoring on King George Island, which had taken place in Seoul, Korea, in April 2013.

(158) ASOC had presented an analysis on the management implications of tourist behaviour, which examined aspects of Antarctic tourist behaviour in the context of current tourism trends. ASOC had called for Parties to take a strategic approach to tourism regulation and management rather than focusing on regulating specific tourist behaviour primarily through site-specific guidelines.

Inspection Reports (CEP Agenda Item 12)

(159) The Chair informed that the Committee had considered three inspection reports:

- A joint inspection by Germany and South Africa of Troll, Halley VI, Princess Elisabeth and Maitri Stations, which recorded no direct contraventions of the Antarctic Treaty or the Environmental

Protocol, although environmental protection measures varied from station to station. The inspection team's environmental recommendations included: replacing ageing incinerators and removing non-functional items, improving prevention of and response to oil spills, monitoring and disposal of treated waste water, implementing measures to prevent the introduction of non-native species, and certifying that necessary permits had been obtained. The team also felt that future inspection teams should draw from past inspection reports as reference points.

- A joint inspection by the United Kingdom, the Netherlands and Spain at 12 permanent stations, three unoccupied stations, three Historic Sites, four cruise ships, one yacht and one wreck site, which recorded no major contraventions of the Antarctic Treaty or Environment Protocol. The inspection team's environmental recommendations included: that new developments and activities should be preceded by an EIA, and that common facilities and services, such as fuel storage, power generation, water production, accommodation, and waste management should be shared by stations where possible to reduce the cumulative impacts of their activities.

- A joint inspection by the Russian Federation and the United States at Maitri, Zhongshan, Bharati, Syowa, Princess Elisabeth, and Troll Stations, which found all stations to be well organised and generally compliant with the Antarctic Treaty and its Environmental Protocol. Recommended improvements included ensuring that station personnel understood the Protocol Annex 1 regarding EIA, and that national Antarctic programmes considered undertaking environmental monitoring of the potential impacts of stations' activities as part of their scientific programmes.

(160) Uruguay and Argentina had recommended that Consultative Parties inform the Secretariat, in addition to notification through diplomatic channels, when they assign Observers to carry out Inspections. It had further recommended that the Secretariat included this information in its database, to be available in Parties' pre-season information exchanges.

(161) Italy and France also had presented responses to the joint inspection by the Russian Federation and the United States in January 2012 at Concordia and Mario Zucchelli Stations.

(162) The ATCM highlighted the importance of inspections under the Environmental Protocol and the Treaty, particularly given the number of environmental recommendations that arose from inspections. The United Kingdom suggested that the ATCM review current and past recommendations from inspection reports to identify consistent issues and possible new tools to address them, and indicated that it would review recommendations in this light with interested Parties over the next year to identify a possible way forward.

General Matters (CEP Agenda Item 13)

(163) The Chair informed that SCAR had urged all Parties to continue to contribute data to the International Bathymetric Chart of the Southern Ocean (IBCSO).

(164) Colombia had described its development of new organisations for supporting its work in Antarctica and had stated that it would soon be able to ratify the Environmental Protocol.

(165) Turkey had explained its growing interest and activities in the Antarctic arena, and had outlined its intention of establishing an Antarctic station in due course.

(166) Portugal had stressed the importance of education and outreach as a potential issue for discussion at the CEP XVII. Portugal had been supported by several other Members, and Brazil had announced its aim to carry on these activities in the next CEP/ATCM in Brasilia and establish a platform for other countries in the coming years. The priority of the Education and Outreach issue had been accordingly elevated in the CEP Five-Year Work Plan.

Election of Officers (CEP Agenda Item 14)

(167) The Committee had elected Dr Polly Penhale from the United States as Vice-chair and had congratulated her on her appointment to the role.

(168) The Committee had warmly thanked Ms Verónica Vallejos from Chile for her term in serving as Vice-chair.

Preparation for CEP XVII (CEP Agenda Item 15)

(169) The Committee had adopted the provisional agenda for CEP XVII contained in Appendix 1 to the CEP's report.

(170) The ATCM thanked Dr Frenot for his excellent chairmanship, and thanked the outgoing Vice-chair Ms Verónica Vallejos for her term in office. The ATCM also acknowledged the achievement of the Committee, in providing consistently sound management advice. The CEP Chair stressed the importance of the CEP having five days to conduct its work.

Item 9:Liability: Implementation of Decision 4 (2010)

(171) The United Kingdom presented IP 8 *Annex VI of the Protocol on Environmental Protection to the Antarctic Treaty: United Kingdom's Implementing Legislation*, regarding the United Kingdom's recently finalised Antarctic Act 2013. The United Kingdom indicated that it had therefore approved all current Recommendations and Measures adopted under Article IX.

(172) Norway presented IP 85 *Norway's Implementing Legislation: Annex VI of the Protocol on Environmental Protection to the Antarctic Treaty and Measure 4 (2004)*, which notified Parties of the measures Norway had taken to implement both Annex VI to the Protocol and Measure 4 (2004), effective 26 April 2013, and of the availability of an unofficial translated version of the Regulations.

(173) Parties provided updated information on the status of their ratification of Annex VI of the Protocol. As of May 2013, nine Consultative Parties (Finland, Italy, Peru, Poland, New Zealand, Russian Federation, Spain, Sweden, and the United Kingdom) had ratified the Annex. Australia and the Netherlands reported that the necessary legislative measures to ratify the Annex had passed Parliament. Consultative Parties confirmed that they were committed to ratifying Annex VI, and attributed any delays in ratification to resource constraints and/or certain implementation challenges. The Meeting invited Consultative Parties that have adopted legislative measures to ratify the Annex to share those measures with other Parties through the ATCM Forum.

(174) On behalf of the CEP, WP 27 *Repair or Remediation of Environment Damage: Report of the CEP intersessional contact group* was introduced. The Meeting thanked the CEP for providing this advice on repair and remediation of environmental damage in the Antarctic Treaty area, requested through Decision 4 (2010). The Meeting agreed to consider the advice as contained in WP 27 at the next ATCM. The Meeting requested the Executive Secretary to present this Working Paper as a Secretariat Paper for consideration by the next ATCM.

Item 10: Safety and Operations in Antarctica, including Search and Rescue

Special Working Group on Search and Rescue

(175) In accordance with Resolution 8 (2012), and informed by intersessional consultations led by the United States, a Special Working Group convened to discuss means of improving search and rescue (SAR) coordination in Antarctica. The Meeting acknowledged the existing SAR arrangements in the Antarctic region, including Rescue Coordination Centres (RCCs) operated by five Parties and the value of the 2008 and 2009 COMNAP workshops on the issue.

(176) The United States introduced WP 25 *Proposed Agenda for the Special Working Group on Search and Rescue,* and thanked Parties, observers and experts for their contributions during the intersessional work.

(177) The special working group adopted the agenda suggested by the United States, as amended by Chile, so that item III.2 of the agenda was as follows: "Further cooperation among ATCPs and with Antarctic RCCs". Following discussion of the status and reporting requirements of the special working group, the chair concluded that the report would be adopted by the Special Working Group and shared with the Operations Working Group.

Current Issues

(178) COMNAP introduced WP 17 *SAR-WG Update on actions resulting from the two COMNAP SAR workshops, "Towards Improved Search and Rescue Coordination and Response in the Antarctic"*. The paper, in accordance with Resolution 8 (2012), provided an overview of updates since COMNAP convened two SAR operational workshops, in August 2008 in Valparaiso/ Viña del Mar and in November 2009 in Buenos Aires.

(179) COMNAP noted that the issue of safety had been under discussion since ATCM I. In 2006 COMNAP began discussions with SAR authorities that confirmed opportunities for greater collaboration. This led to two COMNAP SAR Workshops, in 2008 in Viña del Mar, Chile and in 2009 in Buenos Aires, Argentina. The updates in WP 17 confirm there has been excellent progress in coordination between NAPs, between NAPs and RCCs, and between the RCCs themselves. The paper also noted COMNAP tools including the ATOM, AFIM, SPRS and the AINMRS.

(180) The paper proposed a recommendation for the Special Working Group to consider for COMNAP to endeavour to convene SAR workshops on a regular basis.

(181) New Zealand noted that COMNAP workshops helped consolidate NAP-RCC relationships and fostered improvements in operational procedures. New Zealand noted that shared experiences and improved information on telecommunications and ship reporting had been particularly helpful in the Ross Sea area. Parties highlighted the value of previous workshops and welcomed COMNAP's intention to hold SAR workshops every three years. Following a recommendation from Chile, COMNAP indicated that CCAMLR could be invited to future workshops.

(182) Argentina and Chile stated that the use of the term "overlapping" in WP 17 was not appropriate and requested that the area in question be referred to as an area of collaboration. COMNAP agreed.

(183) Norway emphasised the importance of the four COMNAP products noted in WP 17, both for use today and for future development. Norway further noted the value of SAR tabletop exercises. France highlighted the importance of links between all vessels and the relevant RCC, noting that the IMO's long-range identification and tracking (LRIT) system is another critical SAR tool. IAATO added that COMNAP's Accident, Incident and Near Miss Reports are especially important.

(184) COMNAP noted the contribution of Parties and experts to the success of its workshops. COMNAP added that the 2009 workshop included tabletop exercises, as would future workshops, following Norway's recommendation. COMNAP also noted the value of participating in the SAR tabletop exercise conducted at IAATO's Annual Meeting.

(185) New Zealand presented IP 14 *Search and Rescue Incidents in the Ross Sea Region (2004-2013)*, which outlined 18 SAR incidents within New Zealand's SAR region. These events contributed to the development of New Zealand's response procedures and the strong relationship between the Rescue Coordination Centre New Zealand (RCCNZ), Antarctica New Zealand, and the United States Antarctic Programme (USAP).

(186) The United States presented IP 23 *Summary of International SAR Activities Associated with an Aircraft Incident in the Queen Alexandra Range, Antarctica*, which outlined the activation of the Joint Antarctic Search and Rescue Team operated by the United States and New Zealand in response to the tragic January 2013 crash of a Twin Otter aircraft. The effective

coordination of the United States, New Zealand and Italy was credited largely to the personal contacts and cooperative exchanges facilitated by annual interaction at COMNAP. Italy reiterated the importance of direct communication and common guidelines in SAR incidents.

(187) Australia presented IP 50 *Cooperation between Australia's search and rescue and Antarctic agencies on SAR coordination*, which described the memorandum of understanding on Australia's search and rescue coordination, and delineated the responsibilities for the Australian Search and Rescue Region between the Australian Maritime Safety Authority and the Australian Antarctic Division. It also provided operational procedures to facilitate effective search and rescue coordination. These responsibilities are delivered through Australia's Rescue Coordination Centre (RCC Australia).

(188) Chile presented IP 89 *Support Provided by the Fildes Bay Maritime Station in Emergency Situations in the Antarctic Peninsula Year 2012*, which outlined the station's response to four vessel incidents in the Antarctic Peninsula area. Chile presented IP 90 *Fire and Sinking of Fishing Vessel "Kai Xin"*, regarding the April 2013 rescue of 97 crewmembers of a Chinese flagged fishing vessel, which sank despite rescue efforts. While Chile took action to avoid the dispersal of some quantities of fuel and to retrieve some floating debris, it noted that the environmental impacts had not yet been determined. China thanked Chile for coordinating the rescue of the vessel's crew and said that the lessons learned on communication procedures demonstrated that there was a need for standardised communication procedures between RCC, NAPs, ship owners and others.

(189) New Zealand presented WP 34 *Lessons Learned from Search and Rescue Incidents in the Ross Sea Region*, which outlined best practices from New Zealand's experience in coordinating SAR response, including maintaining close relationships with responsible national programmes, non-government operators, fishing vessels and IAATO. New Zealand also noted the value of developing and sharing clear principles and procedures between the RCCs and national programmes within each SAR region.

(190) Australia presented IP 81 *SAR coordination case study – helicopter incident in Australia's search and rescue region, October 2012*, which shared the results of the debrief on the SAR response to the October 2010 crash of a French AS350 helicopter on a flight from *L'Astrolabe* to Dumont D'Urville, within the Australian Search and Rescue Region. Australia pointed out that the Memorandum of Understanding between the Australian Maritime

Safety Authority (AMSA) and the Australian Antarctic Division (AAD) proved very effective in responding to this incident. Australia highlighted the importance of its agreement with the Rescue Coordination Centre New Zealand (RCCNZ), which further facilitated cooperation with the U.S. Antarctic Program. Australia noted the challenges of handling media across many time zones, the importance of using GPS-enabled devices, which are more accurate and current, and the importance of regularly updating information on NAP activities, resources, and safety equipment.

(191) France thanked Australia for its support in this incident and concurred that direct contact between RCCs and vessel operators ensures a continuous flow of position information to the RCC.

(192) The United States commented that, in practice, its programme did not use the official delineation between the Australia and the New Zealand rescue coordination areas to determine which centre to coordinate with for land-based SAR, and that most activities based out of McMurdo Station were coordinated with New Zealand. The United States noted that each national programme was responsible for SAR coverage for its own activities and that its working relationship with both the New Zealand and Australian RCCs fully supports this approach. The United States highlighted that RCCs can provide important assistance to national Antarctic programmes which allow them to focus on operations and response, including dealing with the media and handling the aftermath of the rescue operation (as outlined in IP 81).

(193) The United States introduced WP 52 *Proposed Development of Regional SAR Standard Operating Procedures*, and WP 53 *Global Search and Rescue (SAR) System: Impacts of New Technologies*, which recognised the value of existing SAR procedures and discussed possibilities for developing standard procedures that might improve SAR coordination and cooperation. The United States presented the International Aeronautical and Maritime Search and Rescue Manual (IAMSAR) action card as an example of a convenient guide to clarify basic SAR information, terminology and procedures to be used by all RCCs, Antarctic stations and private operators. The United States noted that a common guide could be particularly useful for new personnel or operators, or during a particularly complex or rare event. As each SAR incident is unique, shared information can help speeding SAR response.

(194) The United States noted the implications of two types of technology supporting SAR efforts. As mentioned in WP 53, it is important to recognise that purchasing personal locator beacon (PLB) does not mean this beacon is connected to an RCC. It is therefore important that owners register beacons

and understand how the alerting system works, specifically, as IP 81 notes, how to use communications systems in series. Additionally, private operators must ensure their procedures fit RCC processes.

(195) Argentina observed that the IMO IAMSAR Manual had very clear procedures for vessel-related SAR, which vessel captains must follow. Argentina supported the development of SAR procedures through the IMO and ICAO in the Antarctic region.

(196) Chile agreed with Argentina and the United States about the need to discuss concerns about 'SPOT' beacons, which some operators were using in the Antarctic Peninsula area. Chile reported that it contacts commercial providers to ensure its MRCC is listed as a contact point.

(197) IAATO advised the Meeting that some private expeditioners prefer SEND or SPOT devices because they were rechargeable, were trackable online, and allowed two-way communication. However, some were unaware of the limitations of this technology, including sporadic signal delays due to limited satellite coverage and the lack of a ground receiving station in Antarctica. IAATO requests that private expeditioners provide detailed information about beacon types and reporting details. IAATO members also have memoranda of understanding on SAR coordination with other non-government operators.

(198) Australia noted that 406 MHz devices were widely used in Australia, where 270,000 beacons were registered. Australia responded to approximately 1,700 406 MHz beacon incidents annually, which highlighted the importance of accurate registration information, with 35 per cent being PLBs.

(199) Norway, South Africa and the Netherlands reiterated the importance of proper registration of PLBs and ensuring adequate public awareness. Accurate information is essential to respond to SAR incidents and assist in determining if an actual SAR incident existed. Norway added that Parties had the responsibility of warning private/commercial expeditioners with PLBs in Antarctica of the limitations of these systems. Norway and the Netherlands also highlighted the value of inland SAR coordination in Antarctica.

(200) In response to the suggestion of the United Kingdom for improved awareness and information exchange on new commercial technologies, COMNAP agreed it would include this topic in future SAR workshops. This proposal was supported by Norway and the United States. The United Kingdom suggested that it would be useful for commercial suppliers to meet national Antarctic programme operators and MRCC representatives to discuss the

issue of communication and proposed the use of certain locator beacons could be made a permitting condition on private expeditions.

(201) CCAMLR introduced WP 61 *The Commission for the Conservation of Antarctic Marine Living Marine Resources' Vessel Monitoring System and Its Potential to Contribute to SAR Efforts in the Southern Ocean*, which described its satellite-linked vessel monitoring system (VMS), which since 2004 has enabled the CCAMLR Secretariat to remain in near real-time contact with authorised fishing vessels, either directly or through their flag state monitoring centre. The paper described options for strengthening CCAMLR's capacity to assist SAR efforts by making its VMS data available to RCCs for the purposes of SAR efforts. The Executive Secretary noted the ATCM may want to invite CCAMLR to consider such possibilities.

(202) Many Parties welcomed further discussion in CCAMLR on this topic. They emphasised that vessel location information must be used only for SAR purposes and confidentiality should be preserved through an appropriate protocol. France and Chile further highlighted that VMS was not an alert system as such, but a position reporting system that can help to provide a better maritime surface picture, although it could be useful for RCCs as it might identify neighbouring vessels to provide help in case of incidents. The United Kingdom underlined that RCCs need all available data to respond to a SAR incident.

(203) Norway highlighted that its RCC received information from all fishing vessels in its region and from all Norwegian fishing vessels globally. This data system allows it to locate vessels in the vicinity of an incident situation that might support vessels in distress. Similarly, China referred to its national fisheries monitoring system.

(204) ASOC presented IP 63 *An Antarctic Vessel Traffic Monitoring and Information System*, which reiterated ASOC's call for the ATCM to require all vessels in the Treaty Area to operate Automatic Identification Systems (AIS), to transmit long-range information and tracking (LRIT) data to an appropriate data centre, and to develop an Antarctic vessel traffic monitoring and information system to improve SAR efforts, beginning with the Peninsula area.

(205) IAATO presented IP 93 *IAATO Information Submitted Annually to MRCCs with Antarctic Responsibilities*. This information includes emergency assets available on every ship, but IAATO welcomed any feedback from RCCs to improve the system.

(206) The United States noted the value of vessel monitoring and the importance of RCCs being able to access relevant databases, and highlighted the value of IAATO's comprehensive reporting. The United States noted that the ATCM may not be the right forum to add additional mandatory requirements to vessels already subject to IMO regulation. Argentina and Norway supported this view.

Possible Outcomes and ATCM Action

(207) Germany advised that its ice service has data on ice conditions that could be useful in a SAR incident. The United Kingdom highlighted that the free web-based Polar View product is used by some RCCs and many national programmes. Germany noted the International Ice Portal is another tool, and that higher resolution analysis may be available to assist in emergency situations.

(208) In considering procedures among RCCs, national Antarctic programmes and private operators, the Meeting agreed that it was unnecessary at this time to adopt standardised operating procedures across the Antarctic, provided there was sharing of information and best practices and work towards shared goals. New Zealand agreed, noting that it may be useful to develop shared goals rather than a common set of standard operating procedures. COMNAP offered to serve as a central location to share RCC best practices and exchange information through its password-protected website.

(209) IAATO offered to contribute relevant data to such a COMNAP database. The United States suggested that when information is shared, Parties pay particular attention to the advantages and difficulties of new technologies.

(210) The Parties agreed that it was particularly important to educate new actors, such as tourist or fishing vessels, about the RCCs and their responsibilities.

(211) Argentina presented WP 65 *Resources Available on Antarctic Bases for land support in emergency situations: inclusion in EIES*, highlighting the difficulty of land-based SAR efforts and noting that RCCs often depend on available NAP resources. Argentina recommended that the ATCM encourage Consultative Parties to include a description of resources for emergency land support available on their stations in their annual EIES submission. The United States noted that it supported the sharing of information about capabilities, but that it had reservations about using the EIES due to difficulties with data entry and retrieval. France noted that the suggestion to

use the EIES was already recommended by Resolution 6 (2010). COMNAP agreed with France that Resolution 6 (2010) recommended the entry of this information. IAATO advised that its two land-based members supported each other and would exchange information with others.

(212) The Meeting agreed on the importance of having accurate information on resources available for land-based SAR, which should be readily accessible and updated annually. COMNAP advised that it could post such information on its secure website, noting regional groupings already provided quite detailed lists. Uruguay recommended that the EIES be connected to the COMNAP database to avoid duplication of work. Argentina concluded that the exchange of information was critical, whether through COMNAP or EIES.

(213) IAATO presented IP 100 *Joint Search and Rescue Exercise in Antarctica,* jointly prepared with Chile, which outlined the February 2013 SAR exercise among IAATO, Holland America Line NV, and the Maritime Rescue Coordination Centre of Chile. The exercise was the first live SAR exercise involving a tour operator and MRCC authorities in Antarctica. Lessons learned included the challenges of dealing with communication, handling of media inquiries, and building trust. IAATO suggested further steps, such as developing a protocol outlining operators' emergency response centres, coordinating public relations, improving the vessels database and conducting regular exercises.

(214) Several Parties indicated an interest in being involved in future SAR exercises. South Africa suggested that, if live exercises were not feasible, desktop or tabletop exercises could be conducted.

(215) Chile presented IP 109 *Decimoquinta Versión de la Patrulla Antártica Naval Combinada entre Chile y Argentina,* jointly prepared with Argentina, which described the combined Antarctic naval patrol that had operated for the past 15 years. The naval patrol was equipped and trained for rescue and environmental protection operations and undertook regular exercises.

(216) The Meeting requested that the Secretariat provide a copy of this section of the Report to the IMO and ICAO for information.

Main outcomes and proposed ways forward

(217) The Meeting agreed that the ATCM should continue through the Operations Working Group to remain seized of the topic of SAR operations. SAR

processes developed under the auspices of global regimes such as the IMO and ICAO also had relevance for the Antarctic. Parties should continue to engage with these bodies as appropriate regarding SAR in the Antarctic Treaty area.

(218) The Meeting noted CCAMLR's efforts to address fishing vessel safety issues and recommended that CCAMLR consider making its VMS data available to RCCs for SAR purposes only, with appropriate protections for the confidentiality of relevant data. CCAMLR Members were invited to continue this work to improve fishing vessels safety in the Convention Area.

(219) The Meeting also supported COMNAP to take a number of steps to improve effectiveness of SAR coordination and response, including by: 1) holding SAR workshops every three years, open to representatives of RCCs, national Antarctic programmes, CCAMLR, relevant experts, private operators, and commercial providers of SAR alerting and communication tools; 2) establishing a web portal forum to exchange information between RCCs on shared goals and best practices; and 3) ensuring that the latest information on national Antarctic programme resources for land-based SAR was available to RCCs through the COMNAP website. There was also general support for avoiding duplication of information available elsewhere.

(220) The Meeting noted a high level of interest among Parties responsible for SAR in the Antarctic Treaty area in further SAR exercises.

(221) The Meeting adopted Resolution 4 (2013) *Improved Collaboration on Search and Rescue (SAR) in Antarctica*.

(222) ASOC presented IP 59 *Update to Vessel Incidents in Antarctic Waters*, which reviewed vessel incidents and mapped their location. ASOC recommended: specific requirements for equipment, procedures and training for oil spill response; additional training for all personnel on ships in polar waters; support through the IMO Standards of Training and Watchkeeping (STW) Subcommittee for advanced training in ice-covered waters; and inclusion of fishing vessels in the Polar Code.

(223) ASOC presented IP 66 *Discharge of sewage and grey water from vessels in Antarctic Treaty waters*, which expressed concerns that the current system for the management of sewage and grey water waste streams may not be sufficient to provide adequate protection for Antarctic ecosystems and wildlife. ASOC encouraged members to work to include within the Polar Code a prohibition on the release of untreated sewage or untreated grey water in Antarctic waters.

Item 11: Tourism and Non-Governmental Activities in the Antarctic Treaty Area

Review of Tourism Policies

(224) The Netherlands introduced WP 47 *Report of the Informal Contact Group on the Increasing Diversity of Tourism and other Non-Governmental Activities in Antarctica*, which had been established at ATCM XXXV. The report provided examples of the types of activities that are being conducted in the Antarctic and that illustrate the diversification of tourism and other non-governmental activities in Antarctica. Examples were cited under the categories of: airborne and seaborne modes of transportation; expeditions with the primary purpose of accomplishing a certain (often challenging) route; specific categories of activities, including sports and larger expeditions; overnight accommodation for tourism on land; and other non-governmental activities.

(225) The ICG report also summarised participants' responses on domestic experiences relating to the diversification of tourism activities, encompassing governmental authorisation systems, EIAs, examples of prohibited activities, and international cooperation. The report reflected that several participants in the discussions considered the assessment of cumulative impacts and impacts on wilderness values difficult. The report also gave more insight into the domestic systems and the domestic competences that Parties have to authorise or refuse authorisation for activities. In presenting the report, the Netherlands explained that it was the impression on the basis of the work of the ICG that authorisations are seldom refused, but that six examples of refused authorizations had been identified in the report. The Netherlands acknowledged the constructive input of the Consultative Parties which participated, IAATO and ASOC, and thanked the Secretariat for facilitating the discussions.

(226) The Meeting thanked the Netherlands for leading the intersessional discussions, and explored the challenges further. Parties exchanged views on experiences and challenges with applying domestic law with respect of diverse types of activities, for example: the assessment of cumulative impacts and impacts on Antarctica's wilderness values; criteria used to deny authorisation or prohibit a certain activity; whether to pay special attention to the facilities and activities that support land-based activities; and lessons learnt from tourism management in other parts of the world, for example the Arctic and the sub-Antarctic.

(227) On the question of diversity of activities, New Zealand identified at least 13 activities that did not readily fit in the 22 categories included in the post-visit site report form established by Resolution 6 (2005).

(228) In terms of facilities for land-based activities, New Zealand suggested that in addition to an annual report on tourist numbers and operations, IAATO might report more details about the activities of the logistic providers operating on land. On the matter of land-based and adventure tourism, the United States suggested that tourism and non-governmental camping activities would require more exchange between Parties on managing this activity, including best practices, and that the United States would consult with other Parties intersessionally on this topic. The United States added that although the focus of discussions in this context was on comparing domestic procedures, it was more urgent to determine what aspects of tourism (e.g. land-based tourism, or area management as related to tourism) were problematic and then consider what steps should be taken to respond.

(229) The United States and the United Kingdom highlighted that the level of cooperation between competent authorities was worth further consideration. The Russian Federation recalled its proposal of 2010 which would have required competent authorities to share permit information with the Secretariat, which would then have informed "final destination" port authorities. One benefit of this approach would be to provide the ATCM with a clear image of the scale of non-governmental activities in Antarctica.

(230) The Russian Federation was concerned that some Parties had no legislative basis for a permit-based or certification-based system to minimise the risks of non-governmental activities, and that operators based in non-Treaty Parties were active in the Antarctic region. ASOC agreed that Russia raised an important point and asked for more information about the extent of the problem being raised by Russia.

(231) The Netherlands stated that differences in legal systems may provide differing implementations of the Environmental Protocol, which could lead to proponents "forum shopping" in various jurisdictions. France underlined the implications that this could have for the safety of people, as confirmed by the results of the SAR Working Group at ATCM XXXVI. The United Kingdom said that, in this respect, the activity of competent authority exchange, involving a dialogue between CEP and ATCM colleagues on the application of the Environmental Protocol, could prove useful, because it helped to highlight any gaps or inconsistencies. The United States remarked that Parties should focus on the specific issues such as cumulative impacts

and how to minimise them and not necessarily assume that differing application processing methods and legal systems was a problem.

(232) On land-based activities, the United Kingdom recalled that ATCM XXXV Resolution 9 (2012) had adopted questions that competent authorities might use for governing land-based non-governmental activities. France commented that it was important to closely supervise support activities, and cited the example of a base-jumping expedition that had apparently proceeded without any authorisation. ASOC differentiated between the ability to remove land-based infrastructure and the long term occupation of a site, and suggested that competent authorities should assess tourism activities that involved infrastructure ashore on the proposed duration of site occupation over a long term period, as opposed to merely a season in which land-based infrastructure is assembled.

(233) On the issue of challenges relating to the assessment of cumulative impacts, Argentina reminded the Meeting of previous ATCM discussions, including an ICG which developed guidelines to assess cumulative impacts. Argentina suggested that future work on this issue could review the implementation of such guidelines in relation to the cumulative impact. The Netherlands expressed the view that in light of concerns about the cumulative impacts of a diversification of activities and impacts on wilderness values, there is a tendency to consider impacts of individual activities acceptable, while over time the impacts on certain Antarctic values, such as wilderness values, are likely to be significant. The United States noted that effectively regulating, assessing and monitoring the cumulative impacts of tourism was challenging and complex and required policy development within the ATCM. New Zealand suggested that a minor change to the Summarized Report function of the EIES, highlighted in WP 33, would give Parties the ability to better analyse patterns of behaviour at specific sites of interest. The CEP's advice on Recommendation 3 of its 2012 tourism study on site sensitivity methodology would also be crucial to addressing cumulative impacts.

(234) With respect to criteria to deny authorisation for proposed activities, some Parties provided additional examples of proposed activities that were denied authorisation. Several other Parties commented that their competent authorities took an interactive approach to permitting. This included ongoing consultation with potential applicants about environmental and safety considerations, which deterred some applications and improved the standards of others.

(235) However, the need for more prescriptive measures was also discussed. The Netherlands remarked that in some cases more guidance from the ATCM would support the Parties to say "no" to activities that would be considered contrary to the purpose and principles of the Protocol. This was supported by several Parties who remarked that specific domestic laws enabled their competent authorities to take a precautionary approach and deny authorisations to applicants whose activities were associated with a high level of risk, including examples of adventure tourism. Norway commented that, according to its domestic legislation, activities in Antarctica should be executed in a safe and self-sufficient manner. New Zealand noted that there had been examples in the 2010/11 and 2011/12 seasons of private expeditions which were not prepared to operate safely and with insurance, and they had avoided communication with competent authorities rather than be denied authorisation for these reasons.

(236) IAATO noted that its members, who worked with various competent authorities, were aware of the differing approaches taken from country to country, and that it encouraged good dialogue between competent authorities and operators in advance. IAATO also noted the value of its bylaw objective that tourism activities would have no more than a minor or transitory impact and, recalling the comments on land-based activities, referred to its previous submissions on land-based tourism, including IP 84 (ATCM XXXI) and IP 101 (ATCM XXXII).

(237) In sharing lessons from other parts of the world, Norway commented that lessons could be learnt from its experiences of tourism regulation in Svalbard. In the past season, Norway had observed a diversification in tourism in the Arctic, and a tendency towards more adventure tourism. Norwegian policy was to interact with tour operators and notify them of its very strict regulations. New Zealand noted that the management regime in the New Zealand sub-Antarctic islands was comparable to those Antarctic Specially Protected Areas which allowed some tourist activity, and this highlighted the value of area management as a governance tool.

(238) The Meeting welcomed Norway's proposal to facilitate intersessional preparations for a discussion on experiences and challenges identified by competent authorities with regard to diverse types of tourism and non-governmental activities next year.

(239) ASOC presented IP 67 *Management implications of tourist behaviour*, which examined aspects of Antarctic tourist behaviour in the context of current tourism trends, and discussed the implications for regulation and management.

ASOC stated that research on tourist behaviour identified concerns regarding possible environmental impacts resulting from diversification, expansion, potential cumulative impacts and non-compliance. ASOC recommended that Parties should approach tourism regulation and management from a strategic perspective, rather than focusing on regulating specific tourist behaviour primarily through site-specific guidelines. It further stated that behavioural guidelines would usefully complement, but not substitute for, strategic approaches to regulate and manage tourism, including EIAs, site monitoring, and a range of specially managed and protected areas designed to ensure that tourism is concentrated, diverted or dispersed as required.

Supervision and Management of Tourism

(240) New Zealand introduced WP 33 *Report of the Intersessional Contact Group on Information Exchange and the Environmental Aspects and Impacts of Tourism*, which summarised the outcome of discussions between Australia, France, Japan, New Zealand, the United States, the Treaty Secretariat, IAATO, and the WMO. The group identified options for improving the specificity of information exchanged on the subject through modifications to the EIES and post-visit report forms, and proposed key topics for further discussion.

(241) The group recommended amending the exchange of information requirements set out in Resolution 6 (2001) by including the "type of activity" in Non-Governmental Expeditions – Ship-based Operations, and a list of tourism activities from which Parties could select one or more when reporting on activities.

(242) The Meeting discussed the best ways in which to achieve effective data submission and management of tourism, including a number of possible amendments to EIES requirements for the reporting of tourism activities. In doing so, it agreed on the need to avoid duplication of work and to align EIES requirements with data already submitted by operators via post-visit reports.

(243) On specific EIES amendments, several Parties noted the value of providing a list of tourism activities from which to select one or more when reporting on activities. They commented, however, that it would be useful to leave an open field in which activities not already included in the list could be recorded. The Republic of Korea commented that it considered the exchange of information on tourism activities to be of great importance, and encouraged

communication between the ATCM and international organisations dealing with tourism and the environment such as United Nations Educational, Scientific and Cultural Organization (UNESCO). The United States remarked that it would be useful to incorporate information on the date, time of day and number of visitors to a given site in order to relate this to the breeding chronology of birds and seals at that site.

(244) IAATO expressed its willingness to continue to assist the ATCM, by sharing lessons learned from its collection and analysis of data submitted in post-visit reports, and by sharing additional data with Parties. It suggested that Parties might wish to utilise IAATO's data following a third party quality assessment, so that its competent authorities could focus their time and energy on collecting data from non-IAATO sources.

(245) The Meeting agreed to review the list of tourism activities included in post-visit report forms at ATCM XXXVII and consider consolidating or adding other activities identified by the ATCM. The Meeting also asked the Secretariat to report to ATCM XXXVII on its work to develop the following capabilities in the EIES within existing budgetary baselines:

a) a drop down menu of activities in the EIES to correspond with that in post-visit report forms;

b) a tool to search all reported activities within known geographical coordinates in the Summarized Report section of the EIES;

c) a tool to indicate when expeditions receive authorization from more than one Party; and

d) a search of all annual information at one site over a number of years in the Summarized Report section of the EIES.

(246) The Meeting asked the Secretariat to give a presentation to ATCM XXXVII on ATCM information exchange requirements and the functioning of the EIES, including a particular focus on the changes made in Decision 6 (2013) and its work on the search capabilities noted in the paragraph above, without increasing existing budgetary baselines.

(247) The Meeting agreed that it would be important to discuss ways of improving use of the EIES by Parties, and agreed to discuss this matter further at ATCM XXXVII.

(248) New Zealand presented IP 13 *Antarctic Treaty System Information Exchange Requirements for Tourism and Non-Governmental Activities*, which provided an overview of key ATCM Decisions and Resolutions made in

relation to information exchange, with a particular focus on tourism and non-governmental activities.

(249) The Meeting adopted Decision 6 (2013) *Information Exchange on Tourism and Non-Governmental Activities*.

(250) The United States presented IP 20 *Antarctic Site Inventory: 1994-2013*, which provided an update on the findings of the Antarctic Site Inventory through February 2013. The Inventory had collected biological data and site-descriptive information in the Antarctic Peninsula since 1994. The United States further noted that the outcomes of this work could inform recommendations arising from the CEP Tourism Study, particularly with respect to Recommendations 3 on site sensitivity analysis and 6 on tourism trends.

(251) The Meeting thanked the United States and acknowledged Oceanites Inc. for its high quality and pioneering work in long-term monitoring. It noted that the Antarctic Site Inventory was an important primary source of information both regarding CEP Tourism Study recommendations and for developing site guidelines, and more generally for developing a better understanding of environmental changes, including potential tourism impacts.

(252) While expressing its appreciation of the Antarctic Site Inventory, the Netherlands pointed out that IP 20 focused very much on which sites were visited and how often. The Netherlands suggested that the reporting should be focused more on the content and the outcomes of the monitoring work and how this could guide management actions. In commending Oceanites Inc. for its ongoing monitoring, ASOC mentioned that, if possible, it would be useful to analyse and extract information on the impacts of tourism on each site as distinct from other human impacts and natural variability changes.

(253) Argentina presented IP 88 *Areas of tourist interest in the Antarctic Peninsula and Orcadas del Sur Islands (South Orkney Islands) region. 2012/2013 Austral summer season*. The paper reported the distribution of tourist visits to the region according to the voyage plans presented by tour operators that operated through the port of Ushuaia in the 2012/13 season.

(254) IAATO presented IP 97 *Report on IAATO Operator Use of Antarctic Peninsula Landing Sites and ATCM Visitor Site Guidelines, 2012-13 Season*. IAATO noted that the increase in voyages from 2012/13 had a consequential increase in the number of landings; and that while the number of landing sites used had increased by two from the previous year, both were anchorages that were newly recorded from yacht operators. IAATO emphasised that 19 of the 20 most used sites were already covered by visitor site guidelines.

(255) In response to a query, IAATO clarified that it remained interested in the use of the sites covered by guidelines by non-IAATO operators, and other Antarctic activities by non-IAATO operators.

(256) IAATO also referred to IP 98, which provided the *IAATO Guidelines for Short Overnight Stays*. Following the discussions at ATCM XXXV, IAATO's Field Operations Committee had updated IAATO's guidelines. IAATO's guidelines for multi-night coastal camping had also been adopted, and would be tested in the coming season. IAATO advised that in 2012/13, 16 sites saw a total of 61 short overnight stays. The highest passenger-to-guide ratio was 15 passengers to one guide; the average overall was approximately 9:1.

(257) The Meeting thanked IAATO for responding to questions raised previously by Parties, which enabled a clearer understanding of camping activities taking place, as well as their management. In response to a query from ASOC, IAATO confirmed that there had indeed been an increase in camping activities in recent years, and clarified that tourists go ashore after dinner and return to their ships before breakfast.

(258) IAATO presented IP 102 *Barrientos Island Footpath Erosion*, which highlighted issues identified by field staff during IAATO's internal investigation into erosion in moss beds on Barrientos Island in the Aitcho Islands. IAATO was very concerned about the issue and outlined a number of steps they were taking to address the issue.

(259) Ecuador thanked Spain for collaborating on the study of footpath erosion as described in WP 55 *Recovery of moss communities on the tracks of Barrientos Island and tourism management proposal*. Ecuador underlined the importance of monitoring the recovery of the ecosystem of Barrientos Island, an important penguin nesting site, and thanked IAATO for its openness and support throughout the process.

Overview of Antarctic Tourism in the 2012/13 season

(260) IAATO presented IP 103 *IAATO Overview of Antarctic Tourism: 2012-13 season and preliminary estimates for 2013-14 season*. IAATO calculated that the total number of tourists during the 2012/13 season had increased by 29.4 per cent from the previous season, making the total number comparable to the 2009/10 and 2010/11 seasons. IAATO identified several factors leading to this increase, including a mild resurgence of voyages by cruise-only vessels carrying more than 500 passengers from five to seven, accounting for 9,070

passengers, which is approximately 5,000 more than the previous year. Estimations of tourist activity for the 2013-14 season were also provided.

(261) Several Parties thanked IAATO for its detailed reporting and its responsiveness to Parties' concerns. In response to a question from France regarding the flag State of tourist vessels, IAATO explained that tourists came from over 100 different countries and that, while there was no specific policy to encourage vessels to operate under the flag of a Treaty Party, all of its member operators were based in Treaty Parties. It also expressed its intention to be "growth ready" and for tourist activities to have no more than minor and transitory impacts on the Antarctic environment.

(262) In response to a query by ASOC, IAATO confirmed that numbers of air/ cruise visits had doubled the past year and that this was due to a variety of factors, including the increase of "time constrained" visitors that prefer faster travel by air. IAATO explained that this led to new management challenges, such as the decrease in time to educate clients, but also highlighted a good practice by a long-serving Chilean operator in setting up pre-departure briefings for fly-in visitors.

(263) Argentina presented IP 86 *Report on Antarctic tourist flows and cruise ships operating in Ushuaia during the 2012/2013 Austral summer season* and IP 87, *Antarctic tourism through Ushuaia. Comparison of the last five Austral summer seasons*. Argentina has systematically been recording the movement of passengers and vessels that visit Antarctica through the port of Ushuaia since the 2008/2009 season, and providing the ATCM with that information. These papers give details on all tourism voyages from Ushuaia including information on passengers, crew, expedition staff, tour operators, vessel owners and the registration of ships. While particularly focusing on those vessels that call at Ushuaia, the papers provide an alternative and/or complementary source of information to other currently available sources, in order to assist in the assessment of tourist activities in the Antarctic.

(264) The United States, New Zealand and IAATO thanked Argentina for this helpful data, which complemented the information provided by IAATO. In response to a query by New Zealand on guide-to-passenger ratios as presented in IP 86, Argentina explained that the data came from the statements of ships in port where field staff may be recorded on either the crew or passenger list, and so were not readily identifiable.

Yacht and other Activities in the Antarctic

(265) The United Kingdom and IAATO presented IP 54 *Data Collection and Reporting on Yachting Activity in Antarctica in 2012-2013*, which provided an update on data presented in 2012, with the aim of continuing to share information with other Parties about yachts operating in the Antarctic. The data was derived from landings reported by the British team at Port Lockroy, Antarctic Peninsula, and supplemented by additional sightings recorded by IAATO members in the Treaty area. The United Kingdom and IAATO particularly encouraged Parties to share information on any non-IAATO yachts they authorise, in order to increase the level of coordination between Parties about yacht activity in Antarctica. IAATO referred to the positive impact of the outreach campaigns to decrease the number of non-authorised yachts.

(266) The Meeting encouraged Parties to continue to share information on yacht activities in the Treaty area, including for example via the EIES Pre-Season Information facility and via post-visit site reports, in line with Resolution 5 (2005).

(267) Argentina indicated that having this information is useful for drawing attention to the presence of non-authorised yachts in the port of Ushuaia, and that it is interested in contributing to this compilation of information.

(268) ASOC underlined the lack of information on the impact of yacht activity. However, ASOC noted that, according to IP 54, the majority of yachts known to have operated in Antarctica in the 2012/13 season had been authorised whether or not they were IAATO members.

(269) The Russian Federation raised the issue of emergency medical assistance for participants of Antarctic marathons, such as those held on King George Island, and suggested that this required further discussion by the ATCM. It suggested that medical examinations should be a compulsory condition of participation in Antarctic marathons.

(270) In response, IAATO noted that its members were required to follow IAATO guidelines for marathons, which included the requirement to contact national stations in the vicinity of the marathon and cover the issue of medical examinations. IAATO took note of the concerns of the Russian Federation and will report back to the next ATCM on this matter.

Tourism Issues in the Multi-Year Work Plan

(271) Parties discussed how to address the priority issue identified in the multi-year strategic work plan relating to tourism and non-governmental

activities, including: reviewing and assessing the need for additional actions regarding area management and permanent infrastructure related to tourism, issues related to land-based and adventure tourism, and addressing the recommendations of the CEP Tourism Study.

(272) The Meeting agreed to give a particular focus at ATCM XXXVII on one of these areas – issues related to land-based and adventure tourism – as well as to address any initial outcomes arising from the CEP's intersessional work on Recommendations 3 and 6 of the CEP Tourism Study. The Meeting agreed on this more focused approach to ensure a more comprehensive and focused discussion at the next Meeting. To that end, Parties, Observers and Experts were encouraged to prepare working and other papers in relation to these topics. The Meeting also tasked the Secretariat with producing a digest of previous ATCM discussions, as well as Measures and Resolutions, relating to land-based and adventure tourism.

(273) The Meeting agreed to hold discussions at ATCM XXXVII on further actions to address other elements of the priority issue of tourism in the Multi-year strategic work plan.

Item 12: Inspections under the Antarctic Treaty and the Environment Protocol

(274) Germany introduced WP 4 *Inspection by Germany and South Africa in accordance with Article VII of the Antarctic Treaty and Article 14 of the Protocol on Environmental Protection: January 2013,* jointly prepared with South Africa, which reported on inspections of four stations in Dronning Maud Land, 8–29 January 2013. This was the first inspection by South Africa, while Germany has undertaken two other joint inspections (with France in 1989 and the United Kingdom in 1999). While the inspection team observed no direct contraventions of the Antarctic Treaty or the Environmental Protocol, it noted that the inspected stations implemented the standards of the Antarctic Treaty System to varying degrees. South Africa thanked Germany for its initiative and for enabling South Africa to participate in its first full inspection.

(275) Parties whose stations were inspected thanked South Africa and Germany for their report. India acknowledged the recommendations for improvements and confirmed that it intended to address them. Norway expressed the view that a key benefit of inspection reports is that Parties can learn from one

another and discuss recommendations at a higher level. Belgium indicated its willingness to share information on the use of new technologies at stations. The United Kingdom was pleased to welcome the inspection of Halley VI research station and informed Parties that Halley VI became fully operational in February 2013. The station had recently been accepted by the WMO as one of three Antarctic stations serving as a Global Atmospheric Watch (GAW) Station (more information on the science undertaken at Halley VI and the removal of Halley V was available in IP 37). The United Kingdom noted that the inspection report highlighted the use by British Antarctic Survey of its Accident, Incident, Near Miss and Environment (AINME) reporting system, which has been used as model by COMNAP.

(276) Welcoming the inspection team's recommendations relating to preventing the introduction of non-native species, New Zealand noted the excellent work of SCAR and COMNAP in this area. ASOC also recommended that, consistent with its IP 65 *Black Carbon and other Short-lived Climate Pollutants: Impacts on Antarctica*, there should be assessments of the sources of black carbon in the Antarctic, and for black carbon pollution to be added to the inspection report format for stations and vessels.

(277) The United Kingdom introduced WP 9 *General Recommendations from the Joint Inspections undertaken by the United Kingdom, the Netherlands and Spain under Article VII of the Antarctic Treaty and Article 14 of the Environmental Protocol*, jointly prepared with the Netherlands and Spain. The inspections were undertaken in the Antarctic Peninsula region, 1–14 December 2012, and covered 12 permanent stations, three unoccupied stations, three Historic Sites, four cruise ships, one yacht and one wreck site. The inspection team observed no contravention of the Antarctic Treaty and noted the considerable effort at the stations it inspected to comply with the Environmental Protocol. The United Kingdom directed Parties to IP 38 for detailed information.

(278) The United Kingdom commended Brazil's clean-up and demolition following the fire at Comandante Ferraz station. The United Kingdom noted risks to personnel at some of the smaller stations, especially with respect to diving operations, and noted that not all station personnel appeared to have reviewed safety and emergency procedures for fire protection. A general recommendation arising from the inspection was for stations to complete the Antarctic Treaty Inspection checklist, since completed checklists greatly assisted inspectors with their work. The United Kingdom suggest it would be useful for station inspection checklists to be added to the ATS website so they could be read by inspectors prior to their arrival on station.

(279) The Netherlands and Spain also noted the importance of sharing information on station research in order to reduce costs and enhance cooperation. Spain drew attention to the inspectors' general recommendation that stations regularly inspect fuel containers and their handling to reduce the risk of fires. Spain also noted that at the stations inspected, other than a few wind turbines, there was little evidence of renewable energy sources.

(280) The United States expressed appreciation for the inspection team's recommendations regarding Palmer Station in their reports. In response to the general recommendation on the Antarctic Treaty Inspection checklist, the United States reminded the Meeting that the use of the checklist was desirable, but voluntary. In addition, referring to the long list of inspection team recommendations included in the reports, the United States noted that until recommendations made by inspectors were endorsed by the ATCM, they did not reflect the policy of the ATCM. Argentina thanked the Parties that conducted inspections and noted the usefulness of the particular recommendations. Regarding the general recommendations, it agreed with the United States that the use of the checklist was desirable but voluntary and about the need to further discuss those recommendations. France noted that from the national competent authority point of view, such inspections of private vessels were very beneficial.

(281) The Meeting welcomed the inspection reports noting that the mounting of inspections was challenging and resource intensive and that the Parties involved should be commended for their contribution to this key element of the Treaty and Protocol.

(282) In general discussion of inspections as a tool, the United Kingdom and United States encouraged inspection teams to review past reports. If required, the United States could provide archival documents to the Secretariat for this purpose.

(283) Several Parties and ASOC suggested that the ATCM should review previous inspection teams' recommendations annually to assess progress as a means of improving general operations and environmental management at Antarctic stations. Recognising that this required in-depth discussion, initial views on potential processes for reviewing previous inspection recommendations included: the ATCM could develop an inspections recommendations monitoring list similar to the one used to monitor climate recommendations (the Netherlands); an ATME on inspections could elaborate an approach (the Netherlands); since Article 7 imposed no obligation on Parties to follow up recommendations, the ATCM was the appropriate body (Spain).

Uruguay noted that recommendations from inspectors were reviewed by inspected stations and their governments, and views by the inspected stations were taken into account with regard to any actions in response to the recommendations, and considered Party to Party.

(284) The Meeting noted that all the inspection reports discussed had raised concerns over fuel storage and fuel management at Antarctic stations. Several Parties noted that since COMNAP had considerable expertise in the safe handling of fuel, it might be requested by the Meeting to promote its fuel safety and management guidelines.

(285) Uruguay introduced WP 51 rev.1 *Additional availability of information on lists of Observers of the Consultative Parties through the Antarctic Treaty Secretariat,* jointly prepared with Argentina, which recommended that Consultative Parties inform the Secretariat, in addition to notification through diplomatic channels, when they assign Observers to carry out inspections. It further recommended that the ATS should include this information in its contact database, and make it available to Parties.

(286) Ecuador supported the proposal because it would benefit the preparation of future inspections. While the United Kingdom and Italy believed that it was important to continue to notify Parties through diplomatic channels of the list of observers, both Parties had encountered difficulties with the current system, and therefore would support efforts to improve the exchange of information.

(287) The Meeting adopted Decision 7 (2013) *Additional availability of information on lists of Observers of the Consultative Parties through the Secretariat of the Antarctic Treaty.*

(288) Italy presented IP 16 *Status of the fluid in the EPICA borehole at Concordia Station: an answer to the US / Russian Inspection in 2012*, jointly prepared with France, which responded to concerns raised about the potential leakage of drilling fluid from the European Project for Ice Coring in Antarctica (EPICA) borehole providing information on the nature of the drilling fluid and results of measurements conducted on the hole that confirmed that no leakage had occurred, and therefore none was likely to happen in the future. Noting the high scientific interest, Italy confirmed the intention of both nations to keep the borehole accessible as much as possible in the future. The United States thanked Italy for its paper and indicated that it was satisfied with the analysis. The Russian Federation supported the position of the United States.

(289) Italy presented IP 77 *Italy answer to the US / Russian Inspection at Mario Zucchelli Station in 2012*, which presented the regulatory framework of ministerial laws actually in force, and provided more information on the preventive measures, management procedures and environmental monitoring programmes Italy has in place and on future developments concerning transposition of regulations into domestic law.

(290) The Russian Federation presented IP 45 *Report of Russia – US joint Antarctic Inspection, November 29 – December 6, 2012*, jointly prepared with the United States, which reported the inspection of stations located in the Eastern part of Antarctica in Dronning Maud Land, Princess Elizabeth Land and Enderby Land. The inspection covered Maitri (India), Zhongshan (China), Bharati (India), Syowa (Japan), Princess Elisabeth (Belgium), and Troll (Norway). This represented a broad cross section of different stations, including newly-constructed and long-established, small and large, and stations with various levels of government funding. All were found to be well organised and generally compliant with Parties' obligations under the Antarctic Treaty and its Environmental Protocol.

(291) The Russian Federation reminded the Meeting that these inspections were part of the second inspection phase organised jointly with the United States. The first phase, conducted in January 2012 and reported to the previous ATCM, was also conducted under a memorandum of understanding on cooperation in Antarctica signed by their foreign ministers.

(292) The Russian Federation raised a concern regarding the activities conducted by non-governmental entities at some stations, in particular at Belgium's Princess Elisabeth Station and Norway's Troll Station. The Russian Federation noted that the interrelationship between government and non-government actors at government-owned Antarctic research stations and the emerging forms of commercial activities such as satellite information exchanges and bioprospecting raised significant policy issues. The United States thanked the Russian Federation for hosting the second phase of joint inspections, and stressed the efficiency of the DROMLAN (Dronning Maud Land Air Network) in overcoming logistical challenges.

(293) Norway welcomed the thoroughness of the report, which addressed issues including logistics and operations, environmental matters, emergency response capabilities and science. Norway welcomed the opportunity to discuss new types of activities emerging in Antarctica. India reaffirmed its commitment to implement the recommendations in a phased manner from the next austral summer.

Item 13: Science Issues, Scientific Cooperation and Facilitation

(294) SCAR presented IP 5 *The Southern Ocean Observing System (SOOS) 2012 Report,* which highlighted SOOS achievements in 2012, and planned activities for 2013. SCAR reported that the Scientific Steering Committee meeting held in May 2013 in China detailed development and integration of work plans for the six SOOS science themes.

(295) SCAR presented IP 19 *1st SCAR Antarctic and Southern Ocean Science Horizon Scan,* which described the initiation of an Antarctic and Southern Ocean Science Horizon "Scan". SCAR noted that the scan would identify the top 100 Antarctic research questions to be addressed over the next 20 years.

(296) SCAR presented IP 82 *Advancing technologies for exploring subglacial Antarctic aquatic ecosystems (SAEs)*, which supported the SCAR Lecture to the ATCM and provided further information on technological development and deployment to SAEs in Antarctica. The paper outlined the scientific arguments for future technology development and deployment, assessed the current status and application of available technologies, and discussed what is required technologically and environmentally for the future exploration of SAEs. SCAR also summarised the activities of its Advancing TecHnological and ENvironmental stewardship for subglacial exploration in Antarctica (ATHENA) Expert Group.

(297) SCAR presented IP 83 *The International Bathymetric Chart of the Southern Ocean (IBCSO): First Release*, which was the result of a project initiated in 2006 with the objective of designing and implementing an enhanced digital database of bathymetric data available south of 60°S latitude. In April 2013 IBCSO version 1.0 was released by the Alfred Wegener Institute (AWI), in Germany. The map and data are available at: *http://www.ibcso.org.* SCAR urged all Parties to continue to contribute data to this important database.

(298) Belarus presented IP 56 *On planned activities of the Republic of Belarus in the Antarctic*, which reported on its joint expeditions to the Antarctic with the support of the Russian Federation and outlined the plan for the gradual construction of a Belarusian Antarctic station starting in 2014. Belarus noted that the initial EIA will consider many factors but Belarus anticipates that the impact of the station on the environment will be no more than minor or transitory. Several Parties recalled that environmental issues related to the construction of new stations should be carefully considered by the Parties. According to the Protocol, a detailed EIA should be prepared at the right

level required by Annex I in regard to the expected impacts. Those Parties suggested also that it would be useful even if not formally requested by the current procedures that information related to new stations be submitted as papers under the CEP agenda in order to allow the CEP to provide advice to the ATCM.

(299) Japan presented IP 30 *Japan's Antarctic Research Highlights 2012–13*, which illustrated three topics of research activities carried out by the Japanese Antarctic Research Expedition: the Programme of the Antarctic Syowa MST/IS Radar (PANSY) had started continuous observation of the Antarctic lower and middle atmosphere; a meteorite search that was carried out in collaboration with the Belgian Antarctic Research near the Sør Rondane Mountains had collected 420 meteorites totalling 75 kilograms; and a new observation by a balloon-borne unmanned aerial vehicle at Syowa Station.

(300) COMNAP presented IP 33 *Analysis of National Antarctic Program increased delivery of science*, which gave the results of an analysis recently undertaken by one national Antarctic programme, and served as an example of how to minimise environmental impacts while conducting scientific research.

(301) France presented WP 41 *Enhancing consultations in the use of logistical means to serve science in Antarctica*, jointly authored with Chile, on enhancing consultations over the use of logistics to support science in Antarctica. France noted that this proposal was intended to take forward aspects of the work in the ICG discussions on international cooperation led by Chile, and offered that COMNAP could assist by developing a methodology to further international logistics efforts.

(302) In WP 41, France and Chile proposed that information be collated on: opportunities for international cooperation in the use of Antarctic facilities for science; formal and informal logistical cooperation arrangements between national Antarctic programmes; and the current practices of Parties in providing access to facilities for scientists of other nationalities. A number of Parties expressed their commitment to the goals of WP 41. Others indicated that the goals required further discussion. Parties made reference to a range of major multinational scientific projects currently underway and recently completed, including those undertaken in the marine environment, that helped to achieve similar goals.

(303) Australia welcomed and supported the proposal from France and Chile. It noted that the logistic support of science activities was a very important

area of cooperation between the Parties, and one where the Parties had consistently demonstrated their commitment. Australia looked forward to working with France and other Parties on enhancing cooperation in this area.

(304) The Meeting noted that COMNAP and SCAR actively facilitated discussions on international logistic cooperation in support of scientific objectives, and utilised a range of tools to support and coordinate such cooperation. Several Parties suggested avoiding duplication of COMNAP's expert groups.

(305) COMNAP referred Parties to surveys on international cooperation presented in IP 7 from ATCM XXII and XXX and IP 92 from ATCM XXXI, which reported on collaboration between its members and noted the high level of cooperative arrangements that are in place and that go beyond sharing of Antarctic stations, such as vessel use, logistics arrangements and research exchanges in home institutes. Following the proposal of France, the Meeting welcomed COMNAP's offer to provide the ATCM with an update of IP 92.

(306) The Meeting also noted that the ICG on international cooperation, established by ATCM XXXVI under the leadership of Chile, would provide a forum to review the practices currently in place to advance science and logistics cooperation, and to explore further cooperative opportunities for optimizing logistics support for science and thus minimising the impact on the environment.

(307) France along with interested Parties offered to report on details of the cooperative practices that they have with other national Antarctic programmes, as an example of how such information could be presented and further shared.

(308) Other papers submitted under this agenda item included:

- BP 4 *Scientific & Science-related Collaborations with Other Parties During 2012-2013* (Republic of Korea)
- IP 9 *Principales actividades realizadas en materia antártica por la República Bolivariana de Venezuela 2010-2013* (Venezuela)
- IP 11 *Video divulgativo de las relaciones de cooperación antárticas entre la República Bolivariana de Venezuela y la República de Ecuador* (Venezuela)
- IP 57 *Foundation of Austrian Polar Research Institute (APRI) in April 2013* (Austria)

- IP 71 rev.1 *Romanian Scientific Activities proposed for Cooperation within Larsemann Hills ASMA 6 in East Antarctica – Plan for 2013-2014* (Romania)
- BP 4 *Scientific & Science-related Collaborations with Other Parties During 2012-2013* (Republic of Korea)
- BP 5 *CRIOSFERA 1 - A New Brazilian Initiative for the West Antarctic Ice Sheet* (Brazil)
- BP 6 *The Importance of International Cooperation for Brazilian Scientific Research in Antarctica during summer 2012-2013* (Brazil)
- BP 7 *Scientific Results of Brazilian Research in Admiralty Bay* (Brazil)
- BP 12 *Research at Vernadsky station in pursuance of the State Special-Purpose Research Program in Antarctica for 2011-2020* (Ukraine)
- BP 14 *SCAR Lecture: "Probing for life at its limits: Technologies for the exploring Antarctic subglacial ecosystems"* (SCAR)
- BP 19 *Programa de Cooperación Internacional en la Investigación Antártica Ecuatoriana (verano austral 2012-2013)* (Ecuador)
- BP 23 *Conmemoración del vigésimo quinto aniversario de la primera expedición científica del Perú a la Antártida y Realización de la XXI ANTAR (verano austral 2012-2013)* (Peru).

Item 14: Implications of Climate Change for Management of the Antarctic Treaty Area

(309) SCAR introduced WP 38 *The Antarctic Climate Change and the Environment (ACCE) Report: A Key Update,* which updated the original SCAR Antarctic Climate Change and the Environment (ACCE) report (Turner *et al.,* 2009). It summarised subsequent advances in knowledge concerning how the climates of the Antarctic and Southern Ocean have changed in the past, how they might change in the future, and examined the associated impacts on the marine and terrestrial biota. The original ACCE report is available from: *www.scar.org/publications/occasionals/acce.html.* The United Kingdom, the United States and New Zealand thanked SCAR for this important update which was of great relevance to the continuing work of the ATCM on climate change.

(310) Other papers submitted under this agenda item included:

- IP 34 *Best Practice for Energy Management – Guidance and Recommendations* (COMNAP)
- IP 52 *Ocean Acidification: SCAR Future Plans* (SCAR)
- IP 62 *An Antarctic Climate Change Report Card* (ASOC)
- IP 69 *Update: The Future of the West Antarctic Ice Sheet* (ASOC)
- SP 7 *Actions taken by the CEP and the ATCM on the ATME recommendations on climate change* (Secretariat).

Item 15: Education Issues

(311) Argentina introduced WP 57 *International cooperation in cultural projects in Antarctica*, which highlighted the importance of promoting art and cultural projects, especially those that involve artists from different Parties working in Antarctica. Argentina described a proposal designed to raise awareness amongst the general public of the importance of scientific research and the need to protect the Antarctic, through different artistic forms, with international cooperation as a core concept.

(312) The Meeting welcomed the proposal to promote wider public awareness of Antarctica through the development of art projects about Antarctica. The United States, New Zealand, Ecuador, and Australia informed the Meeting of their successes in running artistic fellowship initiatives, which complemented scientific research in Antarctica by raising the profile of Antarctic science with the general public.

(313) The Meeting adopted Resolution 5 (2013) *International Cooperation in Cultural Projects about Antarctica*.

(314) Other papers submitted under this agenda item included:

- IP 10 *Presentación del libro infantil: "La aventura de un osito polar perdido en la Antártida"* (Venezuela)
- IP 17 *El plan científico antártico argentino: una visión para el mediano plazo* (Argentina)
- BP 18 *III Concurso Intercolegial sobre Temas Antárticos, CITA 2012* (Ecuador)

- BP 22 *Examples of educational and outreach activities of the Belgian scientists, school teachers and associations in 2009-2012* (Belgium).

Item 16: Exchange of Information

(315) New Zealand introduced WP 33, *Report of the Intersessional Contact Group on Information Exchange and the Environmental Aspects and Impacts of Tourism,* commenting on the elements of the ICG's work which were relevant to broader discussions on information exchange requirements and the functioning of the EIES, while noting that the specific recommendations would be discussed in detail under agenda item 11). It also referred to IP 13 *Antarctic Treaty System Information Exchange Requirements for Tourism and Non-Governmental Activities,* which provided an overview of relevant ATCM Decisions and Resolutions.

(316) Several Parties thanked New Zealand for the ICG's work and noted that they would provide more detailed comments on its recommendations in the discussion under agenda item 11. Australia noted that the discussion raised broader questions of what information has been and could be included on the EIES, which could form the basis of a more comprehensive discussion by the ATCM in the future.

(317) France introduced WP 43 *Importance of unique and common geo-referencing of toponymic data in the Electronic Information Exchange System,* which sought an agreement on a common principle for the designation of geographic features in Antarctica using, as far as practicable, existing tools. France recalled the necessity to rely on clear geographic data which are necessary to assess environmental cumulative impacts and to assure the success of search and rescue operations in Antarctica.

(318) The Meeting thanked France for its work on this initiative, noting the potential value of this issue for SAR planning and response. The Russian Federation, the United Kingdom, Chile and the United States acknowledged that harmonisation of coordinates would be beneficial, but noted that this would be a difficult task for the Secretariat. Chile stated that it would support the development of a mechanism in the ATS to facilitate the exchange of information on toponomy.

(319) SCAR advised that it had compiled a Composite Gazetteer for Antarctica of all officially submitted place-names used in Antarctica in all languages, and was working to improve the accuracy of the geographical coordinates

used. The Russian Federation, United States and United Kingdom agreed that any additional work on this issue would benefit from further advice on the outcomes of SCAR's work.

(320) The Meeting agreed on the necessity to pursue further discussions. France indicated that it would continue to consult with interested Parties, as it was concerned that there could be serious consequences if it was not addressed.

(321) Another paper submitted under this agenda item was:

- IP 111 *Management of Antarctic Specially Protected Areas: permitting, visitation and information exchange practices* (United Kingdom and Spain)

Item 17: Biological Prospecting in Antarctica

(322) Belgium introduced WP 48 *Biological prospecting in Antarctica – the need for improved information,* jointly prepared with the Netherlands and Sweden, which proposed a method of improving the informational basis relating to commercial uses of Antarctic genetic and living resources. The proposal included further development of databases and geographically referenced data, and suggested that the exchange of information on this topic between Parties be improved and made more easily accessible through the EIES.

(323) Belgium also presented IP 22 *An Update on Status and Trends in Biological Prospecting in Antarctica and Recent Policy Developments at the International Level,* jointly prepared with the Netherlands, which stated that activity in patenting of uses and applications based on Antarctic genetic and living resources had grown. Belgium noted that international discussions had made progress in analysing the issues related to access to genetic resources in the context of Article 10 of the Nagoya Protocol and in the United Nations Ad Hoc Open-ended Informal Working Group to study issues relating to the conservation and sustainable use of marine biological diversity in areas beyond national jurisdiction. The paper recommended that biological prospecting be included in the Strategic Work Plan.

(324) Some Parties welcomed the analysis, but suggested that, because Parties did not share a common understanding of the definition or implications of biological prospecting, the issue should not be prioritised immediately.

(325) Several Parties highlighted the importance of the discussions held in other forums with regard to bioprospecting and benefit sharing. These Parties

reinforced the need to exchange information with other forums so as to learn from these other processes. Some Parties, however, did not support the need to exchange information with other international forums related to bioprospecting and benefit sharing of Antarctic genetic resources.

(326) Some Parties underlined the importance of reaffirming the role of the ATCM in addressing the issue as it related to the Antarctic, by retaining the item as a strategic priority for the ATCM.

(327) The Meeting considered that the ATCM had already decided that it was the competent body to discuss the matter, and therefore it should attest to other forums that it was active on the subject. The Meeting adopted Resolution 6 (2013) *Biological Prospecting in Antarctica*.

(328) Argentina presented IP 18, *Reporte de las recientes actividades de bioprospección desarrolladas por Argentina durante el período 2011-2012*, which gave its support to increased sharing of information on scientific activities.

(329) ASOC presented IP 64 *Biological prospecting and the Antarctic environment*, which examined biological prospecting from the perspective of its environmental impacts. ASOC was concerned that bioprospecting was currently unregulated, and recommended that Parties should declare any intent to conduct biological prospecting in their submissions to the EIES, identify its potential environmental impacts in EIAs, and monitor the environmental effects of these activities. In addition, ASOC recommended that a suitable mechanism be established to identify harvesting of marine living resources in the Southern Ocean related to biological prospecting.

Item 18:Preparation of the 37th Meeting

a. Date and place

(330) The Meeting welcomed the kind invitation of the Government of Brazil to host ATCM XXXVII in Brasilia tentatively between 12-21st May 2014.

(331) For future planning, the Meeting took note that the following likely timetable of upcoming ATCMs:

- 2015 Bulgaria
- 2016 Chile

b. Invitation of International and Non-Governmental Organisations

(332) In accordance with established practice, the Meeting agreed that the following organisations having scientific or technical interest in Antarctica should be invited to send experts to attend ATCM XXXVII: [the ACAP Secretariat, ASOC, IAATO, IHO, IMO, IOC, the Intergovernmental Panel on Climate Change (IPCC), IUCN, UNEP, WMO and WTO].

c. Preparation of the Agenda for ATCM XXXVII

(333) The Meeting approved the Preliminary Agenda for ATCM XXXVII.

d. Organisation of ATCM XXXVII

(334) Pursuant to Rule 11, the Meeting decided as a preliminary matter to propose the same Working Groups at ATCM XXXVII as at this meeting.

e. The SCAR Lecture

(335) Taking into account the valuable series of lectures given by SCAR at a number of ATCMs, the Meeting decided to invite SCAR to give another lecture on scientific issues relevant to ATCM XXXVII.

Item 19: Any Other Business

(336) With regard to incorrect references to the territorial status of the Malvinas Islands, South Georgias Islands and South Sandwich Islands made in documents, cartography and presentations related with this Antarctic Treaty Consultative Meeting, Argentina rejected any reference to these islands as being a separate entity from its national territory, thus giving them an international status that they do not have and affirm that the Malvinas, South Georgias and South Sandwich Islands and the surrounding maritime areas are an integral part of the Argentine national territory. Furthermore, it rejected the shipping register operated by the alleged British authorities thereof and any other unilateral act undertaken by such colonial authorities, which are not recognised and are rejected by Argentina. The Malvinas, South Georgias and South Sandwich Islands and the surrounding maritime areas are an integral part of the Argentine national territory, are under illegal British occupation and are the subject of a sovereignty dispute between the

Argentine Republic and the United Kingdom of Great Britain and Northern Ireland, recognised by the United Nations.

(337) In response, the United Kingdom stated that it had no doubt about its sovereignty over the Falkland Islands, South Georgia and the South Sandwich Islands and their surrounding maritime areas, as is well known to all delegates. In that regard, the United Kingdom has no doubt about the right of the government of the Falkland Islands to operate a shipping register for UK and Falkland flagged vessels.

(338) Argentina rejected the United Kingdom's statement and reaffirmed its well known legal position.

Item 21: Adoption of the Final Report

(339) The Meeting adopted the Final Report of the 36th Antarctic Treaty Consultative Meeting. The Chair of the Meeting, Ambassador Mark Otte, made closing remarks.

(340) The Meeting was closed on Wednesday, 29 May at 14:00.

2. CEP XVI Report

Report of the Committee for Environmental Protection (CEP XVI)

Brussels, May 20–24, 2013

Item 1: Opening of the Meeting

(1)   The CEP Chair, Dr Yves Frenot (France), opened the meeting on Monday 20 May 2013 and thanked Belgium for arranging and hosting the meeting in Brussels.

(2)   The Committee noted that there were no new Members, and that the CEP comprised 35 Members.

(3)   The Chair summarised the work undertaken during the intersessional period, noting that all the planned work decided at the end of CEP XV had been achieved.

Item 2: Adoption of the Agenda

(4)   The Committee adopted the following agenda and confirmed the allocation of 46 Working Papers (WP), 57 Information Papers (IP), 5 Secretariat Papers (SP) and 7 Background Papers (BP) to the agenda items:

1.   Opening of the Meeting
2.   Adoption of the Agenda
3.   Strategic Discussions on the Future Work of the CEP
4.   Operation of the CEP
5.   Cooperation with other Organisations
6.   Repair and Remediation of Environment Damage
7.   Climate Change Implications for the Environment: Strategic approach
8.   Environmental Impact Assessment (EIA)
       a. Draft Comprehensive Environmental Evaluations
       b. Other EIA Matters

9. Area Protection and Management Plans

    a. Management Plans

    b. Historic Sites and Monuments

    c. Site Guidelines

    d. Human Footprint and Wilderness Values

    e. Marine Spatial Protection and Management

    f. Other Annex V Matters

10. Conservation of Antarctic Flora and Fauna

    a. Quarantine and Non-Native Species

    b. Specially Protected Species

    c. Other Annex II Matters

11. Environmental Monitoring and Reporting

12. Inspection Reports

13. General Matters

14. Election of Officers

15. Preparation for Next Meeting

16. Adoption of the Report

17. Closing of the Meeting

Item 3: Strategic Discussions on the Future Work of the CEP

(5)   New Zealand introduced WP 28 *Antarctic Environments Portal: Progress Report*, jointly prepared with Australia, Belgium, Norway and SCAR. It provided an update on the development of the Antarctic Environments Portal since introducing the concept at CEP XV, and addressed issues raised during informal intersessional discussions. It noted that the project aims to facilitate the link between Antarctic science and the CEP by providing ready access to independent, science based information on priority issues. New Zealand demonstrated a prototype of the Portal to the Committee, and outlined the next steps for the project.

(6)   Many Members and ASOC welcomed the progress that had been made and highlighted the value of the Portal as a tool which would provide ready access to scientific syntheses and high quality information to inform decision-making and support the effective implementation of the Protocol, and

thanked New Zealand for its efforts. They endorsed SCAR's demonstrated history of providing independent scientific advice.

(7)   Some Members also raised concerns and comments relating to: governance, decision-making, the composition of the Portal's editorial board, geographic and linguistic representation, assurance that data would be independent and apolitical, status of information published on the Portal, and long-term funding.

(8)   Argentina introduced WP 58 *Contributions to discussions on access to environment-related information and its management within the framework of the Antarctic Treaty System*. The paper emphasised the need for official initiatives concerning information management, such as the Antarctic Environments Portal, to be based on the ATS principle of consensus, particularly with respect to information selection, management and editing, and that it should be in the four Treaty languages. Argentina reiterated other Members' concerns regarding the possible dependence on private funding to support the Portal.

(9)   SCAR set out the system it uses to ensure that the science presented is up to date, accurate, expert, peer reviewed and independent. Stressing that science is constantly changing SCAR underlined the expectation that whatever was uploaded to the Portal would need to be subject to regular review.

(10)   Australia noted that the Portal was envisaged as a tool to assist decision making, and was not intended to make decisions on behalf of the Committee or Parties. It further noted that a possible future scenario was that the Portal would be managed by the Parties, and in that scenario it would be important to address questions regarding content management and funding. For the moment, the Portal project is being managed and resourced by New Zealand, and all interested Members are invited to participate in the ongoing work.

(11)   In order to better explain the aim of WP 58, Argentina made clear that its purpose was mainly to stress the need to set criteria, agreed by consensus, for the selection, editing and general management of information, and was not related to any evaluation of scientific research undertaken by SCAR.

(12)   New Zealand welcomed all the comments and reiterated that the Portal was not intended as an official CEP activity, that it was not intended as a decision-making or political tool, and encouraged feedback and input from interested parties to support the further development of the project.

(13) The Committee welcomed the progress to develop an Antarctic Environments Portal, and encouraged further development on this initiative, asking that an update on progress be given at CEP XVII. Members agreed to provide comments and feedback to the proponents to support the Portal's further development.

(14) ASOC presented IP 61 *Human impacts in the Arctic and Antarctic: Key findings relevant to the ATCM and CEP*, which reported on two international collaborative projects launched at the International Polar Year Oslo Science Conference, 2010, exploring human impacts and future scenarios for the Antarctic environment. It noted that the majority of the reports had concluded that existing environmental management practices and the current system of governance are insufficient today and in the future to meet environmental challenges and the obligations of the Environmental Protocol. ASOC urged Members to undertake full implementation of the Protocol, support global environmental initiatives and to guide their commitment to protect Antarctica with long-term vision and political will.

(15) The Committee thanked ASOC for its contribution. Belgium noted that rapid changes were taking place at a large scale, and that ASOC's paper could be useful in assisting further discussions.

(16) The Russian Federation urged Members to improve the level of implementation of Antarctic regulations in their domestic law, since it was difficult to advance other substantive issues without this. The United Kingdom endorsed the Russian Federation's concerns about effective domestic regulations, and confirmed that it had recently implemented the Liability Annex to the Environmental Protocol.

(17) Argentina highlighted that during its more than 50 years of existence, the Antarctic Treaty had attained important achievements in environmental management and reached high levels of compliance, while preserving its principle of consensus.

(18) The United Kingdom pointed out that the Committee and several of its Members were already engaged in many of the issues that ASOC had raised. While more could be done, the United Kingdom emphasised the importance of taking precautionary approaches, which was a well-embedded practice in the CEP.

(19) The Committee revised and updated its Five-Year Work Plan (WP 7). (Appendix 1)

Item 4: Operation of the CEP

(20)   No papers were submitted under this agenda item.

Item 5: Cooperation with other Organisations

(21)   SCAR presented IP 4 *The Scientific Committee on Antarctic Research (SCAR) Annual Report for 2012/13*. In 2012 SCAR approved five new Scientific Research Projects : a) State of the Antarctic Ecosystem; b) Antarctic Thresholds – Ecosystem Resilience and Adaptation; c) Antarctic Climate Change in the 21st Century; d) Past Antarctic Ice Sheet Dynamics; and e) Solid Earth Response and Cryosphere Evolution. SCAR also introduced IP 19 *1st SCAR Antarctic and Southern Ocean Science Horizon Scan*, on an activity which would assemble the SCAR community and leading Antarctic experts to identify the most important scientific questions to be addressed over the next two decades. Further information was available in BP 20 *The Scientific Committee on Antarctic Research (SCAR) Selected Science Highlights for 2012/13* (SCAR).

(22)   Norway noted the useful approach SCAR was taking in focusing their new research programmes towards management needs and underscored the importance of disseminating results from these programmes in an appropriate manner. In response, SCAR noted that findings from their ongoing research activities would be presented at various events in 2013 onwards and later to the ATCM. The next major SCAR event was the SCAR Biology Symposium in Spain, 15–19 July 2013. Information on SCAR Meetings is available at *www.scar.org/events*.

(23)   Chile presented IP 105 *Report of the CEP Observer to the XXXII SCAR Delegates' Meeting*, providing a brief summary of the meeting, which is presented by SCAR in more detail elsewhere. It stated that the information generated by SCAR is relevant to decision-making processes in the CEP. Therefore, it is expected that the collaboration between the two organisations would be maintained in the future, on the same good terms as at present.

(24)   The SC-CAMLR Observer presented IP 6 *Report by the SC-CAMLR Observer to the Sixteenth Meeting of the Committee for Environmental Protection*. The paper focused on the five issues of common interest to the CEP and SC-CAMLR as identified in 2009 at their joint workshop: a) Climate change and the Antarctic marine environment; b) Biodiversity and non-native species in the Antarctic marine environment; c) Antarctic species

requiring special protection; d) Spatial marine management and protected areas; and e) Ecosystem and environmental monitoring. CCAMLR informed the Committee that the full report of the meeting was available from the CCAMLR website at: *www.ccamlr.org/en/meetings/27*.

(25) Based on catch data reported to the CCAMLR Secretariat, krill fishing had occurred in ASPA 153 (Eastern Dallmann Bay) in 2010 and in 2012, although harvesting was not a permitted activity under the management plan. It was suggested that this was attributable to a lack of awareness of the designated protected area among those responsible for fishing vessels. The Scientific Committee therefore endorsed the need to improve communication, including by linking the management plans of relevant ASPAs and ASMAs to CCAMLR conservation measures, so that management plans could be readily accessed by fishing vessels (CCAMLR Conservation Measure 91-02 (2013). The Scientific Committee also encouraged Members to be proactive in passing on information to fishing vessels under their jurisdiction.

(26) ASOC expressed concern about harvesting events in areas specially managed or protected by the ATCM, expressing the view that protected areas should remain effectively protected.

(27) Belgium presented IP 15 *CCAMLR MPA Technical Workshop*, which summarised the outcomes of a workshop held in Brussels in September 2012. The workshop concluded that there was a need for further systematic conservation planning work towards the development of MPAs. The workshop also recommended that further work should be submitted for consideration by CCAMLR's Scientific Committee and its Working Groups, and that those Members with considerable research history and scientific expertise in the individual domains could take the lead on such projects. The full report of the technical workshop (SC-CAMLR-XXXI/BG/16) was available at *www.ccamlr.org*. The SC-CAMLR Observer informed the CEP that the results of this workshop meant that analyses were now underway in all of the 9 planning domains in the CCAMLR Convention area.

(28) The Committee nominated Dr. Polly Penhale (United States) as CEP Observer to SC-CAMLR-IM-I (Bremerhaven, Germany, 11-13 July 2013) and to SC-CAMLR-XXXII (Hobart, Australia, 23 October – 01 November, 2013).

(29) SCAR presented IP 52 *Ocean Acidification: SCAR Future Plans.* The SCAR Ocean Acidification Action Group intends to: a) define our present

understanding of the contemporary rates and future scenarios of Southern Ocean acidification; b) document ecosystem and organism responses from experimental perturbations and geological records; c) identify present and planned observational and experimental strategies; d) identify gaps in our understanding of the rates and regionality of ocean acidification; and e) define strategies for future Southern Ocean acidification research. The final report would be launched at the SCAR Open Science Conference in August 2014 *(www.scar2014.com)*.

(30) Belgium introduced WP 49 *The Antarctic Treaty System role regarding the development of a comprehensive system of Marine Protected Areas*, jointly prepared with Germany and the Netherlands. It highlighted the responsibility of Parties for environmental protection and the conservation of marine living resources, referring to relevant international commitments. It further noted the work towards the establishment of a representative system of marine protected areas (MPAs) in the CCAMLR Convention area, and referred to IP 15 *CCAMLR MPA Technical Workshop*, which summarised the outcomes of a workshop, held in Brussels in September 2012. Belgium invited the Committee to acknowledge this work and encourage its prompt and positive conclusion.

(31) Several Members acknowledged CCAMLR's efforts to establish a representative system of MPAs in the CCAMLR area, noting that the ATCM and CCAMLR shared a commitment to the protection of the Antarctic environment and associated ecosystems.

(32) Japan reminded Members that CCAMLR had not yet reached a consensus on the details of a system of MPAs, and cautioned against pre-empting discussions to be held at the CCAMLR Special Meeting in Bremerhaven in July 2013.

(33) China and the Russian Federation emphasised that CCAMLR was responsible for considering issues not addressed by the ATCM, such as the rational use of marine living resources, and it was important for the CEP to remain within its mandate in any discussions of this.

(34) Australia agreed that the Parties have an important role in delivering comprehensive environmental protection in the Antarctic Treaty area, including in the marine environment. It recalled the 2009 CEP/SC-CAMLR workshop, which concluded that issues relating to spatial protection and management of Antarctic marine biodiversity were generally best led by

SC-CAMLR at this time, and considered that it was appropriate for the CEP to express its support for the ongoing work within CCAMLR.

(35) South Africa reported that it had declared its first offshore Marine Protected Area around the Prince Edward Islands in the Southern Ocean.

(36) ASOC encouraged the Committee's support for this joint proposal, noting that the CEP had taken similar action with respect to CCAMLR initiatives on Illegal, Unreported and Unregulated Fishing and the development of a Catch Documentation Scheme.

(37) Belgium stated that the intention of its proposal was not to prejudge CCAMLR's Special Meeting or to stimulate discussion on the details of MPAs within the CEP, but rather to acknowledge and show support for CCAMLR's work on MPAs.

(38) Belgium, Germany and Netherlands reminded the meeting of the responsibility of Parties to environmental protection and the conservation of marine living resources under the international agreements that comprise the Antarctic Treaty system and the connection between both. WP 49 noted the work carried out so far towards the establishment of a representative system of marine protected areas (MPAs) in the CCAMLR Convention area, and acknowledged this work and encouraged its prompt and positive conclusion. The CEP welcomed CCAMLR's on-going work on MPAs but in the time available was unable to reach agreement on the text of a resolution.

(39) COMNAP presented IP 3 *The Annual Report for 2012 of the Council of Managers of National Antarctic Programs (COMNAP)*, noting that COMNAP would mark its 25th anniversary with the publication of the book "A story of Antarctic Cooperation: 25 Years of the Council of Managers of National Antarctic Programs". Highlights from the past year included its Sustainable Solutions to Antarctic Challenges Symposium and Innovations in Antarctic Communications Workshop in July 2012; its review of ATCM Recommendations on Operational Matters; its offer of a full COMNAP Antarctic Research Fellowship to Dr Ursula Rack and a half Fellowship to Mr Jenson George; and the development of tools and products such as Accident, Incident and Near-Miss Reporting (AINMR), a Ship Position Reporting System (SPRS), Antarctic Flight Information Manual (AFIM) and an Antarctic Telecommunications Operators Manual (ATOM).

(40) Other papers presented under this Agenda item:

- BP 20 *The Scientific Committee on Antarctic Research (SCAR) Selected Science Highlights for 2012/13* (SCAR)

Item 6: Repair and Remediation of Environment Damage

(41) New Zealand introduced WP 27 *Repair or Remediation of Environmental Damage: Report of the CEP intersessional contact group*, noting that this work had been undertaken in response to a request from the ATCM through Decision 4 (2010). The paper summarised the findings and recommendations of discussions on the practicality of repair or remediation of Antarctic environmental damage, in order to assist the ATCM in considering the resumption of negotiations on further rules relating to liability. The report listed a series of issues that would need to be taken into account when considering repair and remediation activities.

(42) Members thanked New Zealand and congratulated the ICG for the importance and utility of the document.

(43) The Netherlands felt that the precautionary principle should be observed especially as it would not always be possible to repair the damage.

(44) Russia stated that it would not always be possible to disentangle naturally occurring damage from human impacts, and that repair and remediation would need to be site specific as there was no evidence that a single approach would fit all cases.

(45) ASOC stressed that the objectives for repair and remediation should reflect the objectives and provisions of the Environmental Protocol.

(46) Chile reported that, through its Ministry of the Environment, it had developed a methodological guide for the management of soils with potential presence of pollutants. Although it is presented only in Spanish, the guide could be of interest to the Committee, and it would be willing to provide a copy to the Secretariat. The guide considers that a human and an environmental risk assessment must be developed to determine if a place is contaminated, and using a cost/benefit analysis, the decision to remediate the area or not is taken depending on the risk.

(47) The Committee endorsed the findings and recommendations of the ICG and agreed to forward the full WP to the ATCM for its consideration. Members of the New Zealand (Dr Neil Gilbert) and Australian (Dr. Martin Riddle) delegations were nominated to introduce the paper and respond to any questions.

CEP Advice to the ATCM

(48) In response to the request from the ATCM contained in Decision 4 (2010) on the matter of repair or remediation of environmental damage, the Committee endorsed the findings and recommendations contained in WP 27 as its initial advice and stood ready to respond to any further requests from the ATCM.

(49) Australia introduced WP 32 *An Antarctic Clean-Up Manual: report of informal intersessional discussion,* (Australia and the United Kingdom) which reported on the results of informal intersessional discussions to review and revise the draft Antarctic Clean-Up Manual considered by CEP XV. The contributions of several Members and one Observer during the intersessional period had been incorporated into the revised manual.

(50) Australia and the United Kingdom recommended that the Committee:

- considers and endorses the Clean-Up Manual annexed to the draft Resolution presented at Attachment A to WP 32;

- encourages Members and Observers to develop practical guidelines and supporting resources for inclusion in the manual in the future; and

- agrees to convey the attached draft Resolution and annexed Clean-Up Manual to the ATCM for approval.

(51) Australia and the United Kingdom also suggested that, if the Committee agreed with these recommendations, the Secretariat be asked to make the Clean-Up Manual available on the ATS website.

(52) The Committee thanked Australia and the United Kingdom, endorsed the recommendations presented in WP 32, and agreed that the Clean-Up Manual should be made available from the ATS website.

CEP Advice to the ATCM

(53) The Committee endorsed the Antarctic Clean-up Manual, presented in WP 32. It recommended that the ATCM approve the Manual by way of a Resolution.

(54) France introduced WP 42 *The need to take into account the dismantling costs of stations in Comprehensive Environmental Evaluations (CEE) relating to their construction,* prepared jointly with Italy, which illustrated a theoretical cost assessment of deconstructing Concordia Station. The full removal of all the material and components of this station would require approximately 12 years, practically the time needed to construct it, and costs some 25 million euros, almost 75% of its construction costs. France and Italy suggested that a detailed estimate of decommissioning costs should be taken into account when a CEE is prepared for the construction of a new station.

(55) The Committee welcomed the analysis and emphasised the importance of correctly calculating the costs of establishing stations by adopting a life-cycle approach and including the costs of decommissioning. Members drew attention to the possibilities of sharing stations and reopening closed stations rather than opening new ones, and suggested that the potential to decommission a station should be given serious consideration in the design phase. Thanking the authors, ASOC drew attention to the need to examine the environmetal impacts of the whole life cycle of a station prior to construction.

(56) In response to a suggestion from Australia the Committee also agreed to schedule a review of the *Guidelines for Environmental Impact Assessment in Antarctica* in the five-year work plan, including to further consider the recommendations contained in WP 42. It further underlined the role of COMNAP as a centre of expertise with regard to assessing the costs of decommissioning stations. China agreed to the importance of being aware of the cost and duration of dismantling a station in the CEE but pointed out the difficulty of providing a concrete number for the cost of an activity that will happen many years later, and questioned the substantive value of such a number.

(57) France presented IP 36 *Clean-up of the construction site of unused airstrip "Piste du Lion", Terre Adélie, Antarctica,* which reported on the clean-up of the site in fulfillment of the commitments under Annex III, Article 2, of the Environmental Protocol. The work involved three partners: the Terres Australes et Antarctiques Françaises, the French Polar Institute (IPEV)

and a private sponsor, Veolia Environnement France. The total weight of waste was about 300 tons and the total cost of the operation was 305,000 Euro. France noted that the clean-up served as an example of a successful remediation measure, which demonstrated that such an operation is feasible with relatively limited human and financial resources. France, however, also called attention to two major operational constraints: a) this type of work is extremely weather dependent; and b) the limiting factor of the size of the national programme's vessel to remove the waste.

(58) ASOC presented IP 68 *Reuse of a site after remediation. A case study from Cape Evans, Ross Island,* which illustrated how the reuse of a remediated site could undo the effects of remediation, using the case study of a small site at Cape Evans, Ross Island. This paper also made a number of suggestions relevant to assessing cumulative impacts, assessing the effectiveness of remediation, and managing remediated sites.

(59) While thanking ASOC for its presentation, New Zealand noted that a study of the potential recoverability of the site had been undertaken by New Zealand scientists prior to an approval being granted for a multi-season camp site to be established.

(60) Brazil presented IP 70 *Environmental Damage Repair: Disassembling of Ferraz Station, Admiralty Bay, Antarctica,* which outlined the plan for the disassembling of Comandante Ferraz station, which was destroyed by a fire in 2012. An Environmental Management Plan had been elaborated and implemented with the support of several specialised institutions, under the coordination of the Brazilian Ministry of the Environment. Brazil estimated the cost of this operation, excluding human resources, at 20 million USD and referred to IP 78 and IP 95 for more information. It also screened a video to present the Committee with more information on the operations conducted during the 2012-2013 summer.

Item 7: Climate Change Implications for the Environment: Strategic Approach

(61) SCAR introduced WP 38 *The Antarctic Climate Change and the Environment (ACCE) Report: A Key Update*, which represented a major update of the original SCAR Antarctic Climate Change and the Environment (ACCE) report. It summarised subsequent advances in knowledge concerning how the climates of the Antarctic and Southern Ocean had changed, how it might change in the future, and the associated impacts on marine and terrestrial biota.

(62) Members thanked SCAR for its ongoing efforts to update the CEP on the state of knowledge on climate change, and noted SCAR's recommendation to engage with other organisations such as the IPCC and UNFCCC. The Committee noted the pace of change reported in the update and recalled that the ATME on climate change had recommended that '*the CEP consider developing a climate change response work programme*' (Recommendation 19). The United States highlighted the quality of SCAR's peer-reviewed report which had already been published in a scientific journal. Norway remarked that the outcomes of the report might feed well into the Antarctic Environments Portal.

(63) The Russian Federation raised questions regarding the absence in the report of the methods used to calculate sea level rise, and why the contributions of natural phenomena as well as anthropogenic causes to climate change had not been considered. In response, SCAR noted that its report was a review paper and that the individual publications mentioned within it would contain detailed information on specific methodologies.

(64) Colombia, Malaysia and Turkey mentioned that scientists from their national Antarctic programmes were currently conducting research or planning to conduct research with relevance to climate change in Antarctica.

(65) In endorsing SCAR's recommendations, the Committee decided to:

    i. Encourage SCAR and Treaty Parties to engage with the United Nations Framework Convention on Climate Change (UNFCCC) and the Intergovernmental Panel on Climate Change (IPCC) to ensure that climate change issues in the Antarctic and Southern Ocean are fully considered and that both bodies are made aware of the outcomes of the ACCE report and associated updates;

    ii. Focus efforts on implementing the recommendations outlined by the Antarctic Treaty Meeting of Experts (ATME) on climate change and implications for Antarctic management and governance (2010); and

    iii. Convey the key points of the ACCE updated report more broadly to ensure awareness of the critical role of Antarctica and the Southern Ocean in the climate system and the importance of associated impacts on the region.

(66) The Committee decided to establish an ICG on climate change with the following Terms of Reference:

1. Review progress made against ATME recommendations 18 to 29 drawing on SP 8 (CEP XV) and discussions at recent CEP meetings (cf: CEP report 2010 paras 351 - 386);

2. Consider these ATME recommendations in light of recent papers and in particular SCAR's 2013 major update report in order to identify additional actions that may need to be addressed by the CEP;

3. Consider how the recommendations might be addressed by developing a prioritised climate change response work programme;

4. Provide an initial report to CEP XVII.

(67) The Committee agreed that Rachel Clarke of the United Kingdom *(racl@ bas.ac.uk)* and Birgit Njåstad of Norway *(njaastad@npolar.no)* would jointly coordinate and lead the ICG.

(68) The Secretariat introduced SP 7 *Actions taken by the CEP and the ATCM on the ATME recommendations on Climate Change*.

(69) COMNAP presented IP 32 *Cost/energy Analysis of National Antarctic Program Transportation*, which described the results of a case study of transport systems used by the Alfred Wegener Institute (AWI) in Germany. It focused on the analysis of air and sea transportation of people and cargo, using both financial and energy data, as one example of what National Antarctic programmes were doing to reduce costs and fuel use. COMNAP stated that it would share this analysis at its upcoming Annual General Meeting (AGM) in July 2013.

(70) Italy noted that the results of COMNAP's study were similar to the results of a study it had conducted, with respect to the construction of a runway adjacent to Mario Zucchelli Station. The Russian Federation suggested that, while it supported efforts to reduce costs and emissions, future reports should also take into account the risks of national programmes becoming dependent on logistics provided by vessels of other countries. COMNAP agreed to discuss these risks at their AGM.

(71) COMNAP presented IP 34 *Best Practice for Energy Management – Guidance and Recommendations*, which described national programmes' progress on voluntary implementation of the guidance and recommendations, noting that 24 out of 28 countries participated in the survey.

(72)   ASOC presented three interrelated Information Papers on climate change: IP 62, *An Antarctic Climate Change Report Card*, which described the recent findings of climate change research in the areas of environmental and ecosystem changes and indicated the action that Parties could undertake to mitigate their impacts; IP 65 *Black Carbon and other Short-lived Climate Pollutants: Impacts on Antarctica*, which described the potential importance to global warming of black carbon and other short-lived climate pollutants (SLCPs) and suggested that the analysis of the extent of SLCP emissions and impacts on Antarctica, especially from local sources, should be a priority; and IP 69 *Update: The Future of the West Antarctic Ice Sheet*, which updated information reviewed at the 2010 ATME on Climate Change and concluded that: the mass loss of Antarctic ice sheets was accelerating, widespread glacier retreat might have been set in motion, and changes to West Antarctic Ice Sheets were related to anthropogenic climate change. ASOC emphasised the importance of making Antarctica a carbon neutral continent and the role of the Parties in actively promoting the inclusion of Antarctic science in the global climate change dialogue.

(73)   Sweden recalled that ASOC has presented many good and relevant arguments for including work on Short-Lived Climate Pollutants (SLCPs) in the Strategic Work Plan. Sweden has been active in promoting actions to reduce emissions of SLCPs and participated in setting up the Climate and Clean Air Coalition to reduce emissions of SLCPs. Sweden supported the ideas presented by ASOC, and noted that it is important to look further into the impacts of SLCP in the Antarctic and also pay attention to local sources. It also suggested that it could be of interest to SCAR to look further into climate change and short-lived climate pollutants. The Committee noted that these issues could also be considered in the ICG on climate change.

(74)   IAATO presented IP 101 *IAATO Climate Change Working Group: Report of Progress*, which outlined the progress of IAATO's Climate Change Working Group, including additional efforts to raise awareness of climate change in Antarctica through the development of a publicly available powerpoint presentation, and a list of ways in which IAATO Member Operators manage their emissions. IAATO thanked SCAR for their review and comments of the presentation and expressed its commitment to continue to report on this work to the CEP. Other papers presented under this Agenda item were:

   •   BP 21 *Antarctic climate change and the environment: an update* (SCAR)

Item 8: Environmental Impact Assessment

6a) Draft Comprehensive Environmental Evaluations

(75) No papers were submitted under this Agenda item.

6b) Other EIA matters

(76) The Russian Federation introduced WP 24 *Approaches to study of the water layer of sub glacial lakes in the Antarctic*, which explained the techniques used for drilling into subglacial lakes in Antarctica and the challenges that arise. The paper detailed the reasons for selecting the "kerosene-Freon mixture" instead of the "hot water" method to drill into Lake Vostok. The Russian Federation stated that it was impossible for the kerosene-Freon mixture to penetrate the water and impact the lake's ecosystem, whereas it had some concerns over the potential impacts of hot water on microbial life.

(77) In response to a request from Belgium for clarification on whether a permanently frozen layer of water would remain at the end of the borehole to prevent the penetration of kerosene-Freon into Lake Vostok, the Russian Federation confirmed that a standard operating procedure was to increase the thickness of the ice cork in the borehole after research work is concluded. In response to France's request about an earlier SCAR suggestion to insert a silicon fluid interlayer at the end of the borehole to protect the water in the lake, which the Russian Federation had previously considered a possibility, the Russian Federation said that it had decided against this technique, due to concerns over potential cross-contamination between the fluids.

(78) The Russian Federation presented IP 42 *To* [sic] *discovery of unknown bacteria in Lake Vostok,* which reported the discovery of an unknown group of bacteria (phylotype) in the first small sample of Lake Vostok water to be laboratory tested. The bacteria could not be identified according to existing data bases and classification methods. Acknowledging the concern about this issue, the Russian Federation stressed that the unknown microbial organism posed no threat to humankind, since it could not survive outside of its natural environment.

(79) The Russian Federation also presented IP 49 *Results of studies of subglacial lake Vostok and drilling operations in deep ice borehole of Vostok station*

in the season 2012-2013, which gave a technical overview of the drilling activities. France thanked the Russian Federation for sharing this information and encouraged it to continue to provide updates on the work to the Committee in the future.

(80) China presented IP 21 *Initial Environmental Evaluation for the Construction of Inland Summer Camp, Princess Elizabeth Land, Antarctica*. The main purposes of the camp are to provide logistics support and emergency rescue protection, and to support local observation. China stated that the camp construction would have no more than minor or transitory environmental impact.

(81) In thanking China for the information, France, Belgium and Germany raised questions on the environmental impacts of the new camp, estimated by China as no more than minor and transitory despite the size, number of people hosted and planned duration of activity. In response to a question from Germany about why it had not undertaken a comprehensive environmental evaluation, China stated that an IEE is sufficient for the construction of a summer camp. China replied to the question from France and Belgium that it was willing to exchange opinions in respect of the results of its IEE, and that it would present further information on the camp construction progress at CEP XVII. Spain recalled Article 8 of the Environmental Protocol and stated that China appeared to have acted in accordance with its obligations.

(82) The Republic of Korea presented IP 24 *Progress of the Jang Bogo Station during the first construction season 2012/13*, which described the Jang Bogo Station construction activities. Construction started in December 2012 and would continue for two Antarctic summer seasons. Korea reported on material transportation, construction activities, waste management and environmental monitoring, and outlined its response to incidents. An informative presentation on the station construction was shown to delegates. Korea also referred to IP 25 *Mitigation measures of environmental impacts caused by Jang Bogo construction during 2012/13 season*, which explained the implementation of the mitigation measures proposed in the CEE presented in 2011 and suggested by the Parties, to reduce the impacts of construction.

(83) Korea informed the Committee of the steps it had taken to apply environmental management standards in the construction of its new base: by conducting a comprehensive Environmental Impact Assessment (EIA),

training all expedition members in environmental education, and strictly applying the Non-Native Species Manual. Further, all necessary measures had been taken to address a fuel spill accident which had occurred during bad weather at the construction site, according to the "Jang Bogo Station Fuel Spill Prevention and Contingency Plan". The majority of the total of 1,100 litres of spilled diesel was recovered and the site would continue to be monitored.

(84) Korea expressed its gratitude to the Russian Federation, Italy, the United States, Australia and New Zealand, for sharing their knowledge and experience and for providing logistical and technical support.

(85) Several Members congratulated the Republic of Korea for its comprehensive report on such a challenging project, and the Committee expressed its sincere condolences regarding the fatal accident that occurred last season during the station's construction. India was very impressed by the way the whole structure was pre-constructed in Korea. In response to a query from New Zealand regarding external environmental audits, the Republic of Korea said that it would provide further information to CEP XVII.

(86) The Russian Federation presented IP 48 *Permit for the Activity of the Russian Antarctic Expedition in 2013-17*, on the legal requirements and permits granted by the Russian Federation for the declared activities. The paper described in particular the IEE prepared for the activities planned for the five-year period from 1 January 2013 to 31 December 2017. The IEE covers all types of activity planned for the Russian Antarctic Expedition for the next five years. Separate IEEs will be prepared for any new types of activity not covered by the present IEE.

(87) Brazil presented IP 58 *Terms of Reference of the Initial Environmental Evaluation (IEE): Reconstruction and Operation of Ferraz Station (Admiralty Bay, Antarctica)*, which provided an update on Brazilian efforts to rebuild its station, including the selection of a conceptual project for the station construction from amongst the 74 entrants in an international competition and preparations for a forthcoming IEE. Brazil pointed out that, during the 2012-2013 summer, representatives of Brazilian environmental institutions collected samples for environmental analysis. The results of such analysis will guide the implementation of the Remediation Plan for the area, which will be implemented prior to reconstruction works.

(88) The Committee commended Brazil for its transparency and willingness to cooperate with other partners, and for upholding high environmental standards. Several Members acknowledged that the recovery of Comandante Ferraz station was consistent with necessary requirements under the Environmental Protocol.

(89) India presented IP 75 *Initial Environmental Evaluation for Establishment of the Ground Station for Earth Observation Satellites at the Indian Research Station Bharati at Larsemann Hills, East Antarctica,* noting that this ground station would help with communication and remote sensing, and would contribute to global research on climate change.

(90) Italy presented IP 80 *First steps towards the realization of a gravel runway near Mario Zucchelli Station: initial considerations and possible benefits for the Terra Nova Bay area.* Italy began by noting that increasing difficulties with its present fast ice runway, required a more reliable longterm solution. Reiterating points raised by COMNAP in IP 32, regarding transport costs and energy use, Italy remarked that it intended to share the runway with other national Antarctic programmes, which would lower costs as well as the overall human footprint. While building the runway would only have a temporary impact over a period of four years, Italy acknowledged that the facility would likely result in a more than minor or transitory impact, and would therefore be subject to a CEE.

(91) Germany appreciated the Italian conclusion that building such a permanent infrastructure would be subject to a CEE. It noted that the runway would also be of advantage for the Parties who have facilities in this area, like Germany which has a summer hut in the locality, and could lead to enhance cooperation and scientific research. In addition, Germany stated that cumulative impacts should be taken into account when carrying out a CEE. In response to a question from Germany, Italy stated that the runway would not be used for tourism.

(92) In view of the IEEs discussed, the Netherlands raised several issues, including: the assessment of cumulative impacts; the lack of common agreement on the EIA process; the prospect of operating joint scientific facilities; the need to assess gaps in knowledge; assessing impacts on wilderness; and the possibility that facilities established for science would later be used for other activities, for example tourism. The Netherlands commended China for taking wilderness values into account in the preparation of their IEE (IP 21), and encouraged other Members to do the same.

(93) IAATO stated that it did not support the building of permanent infrastructures for tourism purposes as this would contradict the organisation's vision and mission of having a no more than minor or transitory impact.

(94) Ukraine mentioned recent improvements to Vernadsky Station, including the installation of more environmentally friendly generators, and a larger fuel tank.

(95) ASOC registered its concern over the increased human footprint and reduction of Antarctic wilderness as a result of the expansion of human activities in Antarctica. It also said that there is a lack of common agreement on the criteria to determine if an IEE or CEE is necessary for a particular activity, that there was generally a poor level of follow-up on these, and that inspection reports have shown that there was a lack of knowledge of the EIA process at research stations. Referring to SP 5, ASOC observed that only 14 Parties had submitted EIAs to the Secretariat for inclusion in the list.

(96) Other papers submitted under this agenda item included:

- SP 5 *Annual list of Initial Environmental Evaluations (IEE) and Comprehensive Environmental Evaluations (CEE) prepared between April 1st 2012 and March 31st 2013*

- BP 2 *Assessing the vulnerability of Antarctic soils to trampling* (New Zealand).

Item 9: Area Protection and Management Plans

9a) Management Plans

i) Draft Management Plans which have been reviewed by the Subsidiary Group on Management Plans

(97) Norway introduced WP 56 *Subsidiary Group on Management Plans – Report on 2012/13 Intersessional Work*, on behalf of the Subsidiary Group (SGMP). The Group had in the intersessional period reviewed eight revised management plans, and recommended that the Committee approve three of these revised management plans.

(98) With respect to ASPA No 132: Potter Peninsula (Argentina) and ASPA No 151: Lions Rump, King George Island, South Shetland Islands (Poland),

the SGMP advised the Committee that the final revised management plans were well written, of high quality and adequately addressed the key points raised during the review.

(99) Accordingly, the SGMP recommended that the Committee approve these revised plans.

(100) With respect to the proposal for a new ASPA at Cape Washington and Silverfish Bay (USA and Italy), the SGMP advised the Committee that the plan adequately addressed the provisions of Annex V and relevant CEP guidelines, and was likely to be effective in achieving the stated aims and objectives for management of the Area. Accordingly, the SGMP recommended that the Committee approve the management plan for this new ASPA.

(101) In addition, the SGMP advised the Committee that further intersessional work would be conducted with regards to five management plans submitted for intersessional review:

    i.   ASPA No 128: Western Shores of Admiralty Bay, King George Island, South Shetland Islands (Poland/USA)

    ii. ASPA No 144: "Chile Bay" (Discovery Bay), Greenwich Island, South Shetland Islands (Chile)

    iii. ASPA No 145: Port Foster, Deception Island, South Shetland Islands (Chile)

    iv. ASPA No 146: South Bay, Doumer Island, Palmer Archipelago (Chile)

    v. New ASPA: High altitude geothermal sites of the Ross Sea region (New Zealand)

(102) In response to a question raised by the Russian Federation on the possibility that during a revision the elements requiring protection might need to be changed, Norway stated that the SGMP had reviewed all revised management plans in accordance with the "Guide to the Preparation of Management Plans for Antarctic Specially Protected Areas."

(103) The Committee endorsed the SGMP's recommendation and agreed to forward the revised management plans for ASPA 132, ASPA 151 and a new ASPA at Cape Washington and Silverfish Bay to the ATCM for adoption.

(104) IAATO thanked Italy, the United States and the SGMP for taking the views of IAATO into consideration while developing the ASPA at Cape Washington and Silverfish Bay and showed its appreciation for the effort to amend the boundary to allow for some visitation within the general vicinity of the colony. Nonetheless, IAATO expressed its disappointment that visits from responsible tourism would no longer be possible, particularly as the levels of this visitation were very low and there were few realistic alternative options for visits to emperor penguin colonies in the area. IAATO noted that visits to Franklin Island, which was provided as an alternative visitor site for emperor penguins, are for viewing Adelie penguins, not emperor penguins. IAATO further suggested to the Committee that, given the level of activity in the area, there would be value in considering an ASMA for the region.

ii) Draft revised Management Plans which had not been reviewed by the Subsidiary Group on Management Plans

(105) The Committee considered revised management plans for 12 Antarctic Specially Protected Areas (ASPAs) and two Antarctic Specially Managed Areas (ASMAs) under this category:

- WP 2 *Revised Management Plan for Antarctic Specially Protected Area No 137 Northwest White Island, McMurdo Sound* (United States)

- WP 3 *Revised Management Plan for Antarctic Specially Protected Area No 123 Barwick and Balham Valleys, Southern Victoria Land* (United States)

- WP 5 *Revised Management Plan for Antarctic Specially Protected Area No 138 Linnaeus Terrace, Asgard Range, Victoria Land* (United States)

- WP 6 *Revision of the Management Plan for Antarctic Specially Protected Area No 141 Yukidori Valley, Langhovde, Lützow-Holm Bay* (Japan)

- WP 11 *Revised Management Plan for Antarctic Specially Protected Area No 108 Green Island, Berthelot Islands, Antarctic Peninsula* (United Kingdom)

- WP 12 *Revised Management Plan for Antarctic Specially Protected Area No 117 Avian Island, Marguerite Bay, Antarctic Peninsula* (United Kingdom)

- WP 13 *Revised Management Plan for Antarctic Specially Protected Area No 147 Ablation Valley and Ganymede Heights, Alexander Island* (United Kingdom*)*

- WP 14 *Revised Management Plan for Antarctic Specially Protected Area No 170 Marion Nunataks, Charcot Island, Antarctic Peninsula* (United Kingdom)

- WP 29 *Revision of Management Plan for Antarctic Specially Protected Area No 154 Botany Bay, Cape Geology, Victoria Land* (New Zealand)

- WP 30 *Revision of Management Plan for Antarctic Specially Protected Area No 156 Lewis Bay, Mount Erebus, Ross Island* (New Zealand)

- WP 36 *Review of Management Plans for Antarctic Specially Protected Areas (ASPAs) 135, 143 and 160* (Australia)

- WP 54 rev.1 *Review of the Management Plan for ASMA No 1: Admiralty Bay, King George Island, South Shetland Islands* (Brazil, Ecuador, Peru, Poland)

- WP 59, *Revised Management Plan for Antarctic Specially Protected Area No 134 Cierva Point and offshore islands, Danco Coast, Antarctic Peninsula* (Argentina)

- WP 60, *Revision of Management Plan for Antarctic Specially Protected Area No 161 Terra Nova Bay, Ross Sea* (Italy).

(106) The Russian Federation recalled its proposal from 2012 (ATCM XXXV WP 35), that the Committee should consider the Revised Management Plans of ASPAs and ASMAs for which fauna or flora were the main values, only when information was submitted on the results of monitoring of the state of values that were a cause for designating such an area. The Russian Federation underlined its belief in the need for a scientifically justified approach to the choice of the ASPAs and ASMAs.

(107) With respect to WP 2 (ASPA 137), WP 3 (ASPA 123) and WP 5 (ASPA 138), the United States explained that revisions were minor and aimed at bringing these management plans in line with Resolution 2 (2011) *Revised Guide to the Preparation of Management Plans for Antarctic Specially Protected Areas.* Changes included the addition of an introduction and the improvement

of the maps. In response to a query from the Russian Federation, the United States clarified that all plans included, in the reference section and when appropriate, the monitoring results of a site review.

(108) With respect to WP 6 (ASPA 141), in response to a question from the Russian Federation, Japan confirmed that its preparation of the management plan was in accordance with the "Guide to the Preparation of Management Plans for Antarctic Specially Protected Areas", and included a biennial vegetation survey in the Yukidori Valley, but did not currently include avian surveys.

(109) With respect to WP 11 (ASPA 108), WP 12 (ASPA 117), WP 13 (ASPA 147) and WP 14 (ASPA 170), the United Kingdom said that only minor changes had been made to the management plans. Some of these changes were: the addition of an introduction, a range of minor editorial amendments, the incorporation of improved maps, reference in the introduction to the Environmental Domains Analysis (Resolution 3 (2008)) and the Antarctic Conservation Biogeographic Regions (Resolution 6 (2012)), visitor management requirements related to the introduction of non-native species, and a redefinition of Area boundaries.

(110) In introducing WP 29 (ASPA 154) and WP 30 (ASPA 156), New Zealand explained that all revisions were minor. ASPA 154 was protected for its unique biodiversity, science and historic values, and ASPA 156 was designated as a tomb to prevent unnecessary disturbance as a mark of respect in remembrance of the victims of an aircraft crash. In response to a query from Japan, New Zealand assured the Committee that there was no negative impact caused by recreational visits to ASPA 156.

(111) Argentina informed the Committee that it had reviewed the Management Plan for ASPA 134 (WP 59) and that only minor adjustments had been made. These included the addition of: information concerning the reasons for designation, considerations related to the prevention of introduction of non-native species, two new sections in response to Resolution 2 (2011), and an update and expansion of the description of the values of the Area.

(112) With respect to WP 60 (ASPA 161), Italy informed the Committee that there had been no substantial changes to the Management Plan, and that boundaries, maps and descriptions remained the same.

(113) Introducing WP 36 (ASPAs 135, 143 and 160), Australia said that only minor amendments were made to the management plans, and noted that in

each case the revision was prepared with reference to the revised guide in Resolution 2 (2011).

(114) With regard to WP 54 rev.1 (ASMA 1), Brazil said that the plan had been updated to include two new aims, two new Appendices, four scientific values and two new maps. Brazil explained that the United States, as a member of the Management Group for ASMA 1, had participated in the review process. It recommended that the CEP should ask the Subsidiary Group on Management Plans to undertake an intersessional review. The proposer will also submit the current draft to CCAMLR WG-EMM/CCAMLR, in order to receive contributions to the final version, which would be presented to CEP XVII.

(115) In noting the important links between CCAMLR and the CEP in respect of ASMAs and ASPAs with a marine component France suggested that the Committee should establish a mechanism for regular reports from the Scientific Committee of CCAMLR to the CEP on any harvesting of living resources in such areas. The SC-CAMLR Observer noted that such information was contained in IP 6 and confirmed that if further information was required by the CEP this could be provided in future. The Committee welcomed the information provided and encouraged the development of improved mechanisms for timely and efficient information exchange between CEP and SC-CCAMLR. New Zealand also noted the importance of delegations sharing ASPA and ASMA information directly with their CCAMLR colleagues within their own governments.

(116) ASOC expressed its support for such a mechanism and declared that in its opinion there should be no fishing in ASMAs or ASPAs.

(117) The Committee decided to refer the revised management plans for ASPA 141 and ASMA 1 to the SGMP for intersessional review, and agreed to forward the other revised management plans to the ATCM for adoption.

iii) New draft management plans for protected/managed areas

(118) The Committee considered one proposal to designate a new Antarctic Specially Managed Area and one new Antarctic Specially Protected Area:

- WP 8 *Proposal for a new Antarctic Specially Managed Area at Chinese Antarctic Kunlun Station, Dome A* (China).

- WP 63 *Draft Antarctic Specially Protected Area (ASPA) Management Plan for Stornes, Larsemann Hills, Princess Elizabeth Land* (Australia, China, India, and the Russian Federation).

(119) In introducing WP 8, China noted that it had conducted a Comprehensive Study in the Dome A area, and had prepared a draft management plan that aimed to enhance the protection of its scientific, environmental and logistical values. China proposed that the draft management plan be considered by the SGMP during the intersessional period, and invited Members to participate in this process.

(120) While congratulating China for the comprehensive report, several Members questioned the justification of designating a new ASMA at Dome A. Some Members noted that Kunlun station was constructed only recently, and suggested that it might be premature to designate the area as an ASMA. The United Kingdom inquired whether the proposal made by China was aligned with the purposes of ASMAs as defined by Annex 5 of the Environmental Protocol where principal objectives were to avoid conflict and improve collaboration between different users of an area. The Russian Federation and Norway also asked what were the threats envisaged to this remote area. France noted that other sites had now been identified with deeper ice-coring potential. Germany questioned the advantages of designating an ASMA in such a remote region with a low level of biodiversity. The United States also suggested that further discussion among Members may be useful. While recognising the scientific value of Dome A and expressing its gratitude for the support of Chinese colleagues in the region, Australia agreed with the need for further consideration.

(121) China quoted the Article 4 of Annex 5 to the Environmental Protocol and pointed out that its proposal for the designation of an ASMA did not conflict with the statement in this Arcticle, especially the wording of "where activities are being conducted or may in the future be conducted". China generally responded to the questions from some Members that its consideration of "planning and co-ordination" statement in Article 4 is based on solid information from the science community of the intention of carrying out scientific research in Dome A area by some countries and even non-governmental activities such as extreme sports could be anticipated, so that the precautionary principle was applied in this proposal. ASOC welcomed the intention by China to take a precautionary approach to area management.

(122) China thanked Members for their comments and suggestions. China reiterated that its proposal was based not on the premise that more than one Party would necessarily be using the site but on a precautionary approach to likely future activities and interest in the region, and on the values to be protected.

(123) The Committee accepted China's offer to lead further discussions on the proposed ASMA during the intersessional period, and encouraged Members to participate.

(124) Norway suggested that the debate highlighted the need for the Committee to review and reconsider the overall process of designating ASPAs and ASMAs, and recommended that Members engage in a broad discussion of the topic. Many Members expressed their support for this suggestion. Norway noted that it would work intersessionally with interested Members on this topic with a view to developing concrete proposals.

(125) In introducing WP 63, Australia stated that the proposed ASPA in the Larsemann Hills aimed to protect the area's unique geological features, specifically the rare mineral occurrences and the highly unusual host rocks in which they occur. It noted that this was consistent with Article 3.2(f) of Annex V which provides for examples of outstanding geological, glaciological or geomorphological features to be included in the series of ASPAs.

(126) The Russian Federation noted that the draft ASPA management plan had been discussed at a Larsemann Hills ASMA Management Group meeting in St Petersburg in April 2013. Further details of the Management Group's activities are provided in IP 46.

(127) Belgium suggested that the Grovenes and Broknes peninsulas, where Belgian and British scientists have identified the presence of endemic algal communities, might also be included within the boundary of future ASPAs.

(128) The Committee agreed to forward the draft management plan for an ASPA at Stornes, Larsemann Hills, Princess Elizabeth Land, to the SGMP for review during the intersessional period.

CEP Advice to the ATCM

(129) The Committee agreed to forward the following management plans to the ATCM for adoption:

#	Name
ASPA 137	Northwest White Island, McMurdo Sound
ASPA 123	Barwick and Balham Valleys, Southern Victoria Land
ASPA 138	Linnaeus Terrace, Asgard Range, Victoria Lands
ASPA 108	Green Island, Berthelot Islands, Antarctic Peninsula
ASPA 117	Avian Island, Marguerite Bay, Antarctic Peninsula
ASPA 147	Ablation Valley and Ganymede Heights, Alexander Island
ASPA 170	Marion Nunataks, Charcot Island, Antarctic Peninsula
ASPA 154	Botany Bay, Cape Geology, Victoria Land
ASPA 156	Lewis Bay, Mount Erebus, Ross Island
ASPA 135	North-East Bailey Peninsula, Budd Coast, Wilkes Land, East Antarctica
ASPA 143	Marine Plain, Mule Peninsula, Vestfold Hills, Princess Elizabeth Land
ASPA 160	Frazier Islands, Windmill Islands, Wilkes Land, East Antarctica
ASPA 134	Cierva Point and offshore islands, Danco Coast, Antarctic Peninsula
ASPA 161	Terra Nova Bay, Ross Sea
ASPA 132	Potter Peninsula, King George Island
ASPA 151	Lions Rump, King George Island
NEW ASPA	Cape Washington, South Victoria Land

(130) With respect to WP 56 regarding the SGMPs terms of reference 4 and 5, Norway, as convenor of the SGMP, recalled that CEP XIV had supported the recommendations of the 2011 Workshop on Marine and Terrestrial Antarctic Specially Managed Areas, and had encouraged interested Members "to review the provisions of existing ASMA management plans, with a view to preparing a suggested work plan and supporting materials to support work by the SGMP to develop guidance for establishing ASMAs and for preparing and reviewing ASMA management plans" and asked the Committee's views on whether this was an issue to be brought forward by the SGMP in the coming intersessional period. The Committee noted the importance of the topic, in particular in light of the discussions, but also noted the high work load of the SGMP, and suggested this issue be postponed to a future time.

(131) The Committee agreed that the work plan for the SGMP during the 2013/14 intersessional period should be as follows:

Terms of Reference	Suggested tasks
ToR 1 to 3	Review draft management plans referred by CEP for intersessional review and provide advice to proponents (including the five postponed plans from the 2012/13 intersessional period)
ToR 4 and 5	Work with relevant Parties to ensure progress on review of management plans overdue for five-yearly review
	Review and update SGMP work plan
Working Papers	Prepare report for CEP XVII against SGMP ToR 1 to 3
	Prepare report for CEP XVII against SGMP ToR 4 and 5

iv) Other matters relating to management plans for protected/managed areas

(132) The Republic of Korea presented IP 26 rev.1 *Management Report of Narebski Point (ASPA No 171) during the 2012/2013 period*. In accordance with the provisions of the Management Plan for ASPA 171, scientific studies and management activities had been undertaken, and the paper outlined lessons learned and recommendations. The Republic of Korea noted that the population of penguins in the region had increased, but that the reason for this was unclear. The management plan would be reviewed in 2014.

(133) Chile thanked the Republic of Korea for their document that includes new scientific information about the penguin colonies in the area. Chile also stated that it wished to include data on that research in the future. Chile reminded Parties that it will present a revision of ASPA 150 to the next CEP and will ask the Republic of Korea for their comments during the review process.

(134) China reported that it planned a site visit to ASPA 168 in the 2013/14 season, and that China would report on a possible revision of the management plan to CEP XVII.

(135) Norway, on behalf of Argentina, Chile, Spain, the United Kingdom and United States, presented IP 74 *Deception Island Specially Managed Area (ASMA) Management Group Report*, which summarised the activities undertaken within the ASMA, and the work of the Management Group to fulfil the objectives and principles of its Management Plan during the intersessional period (2012/13).

The following papers were also presented under this Agenda items:

- SP 6 *Status of Antarctic Specially Protected Area and Antarctic Specially Managed Area Management Plans*

9b) Historic Sites and Monuments

(136) Germany introduced WP 18 rev.1 *Proposal to add the site commemorating the location of the former German Antarctic Research Station "Georg Forster" to the List of Historic Sites and Monuments*. It noted that the site, which had contained Germany's first permanent Antarctic research base, had been cleaned and remediated following the station's removal in 1996.

(137) Several Members commended Germany for its successful station clean-up and removal, noting that this provided a model for other Parties to follow.

(138) The Committee approved the proposal to add the site, noting that the designation applied to the site of the former German Antarctic Research Station "Georg Forster", and not to the plaque commemorating the location, to the List of Historic Sites and Monuments, and agreed to forward it to the ATCM for adoption.

(139) The Russian Federation introduced WP 23 *Proposed addition of the Professor Kudryashov's drilling complex building at the Russian Antarctic Vostok station* to the List of Historic Sites and Monuments. The Russian Federation noted its proposal was aimed at commemorating the unique achievement of the Russian drillers and glaciologists in the field of drilling deep ice boreholes, reconstruction of paleoclimatic changes based on ice core data, microbiological studies of these ice cores, and ecologically clean unsealing of the subglacial Lake Vostok. Professor Kudryashov had made a major contribution to Antarctic science, and the drilling complex that carries his name hosted an important event in Antarctic history when Russian scientists unsealed the subglacial lake. In response to a query by the United Kingdom, the Russian Federation clarified that its proposal referred exclusively to the building not including the equipment and the borehole. It planned to remove the drilling fluid once the drilling activities at the site were concluded.

(140) The Committee approved the proposal and agreed to forward it to the ATCM for adoption.

(141) The United Kingdom introduced WP 62 *New Historic Sites and Monuments: Mount Erebus camp sites used by a contingent of the Terra Nova Expedition in December 1912*, jointly prepared with New Zealand and the United States.

While information about the sites was limited, the proponents considered the locations of the camps to be of significant interest to Antarctic historians, and that access to the sites should be controlled, in order to prevent disturbance of the recently discovered historic remains.

(142) In response to queries, the United Kingdom clarified that the scope of their proposal included two separate new historic sites, corresponding to each of the camps described in WP 62.

(143) The Committee approved the proposal and agreed to forward it to the ATCM for adoption.

(144) Norway suggested that the Committee might consider at some time in the future engaging in a broader discussion on Historical Sites and Monuments designations. Norway pointed out that many constructions in Antarctica might be considered to have historical value and that this could lead to the designation of a large number of historic sites in the future, which might be seen to contradict the Environmental Protocol's provision regarding clean-up of past activities in Antarctica. In supporting Norway's proposal, Germany suggested that intersessional discussions could be valuable.

(145) While several Members supported the point raised by Norway, Argentina and the United States recalled the contributions of Chilean Ambassador Jorge Berguño to the management of Historic Sites and Monuments, the Committee did not view the issue as an urgent priority. Rather, a review of the procedure of designating Historic Sites and Monuments would be noted in the Five-Year Work Plan.

CEP Advice to the ATCM

(146) After considering proposals for four Historic Sites and Monuments, the Committee agreed to forward them to the ATCM for adoption:

#	Name of site/monument
NEW HSM	Location of the first permanently occupied German Antarctic research station "Georg Forster" at the Schirmacher Oasis, Dronning Maud Land
NEW HSM	Professor Kudryashov's Drilling Complex Building, Vostok Station
NEW HSM	Upper "Summit Camp", Mount Erebus
NEW HSM	Lower "Camp E", Mount Erebus

9c) Site Guidelines

(147) The United Kingdom introduced WP 15 *Policy Issues Arising from the 2013 On-Site Review of Guidelines for Visitor Sites in the Antarctic Peninsula,* WP 16, *Site Guidelines for i) Orne Harbour and ii) Orne Islands,* and WP 20, *On-Site Review of Guidelines for Visitor Sites in the Antarctic Peninsula: summary of programme and suggested amendment of eleven Guidelines,* jointly prepared with Australia, Argentina and United States. These papers, as well as a short presentation by the United Kingdom, described the organisation and outcomes of an on-site review of Site Guidelines carried out by the co-authors and IAATO in January 2013.

(148) The United Kingdom reported that the review team had identified no significant visitor impacts on the sites other than those which had been the subject of previous discussion by the Committee. Evidence from this relatively short, but focused and intensive, series of visits suggested that the Guidelines were successful in directing the way that most organised groups of visitors were using the sites, in order to avoid any adverse environmental impacts. At the same time, it noted that Site Guidelines remained only one of a range of potential tools to manage visitation.

(149) The Committee congratulated the proponents and acknowledged IAATO's constructive role in the review, and several Members noted the close relationship between the recommendations arising from this review and those adopted by the CEP and the ATCM via the CEP Tourism Study (2012). The Russian Federation viewed the on-site survey as an excellent model of a coordinated effort that could also be applied to other areas in Antarctica where humans were present. Germany endorsed the recommendation to collate generic and specific site guidelines into a practical package format and thus strengthening the generic site guidelines. IAATO added that the on-site review had been a useful public relations exercise, as it had involved close interaction between Committee Members and tour operators as well as tourists.

(150) Several Members expressed their strong support for the recommendation for ongoing monitoring of sites to identify any visitor impacts, and suggested that the Committee should discuss how this might be achieved. On this note, New Zealand reiterated the value of the long-term data available from the Antarctic Site Inventory of Oceanites Inc. Norway also noted that

experiences from the Arctic might be relevant when considering issues related to methodologies for assessing site sensitivities.

(151) ASOC acknowledged the value of site specific guidelines, but also urged the Committee to take a strategic approach to tourist management, consistent with Resolution 7 (2009).

(152) In response to a question from Germany, the United Kingdom commented that, although there was less site-specific detail in the Site Guidelines for Orne Islands than for some other sites, it was considered a sufficiently important site to justify its own set of Guidelines given its location.

(153) The CEP discussed the recommendations presented in WP 15:

The CEP noted and endorsed Recommendation 1 that*: Parties continue to make efforts to ensure that all visitors to sites covered by ATCM Site Guidelines are aware, and make use of, the Guidelines.* This should include recreational visits by National Antarctic Programme (NAP) personnel as well as visitors participating in private or non-commercial activity.

The CEP considered Recommendation 2: *For the CEP to consider the value of a survey to establish the level of recreational visits from NAP staff to sites with Site Guidelines in place.* The CEP encouraged members to bring forward information on recreational visits to sites subject to site guidelines, by NAP personnel. The United Kingdom offered to coordinate an informal process to seek and collate information for reporting to CEP XVII. The CEP further noted work underway in the ATCM with respect to the CEP tourism study recommendations on development of visitation databases, and encouraged Parties to consider ways to ensure visits by NAP personnel are included in such systems as they are developed.

The CEP noted and endorsed Recommendation 3: *That Parties continue to carry out on-site reviews of Site Guidelines, as determined by the individual requirements of the sites.* The CEP encouraged Parties to focus on including appropriate site-specific information within new or amended Site Guidelines.

The CEP considered Recommendation 4: *Parties work to establish an appropriate site monitoring programme, including a recommended set of criteria for such a programme.* The CEP noted that this recommendation coincides with the recommendations 6 and 7 of the CEP tourism study relating to monitoring.

The CEP considered Recommendation 5: *In view of the assessment from this year's on-site review program that there are sites which are particularly sensitive to visitation, the CEP consider whether monitoring for visitor impacts would be useful in these particular locations.* The CEP noted that this recommendation coincides with the recommendations 3, 6 and 7 of the CEP tourism study relating to monitoring.

The CEP considered Recommendation 6: *That any CEP discussion of monitoring sites should include consideration of including non site-specific impacts (for example, litter or other objects).* The CEP noted that this recommendation relates to the recommendations of the CEP tourism study on monitoring, and encouraged Parties to consider this area in their future discussions

The CEP noted and endorsed Recommendation 7: *That Parties should continue to seek input from IAATO and other non-governmental operators as appropriate, when revising or creating new Site Guidelines. Operators should alert Parties to changes at sites that merit review and possible revision of the Site Guidelines.*

The CEP noted and endorsed Recommendation 8: that, where possible:

- illustrated photo-maps should be used to assist in on-site interpretation of the provisions of the Site Guidelines;

- a standardised map format should be developed for use across Site Guidelines;

- that the Site Guidelines should include information on the date of their adoption and any subsequent revision; and

- that the CEP considers the benefit of bringing all the Site Guidelines together with the similarly formatted General Guidelines as part of the practical package of information for visitors to Antarctica.

The CEP noted and endorsed Recommendation 9: *That the CEP encourages the development, by IAATO and other non-governmental operators, of best-practice training assessment and/or accreditation schemes for Antarctic guides and expedition leaders, noting the CEP discussions in 2005 and 2006.* The CEP further noted the desirability of ATCM engagement in this work.

The CEP considered Recommendation 10: *Noting that visible signs of disturbance are important in avoiding disturbance of wildlife, that CEP members give consideration to the production of visitor-focused guidelines detailing such signs.* The CEP encourages members to bring forward, in consultation with SCAR, proposals relating to this recommendation.

(154) In considering the connections between the recommendations in WP 15 and the recommendations of the CEP tourism study, it was noted that the ATCM had requested the CEP to address Recommendations 3, 4, 6 and 7, where recommendations 3 and 6 had been identified as priority areas.

(155) The United States introduced WP 26 *Proposed Amendment for Antarctic Treaty Site Guidelines for Visitors to Torgersen Island*, which proposed an amendment to the existing guidelines in response to significant declines in the Adélie penguin population. In response to a query from France, the United States commented that, as site guidelines were voluntary, it was more appropriate for the Torgersen Island site guidelines to strongly discourage, rather than to prohibit, early season visitation to the island. In response to a query from Norway regarding the absence of a reference to ship size, the United States noted that it was the timing of visits, rather than overcrowding, that was of most concern at this site. The Committee approved the revised Site Guidelines for this site.

(156) Thanking the United States, ASOC noted that it was a good example of the practical application of the Precautionary Principle to site management.

(157) The United States introduced WP 46 *Proposed Amendment for Antarctic Treaty Site Guidelines for Visitors Baily Head, Deception Island*, jointly prepared with Argentina, Chile, Norway, Spain, United Kingdom, ASOC and IAATO. It noted that the Deception Island Management Group had been prompted to review these guidelines following the report of a significant decline of more than 50 per cent in the abundance of chinstrap penguins breeding at Baily Head since the last comprehensive census in 1986/1987. The Committee approved the revised Site Guidelines for this site.

(158) Ecuador introduced WP 64 *Updated Map of Barrientos Island*, which it proposed should be included in the current Site Guidelines for Barrientos Island. Several Members thanked Ecuador for their work, and IAATO remarked that the updated map was comprehensive and user-friendly. After minor modifications of the maps based on comments during the discussion the Committee approved the revised Site Guidelines.

CEP Advice to the ATCM

(159) After considering two new site guidelines and fourteen revised site guidelines, the Committee agreed to forward the following site guidelines to the ATCM for adoption:

- Yankee Harbour
- Half Moon Island
- Brown Bluff
- Hannah Point
- Cuverville Island
- Danco Island
- Neko Harbour
- Pleneau Island
- Petermann Island
- Damoy Point
- Jougla Point
- Baily Head, Deception Island
- Torgersen Island
- Barrientos Island
- Orne Harbour (new)
- Orne Islands (new)

(160) The United States presented IP 20 *Antarctic Site Inventory 1994-2013*, which provided an update on results of the Antarctic Site Inventory undertaken by Oceanites Inc. through February 2013. Key trends that this long-term dataset has identified are the rapid increase and southward expansion of gentoo penguin populations, and significant declines in chinstrap and Adélie penguin populations on the western Antarctic Peninsula.

(161) IAATO presented IP 97 *Report on IAATO Operator Use of Antarctic Peninsula Landing Sites and ATCM Visitor Site Guidelines, 2012-13 Season*, noting that traditional ship-based tourism represented over 95 per cent of

all landed activity, that the 20 most-visited sites represented 72 per cent of the total number of landings made, and that all but one of these most-visited sites – Portal Point – were covered by site specific management plans. In response, the United Kingdom offered to assist in the drafting of new site guideline for Portal Point should Members consider this necessary.

(162) IAATO presented IP 102 *Barrientos Island Footpath Erosion*, which summarised the results of an internal investigation conducted by IAATO in relation to the erosion in moss beds on Barrientos Island. IAATO reported that its members would continue to prohibit walks through Closed Area B on Barrientos Island until additional information was available, and that it would review options to strengthen feedback from field staff. IAATO also commented that while Site Guidelines were perceived as very beneficial, the Barrientos Island example showed that more detailed information was needed where more precise management practices were promoted.

(163) Ecuador thanked IAATO for its investigation, and informed the Committee that it had observed full compliance with Resolution 5 (2012) and that it would continue to update the Committee on this issue.

9d) Human Footprint and Wilderness Values

(164) The Committee discussed proposals for revised site guidelines for one site New Zealand introduced WP 35 *Possible guidance material to assist Parties to take account of wilderness values when undertaking environmental impact assessments* and IP 39 *Intersessional report on the provision of guidance material to assist Parties to take account of wilderness values when undertaking environmental impact assessments*. New Zealand proposed that Parties use this material within the Guidelines for Environmental Impact Assessment in Antarctica, and possibly as part of a wider update of those Guidelines.

(165) Members acknowledged New Zealand's ongoing leadership of the Committee's discussions of wilderness values. Many members expressed their support for the proposal and for continuing discussions of wilderness values. France remarked on some of the complexities concerning wilderness values, including the question of scale in establishing wilderness areas, and the differences between tangible and intangible values, and between aesthetic and wilderness values.

(166) Japan encouraged members to provide concrete examples of how to take wilderness values into account for area protection.

(167) In light of the discussions, New Zealand confirmed that it will aim to continue work on wilderness. This will include technical refinements and collaboration with interested Parties with a view to contributing to a review of the EIA guidelines in due course. New Zealand pointed out that the ASOC posting on the CEP Forum contained examples of how to take wilderness values into account in EIAs.

(168) ASOC presented IP 60 *Mapping and modelling wilderness values in Antarctica: contribution to CEP's work in developing guidance material on wilderness protection using protocol tools*, which summarised the recommendations of a report produced by the Wildland Research Institute. Based on a literature review on how wilderness quality is mapped and modelled worldwide, using Geographical Information Systems (GIS), the paper recommended, *inter alia*, that the CEP adopt the universal basic premise that wilderness conditions are seen to exist where a location is remote from settlement and mechanised access, and relatively free from human-induced changes to land cover. ASOC called for Parties to use existing tools of the Environmental Protocol to take concrete steps to protect Antarctica's wilderness values.

(169) The Netherlands supported ASOC's recommendations and suggested that a broader view of wilderness from across the world would also be helpful. In response to a query from the Russian Federation, ASOC clarified that their literature review had not included the development of a quantitative measure for Antarctic wilderness.

(170) COMNAP presented IP 33 *Analysis of national Antarctic program increased delivery of science,* which presented the results of an analysis undertaken by the Chilean National Antarctic Program, Instituto Antartico Chileno (INACH). This analysis identified procedures and strategies to continue to deliver more science while reducing its programme's Antarctic footprint.

9e) Marine Spatial Protection and management

(171) The following papers were presented under this Agenda item:

- IP 34 *Using ASMAs and ASPAs when necessary to complement CCAMLR MPAs* (IUCN)

9f) *Other Annex V matters*

(172) The United Kingdom introduced WP 10 *Identification of potential climate change refugia for emperor penguins: a science-based approach,* which stated that climate change was likely to impact upon emperor penguin distribution range and breeding success. The United Kingdom suggested that the remote sensing techniques outlined in the paper could make a step-change contribution in improving the evidence base for the monitoring of vulnerable sites, including ASPAs, and recommended that the CEP: a) acknowledge the significant value offered by remote sensing as a technique for gathering detailed evidence on emperor penguin population variability, linked to localised climate change; b) endorse the proposal laid out in this paper as an appropriate method of identifying potential climate change refugia for emperor penguins; and c) encourage Parties with work programmes related to emperor penguins to consider collaboration with the United Kingdom in further developing and applying these monitoring techniques across the wider Antarctic region.

(173) Members thanked the United Kingdom for its Paper and acknowledged the benefits of the proposed techniques. Several Members noted that although remote sensing was very useful, other complementary techniques had to be taken into account, including ground studies to validate remote sensing. France recalled some limits to only using satellite imagery and that individual tracking of emperor penguins in Dumont d'Urville provide useful information on the demographic parameters that help to improve our understanding of the variations in the size of colonies in connection with climate change. Germany and Argentina reminded Members of the activities of SCAR's Action Group on Remote Sensing, and proposed collaborative work with SCAR. Australia mentioned that its scientists were also engaged in remote sensing research, and expressed its will to collaborate with the United Kingdom and exchange information.

(174) While congratulating the United Kingdom for its precautionary approach, China underlined that many factors impact the size of penguin colonies, and that potential shortcomings of data from remote sensing included the limited time of the observation, and that some data could only be registered by on-ground research. The Russian Federation agreed that changes in populations of birds and other species were not only related to climate change but also to other variables. It suggested that it would be interesting to compare the

situation of penguin colonies in East and West Antarctica, where the impacts of climate change are different.

(175) SCAR advised that its newly formed Action Group on Remote Sensing would meet during the SCAR Biology Symposium in Barcelona in July 2013. ASOC noted that there is little knowledge on how the biology of emperor penguins might be affected by climate change and supported the United Kingdom's proposal to conduct large-scale and long-term studies.

(176) In conclusion, the Committee endorsed the monitoring of emperor penguin colonies using remote sensing techniques to identify potential climate change refugia, and encouraged Members to undertake similar work in other regions of Antarctica. The Committee also noted that other techniques should be used to complement remote sensing, and welcomed the offer of the United Kingdom to lead informal discussions on the issue during the intersessional period.

(177) In introducing WP 21 *Analysis of the ASPA and ASMA wildlife values*, the Russian Federation recalled its proposal to require monitoring programmes, particularly of Antarctic wildlife, in areas with existing or proposed management plans, in order to gather scientific evidence that would inform decisions about management plans.

(178) In response, a number of Members reiterated the reservations they had stated at previous meetings regarding the proposal to make such monitoring mandatory, including CEP XV.

(179) The Russian Federation thanked Members for their comments and suggestions, and noted that while its proposal was in full compliance with Resolution 2 (2011), it would revise its proposal, to remove the mandatory elements.

(180) The Committee did not reach a consensus regarding the proposal of the Russian Federation regarding environmental monitoring related to protected areas. While the Committee expressed its gratitude towards the Russian Federation for raising an important issue, several Members still held concerns regarding the substance of the proposal. Accordingly, the Committee agreed to continue its discussion of monitoring at CEP XVII.

(181) The Committee welcomed the Russian Federation's offer to lead informal intersessional discussions on this subject. It encouraged participation by interested Members and SCAR.

(182) The Russian Federation introduced WP 22 *Russian Antarctic biogeographic regioning as compared with the New Zealand classification*, which noted that Russian scientists have generated classifications of major landscape types on the basis of environmental parameters. The Russian Federation noted that this work could build on and complement existing classifications, such as the Environmental Domains Analysis adopted under Resolution 3 (2008) and the Antarctic Conservation Biogeographic Regions adopted under Resolution 6 (2012).

(183) Many Members thanked the Russian Federation for its work and expressed their strong support for the proposal. Australia recalled ATCM XXXV-WP 23, which it had submitted jointly with New Zealand and SCAR, which identified 15 biologically distinct Antarctic Conservation Biogeographic Reions and noted that the inclusion of more data could allow further analyses and possibly result in refinements to the classification. New Zealand highlighted the importance of continual refinement of biogeographic regions and associated scientific tools, and acknowledged the Russian Federation's contribution in this regard.

(184) SCAR welcomed the paper from the Russian Federation. It recalled ATCM XXXV-WP 23 rev.1 presented last year by Australia, NZ and SCAR, which noted that the Antarctic Conservation Biogeographic regions are based both on the original environmental domains analysis of the full Antarctic prepared by New Zealand. What the scientific analysis did to arrive at these regions was to include expert opinion and data on the distribution of organisms. SCAR welcomed the additional views from the Russian Federation, which help further develop biogeographic understanding of the region. The additional biodiversity data that are available are also welcome, and could be contributed to the SCAR biodiversity database hosted by Australia. The development by Australian scientists of an Antarctic Near Shore and Terrestrial Observing System will also help the CEP with its work. These new data, especially from genetic studies, will also help in understanding the influence of history on biogography. Two new SCAR Research Programmes, State of the Antarctic Ecosystem and Antarctic Thresholds Ecosystem Resilience and Adaptation, provide a means to integrate biogeographic information both from scientists from the Russian Federation and those from elsewhere.

(185) The Committee agreed that the work undertaken by the Russian Federation was complementary to previous work by Australia, New Zealand and SCAR, and that it provided useful data.

(186) Belgium introduced WP 39 *Human footprint in Antarctica and the long-term conservation of terrestrial microbial habitats*, prepared jointly with SCAR, South Africa and the United Kingdom, which highlighted potential threats to the conservation of terrestrial microbial ecosystems in Antarctica, and to future scientific research on these ecosystems. Belgium pointed out that recent advances in molecular biology techniques had identified diverse microbial communities and species endemic to Antarctica. The proponents accordingly recommended: a) that microbial contamination of pristine sites are considered by Parties in their EIAs for activities in locations unlikely to have ever been visited; and b) that the protected area system should be used more actively to protect microbial habitats for future science and for their own intrinsic value, including through the designation of areas kept inviolate from human interference.

(187) Members thanked Belgium and its co-authors for their contribution, supported by extensive scientific data, and recognised the importance of this question. Moreover they raised several questions, including: the difficulty of controlling the transportation of microbial organisms; the definition of "pristine area" as applied to micro-organisms in Antarctica; the possibility of establishing prohibited areas; and the current lack of decontamination methods. The inclusion of aquatic micro-organisms was proposed; and the significance of ecological research was proposed.

(188) Some members noted the importance of work to protect microbial habitats and expressed general support for the recommendations in WP 39.

(189) The United Kingdom introduced IP 111 *Management of Antarctic Specially Protected Areas: permitting, visitation and information exchange practices*, jointly prepared with Spain, which presented information on Parties' information exchange practices associated with visits to ASPAs. Parties had interpreted and implemented the protected area legislation in different ways. Some Parties had not provided full information on ASPA visitation through the EIES within the required annual time limits. Estimated levels of visitation to ASPAs varied considerably, with, on average, the greatest level of visitation to (i) ASPAs within the Antarctic Peninsula and Ross Sea regions and (ii) those ASPAs designated for the protection of historic

values. The United Kingdom and Spain concluded that ASPA visitation data were likely to be of limited use for informing general and ASPA-specific environmental management practices without full and consistent disclosure by Parties.

(190) Several Members expressed their concern at the lack of ASPA visitation data available in the EIES and recommended full and comprehensive information sharing in accordance with the requirements of Article 10 of Annex I of the Madrid Protocol, to enable more coordinated and effective management of activities within ASPAs. They also noted that consideration could in the future be given to reviewing and where appropriate revising the information exchange requirements to ensure that Parties' reports provide data of most relevance to informing protected area management. ASOC also noted that limitations in the exchange of information were an issue of broader relevance in the ATCM and CEP, for example with regard to inspections and biological prospecting.

(191) Ecuador introduced WP 55 *Recovery of moss communities on the tracks of Barrientos Island and tourism management proposal*, jointly prepared with Spain, which described the results of the visitor monitoring system and an assessment of the state of the vegetation cover on the tracks of Barrientos Island. The paper proposed to conduct additional monitoring on both central and coastal paths, and encouraged Parties to develop specific visitor management measures for the western tip of the island.

(192) The United Kingdom, France, and Argentina suggested keeping the discussed paths closed and expressed their willingness to contribute to management guidelines. In response to a query by France, Ecuador clarified that the known instances of the use of central and coastal paths were likely to have been due to a misunderstanding of the area maps. IAATO stated that its members had decided to refrain from using the paths, and IAATO was also ready to contribute to management guidelines. ASOC regarded the approach taken by Spain and Ecuador as a model for the management of areas with regular visits.

(193) The following papers were also presented under this Agenda item:

- IP 35 *The non-native grass Poa pratensis at Cierva Point, Danco Coast, Antarctic Peninsula – on-going investigations and future eradication plans* (Argentina, Spain and United Kingdom)

- IP 46 *Report of the Antarctic Specially Managed Area No 6 Larsemann Hills Management Group* (Australia, China, India and Russian Federation)

- IP 73 *Antarctic trial of WWF's Rapid Assessment of Circum-Arctic Ecosystem Resilience (RACER) Conservation Planning Tool: initial findings* (United Kingdom and Norway)

- BP 10 *Update on Developing Protection for a Geothermal Area: Volcanic Ice Caves at Mount Erebus, Ross Island* (Unites States and New Zealand)

Item 10: Conservation of Antarctic Flora and Fauna

10a) Quarantine and Non-native Species

(194) Germany introduced WP 19 *Report on the Research Project "The Impact of Human Activities on Soil Organisms of the Maritime Antarctic and the Introduction of Non-Native Species in Antarctica"*, regarding biosecurity measures to prevent the transfer and introduction of non-native soil organisms, and referred to IP 55 and related information included in the final report of the research project which is available at *http://www.umweltbundesamt.de/ uba-info-medien/4416.html*.

(195) Many Members expressed their appreciation of Germany's scientific efforts and highlighted factors which could increase the risk of introduction of non-native organisms, including increasing visitor numbers and climate change. New Zealand underlined the importance of continuing work on the issue of non-native species in Antarctica, and in taking a precautionary and preventative approach to managing risks. SCAR recalled the findings of its "Aliens in Antarctica" study presented to the ATCM in 2012, which concluded that on a per capita basis, scientists have been found to transport more plant propagules than other types of visitors; therefore all categories of visitors should be considered capable of transferring non-native species to the region.

(196) The Committee commended Germany for its research and endorsed the recommendations contained therein. The Committee agreed to take the work forward, under the leadership of Germany, via an open and informal working group. The Committee noted the readiness of SCAR, IAATO and ASOC to contribute to this work.

(197) Other papers submitted under this agenda item were:

- IP 28 *Colonisation status of known non-native species in the Antarctic terrestrial environment (updated 2013)* (United Kingdom)

- IP 35 *The non-native grass* Poa pratensis *at Cierva Point, Danco Coast, Antarctic Peninsula – on-going investigations and future eradication plans* (Argentina, Spain, United Kingdom).

- BP 9 *Australia's new Antarctic cargo and biosecurity operations facility* (Australia)

10b) Specially Protected Species

(198) No papers were submitted under this Agenda item.

10c) Other Annex II Matters

(199) COMNAP presented IP 31 *Use of hydroponics by national Antarctic programs*, which reviewed the potential environmental impacts of hydroponics of the national Antarctic progammes of Australia, New Zealand and the United States, and the risk-based management measures in place.

Item 11: Environmental Monitoring and Report

(200) Belgium introduced WP 37 *www.biodiversity.aq: The new Antarctic Biodiversity Information Network*, jointly prepared with SCAR, which described the renewed international Antarctic Biodiversity Portal which built on the legacy of the SCAR Marine Biodiversity Information Network and the Antarctic Biodiversity Information Facility. SCAR demonstrated how the Portal provided access to both marine and terrestrial Antarctic biodiversity data.

(201) Australia welcomed the Biodiversity Portal initiative, and indicated that it would work closely with Belgium to maximise synergies with the Biodiversity Database, which is managed by the Australian Antarctic Data Centre on behalf of SCAR.

(202) Many Members expressed their support for the Biodiversity Portal, and thanked Belgium and SCAR for the work, which makes biodiversity data more accessible to the science community and the general public.

(203) Several members raised questions, related to: the interaction with the Antarctic Environments Portal; long term funding; private funding; mapping; and the Committee's involvement with the portal.

(204) In response to a question from Germany and Brazil, SCAR and New Zealand reiterated that the biodiversity portal was a depository of primary raw data, whereas the Antarctic Environmental Portal managed by New Zealand would provide summary information based on published peer-reviewed science that is relevant to the CEP priority issues.

(205) Argentina expressed concern regarding dependence on private sources of funding, and over the scope of some maps included in the portal, which exceeded the area of the Antarctic Treaty. It also recalled the presentation of its WP 58 *Contributions to discussions on access to environment-related information and its management within the framework of the Antarctic Treaty System.*

(206) Peru shared the concern of Argentina in connection with the geographical scope of the Antarctic Biodiversity Portal. Furthermore, Peru expressed that it could not support the Resolution that was proposed in WP 37 due to the fact that one of the associated institutions to *www.biodiversity.aq*, called Ocean Biogeographic Information System (OBIS), presented incorrect maps of Peru.

(207) The Committee noted the initiative and acknowledged the great value of *www.biodiversity.aq*.

(208) SCAR presented IP 19 *1st SCAR Antarctic and Southern Ocean Science Horizon Scan*, which aimed to assemble 50 of the world's leading Antarctic scientists, policy makers, leaders, and visionaries to identify the most important scientific questions that should be addressed by research in and from the southern polar region over the next two decades, in order to assist in aligning international programmes, projects and resources.

(209) The Republic of Korea presented IP 27 *Korean/German Workshop about Environmental Monitoring on King George Island*, jointly prepared with Germany, which summarised the proceedings of the workshop that took place in Seoul, Korea, in April 2013. It noted that King George Island was a suitable site for studies of climate changes and human impacts. It also noted that long-term data collection via an integrated monitoring scheme was needed. The dialogue between Korea and Germany would be carried out on a regular basis, for example through annual meetings, with all interested

scientists who could contribute to monitoring and research activities in Maxwell Bay would be welcome to join.

(210) ASOC presented IP 67 *Management implications of tourist behavior*, which examined aspects of Antarctic tourist behaviour in the context of current tourism trends. The paper suggested a strategic approach to tourism regulation and management, including through using specially managed and protected areas as tourism management tools, rather than focusing on regulating specific tourist behaviour primarily through site-specific guidelines.

(211) Other papers submitted under this agenda item were:

- IP 5 *The Southern Ocean Observing System (SOOS) 2012 Report* (SCAR)

- IP 29 *Remote sensing for monitoring Antarctic Specially Protected Areas: Progress on use of multispectral and hyperspectral data for monitoring Antarctic vegetation* (United Kingdom)

- IP 59 *Update to Vessel Incidents in Antarctic Waters* (ASOC)

- IP 66 *Discharge of sewage and grey water from vessels in Antarctic Treaty waters* (ASOC)

- IP 76 *Report on the accident occurred to an excavator vehicle at Mario Zucchelli Station, Ross Sea, Antarctica* (Italy)

- IP 107 *Antarctic Center for Research and Environmental Monitoring, CIMAA: Advances in water quality monitoring and opportunities for cooperation* (Chile).

Item 12: Inspection Reports

(212) Germany introduced WP 4 *Inspection by Germany and South Africa in accordance with Article VII of the Antarctic Treaty and Article 14 of the Protocol on Environmental Protection: January 2013* and referred to IP 53 jointly prepared with South Africa. The inspections of Troll (Norway), Halley VI (United Kingdom), Princess Elisabeth (Belgium) and Maitri (India) stations on 8–29 January 2013 had observed no direct contraventions of the Antarctic Treaty or the Environmental Protocol, although environmental protection measures varied from station to station. The inspection team's environmental recommendations included: replacing ageing incinerators and removing non-

functional items, improving prevention of and response to oil spills, monitoring and disposal of treated waste water, implementing measures to prevent the introduction of non-native species, and certifying that necessary permits had been obtained. The team also felt that future inspection teams should draw from past inspection reports as reference points.

(213) South Africa expressed appreciation for the hospitality and cooperation received at all the stations that were inspected, and reiterated the value of such inspection in the furtherance of the implementation of the provisions of the Treaty and Protocol. Members whose stations had been inspected thanked Germany and South Africa for their report, confirmed that they intended to implement the recommendations, and noted that these inspections inspired improvement and were important checks for national Antarctic programmes.

(214) Norway thanked Germany and South Africa for their thorough inspection report and noted the importance of inspections in Antarctica, both for ensuring maintenance of the principles of the Antarctic Treaty, and as a check and balance for the individual operators. Norway noted that the inpection had provided good input for further development of environmentally sound operations at Troll. Norway furthermore underscored that necessary permits had been obtained and were carried by Norwegian scientists conducting work in ASPA 142, although a copy of this permit was not available at the Troll Station at the time of the inspection. With regard to the general recommendations from the inspection Norway lent in particular its support to the importance of shared use of facilities and infrastructure from an environmental perspective.

(215) On Maitri Station, India commented that some logistical issues had prevented its staff from offloading several pieces of machinery. India informed about the elaboration of a plan which aims at the introduction of best practice environmental standards at its research stations. For the next season, the incinerator at Maitri is proposed to be fitted with an emissions control mechanism. Containment of fuel tanks will be enhanced and the treatment of sewage water improved in a phased manner.

(216) In referring to ATCM XXXVI-IP 37 on Halley VI Station, the United Kingdom confirmed that the new station was now open and fully operational. The station had recently been awarded enhanced status within the WMO's Global Atmosphere Watch programme. The United Kingdom reiterated

other Members' support for the sharing of facilities in order to minimise cumulative environmental impacts.

(217) The United Kingdom introduced WP 9 *General Recommendations from the Joint Inspections undertaken by the United Kingdom, the Netherlands and Spain under Article VII of the Antarctic Treaty and Article 14 of the Environmental Protocol* and referred to IP 38 *Report of the Joint Inspections undertaken by the United Kingdom, the Netherlands and Spain under Article VII of the Antarctic Treaty and Article 14 of the Environmental Protocol,* jointly prepared with the Netherlands and Spain. The inspections undertaken in 1–14 December 2012 of 12 permanent stations, three unoccupied stations, three Historic Sites, four cruise ships, one yacht and one wreck site had observed no major contraventions of the Antarctic Treaty or Environment Protocol. The inspection team's environmental recommendations included: that new developments and activities should be preceded by an EIA, and that common facilities and services, such as fuel storage, power generation, water production, accommodation, and waste management should be shared by stations where possible to reduce the cumulative impacts of their activities.

(218) Spain and the Netherlands thanked the United Kingdom for organising the inspection and extended their appreciation to all those inspected for their hospitality and cooperation. Spain reiterated the report's recommendation for frequent testing of fuel storage tanks for leakage and corrosion.

(219) Brazil, China, Chile, Poland, the Republic of Korea, Argentina and the Russian Federation informed the Committee that they were each in the process of considering and implementing specific recommendations relating to their stations if appropriate.

(220) While acknowledging the benefits of stations sharing facilities and resources, the Russian Federation remarked that this might be difficult to achieve, given practical problems and the fact that domestic legislation to implement the Environmental Protocol differed between Parties.

(221) With respect to a recommendation regarding maximum visitor capacity for the most frequently visited sites, IAATO commented that it considered that the range of activities and visitor behaviour at a site were more relevant to the potential environmental impact.

(222) Malaysia commented that it had been a beneficiary of international cooperation in Antarctica and noted that, while Malaysia did not have its own Antarctic station, Malaysian students had produced many PhDs and Masters degrees in Antarctic fields with the support of other Treaty Parties.

(223) The Russian Federation presented IP 45 *Report of Russia – US joint Antarctic Inspection, November 29 – December 6, 2012,* jointly prepared with the United States. It reported on inspections conducted of Maitri (India), Zhongshan (China), Bharati (India), Syowa (Japan), Princess Elisabeth (Belgium), and Troll (Norway) stations, 29 November–6 December 2012. All stations were found to be well organised and generally compliant with the Antarctic Treaty and its Environmental Protocol. Recommended improvements included ensuring that station personnel understood the Protocol Annex 1 regarding EIA, and that national Antarctic programmes considered undertaking environmental monitoring of the potential impacts of stations' activities as part of their scientific programmes.

(224) The United States thanked Russia for its cooperation and extended its appreciation to all personnel involved in the inspection.

(225) All inspected Parties noted their appreciation to Russia and USA for the thorough inspection conducted by the two Parties. India explained that it was implementing a plan to address all the report's recommendations and that it would update the Committee on its progress. Japan confirmed that it was addressing the waste management issues mentioned in the report. Norway noted with interest the recommendation on making the monitoring of the impacts of station operations a part of science programmes.

(226) ASOC pointed out that the negative aspects shown in the report were very similar to the ones shown in the past. It was concerned that there was a gap between Parties that implemented the Protocol stringently and others that did not. ASOC observed that the ongoing practice of inspections would contribute to improve standards of Protocol implementation.

(227) China drew the attention of the Committee to the fact that the inspection team had arrived on the day of their station resupply, and that the entire staff had therefore been occupied with this task. It noted that some other issues raised in the report had been addressed in the meantime.

(228) Uruguay introduced WP 51 rev.1 *Additional availability of information on lists* of Observers of the Consultative Parties through the Antarctic Treaty Secretariat, jointly prepared with Argentina, which recommended that Consultative Parties inform the Secretariat, in addition to notification through diplomatic channels, when they assign Observers to carry out Inspections. It further recommended that the ATS included this information in its database, to be available in Parties' pre-season information exchanges.

(229) Italy drew the attention of the Committee to IP 77 *Italy answer to the US / Russian Inspection at Mario Zucchelli Station in 2012* (Italy) and IP 16 *Status of the fluid in the EPICA borehole at Concordia Station: an answer to the US / Russian Inspection in 2012* (France and Italy), which answered some questions raised by the joint US-Russian inspection which took place in 2012, mainly related to the transposition of regulations into domestic law and the status of the drilling fluid in the EPICA borehole at Concordia Station. Italy highlighted that this presented a good example of how inspections can be an effective tool also to increase internal political awareness.

Item 13: General Matters

(230) SCAR presented IP 83 *The International Bathymetric Chart of the Southern Ocean (IBCSO): First Release*, and urged all Parties to continue to contribute data to the IBCSO database. The map and data were available for download, and more details could be found at: *www.ibcso.org*.

(231) In presenting IP 104 *Colombia en la Antártida*, Colombia described its development of new organisations for supporting its work in Antarctica. Colombia said that they would soon be able to ratify the Environmental Protocol and join other countries in active research.

(232) Turkey explained its growing interest and activities in the Antarctic arena, and outlined its intention of establishing an Antarctic base. Turkey expressed its wish to cooperate strongly with other Members in this respect.

(233) Portugal stressed the importance of education and outreach as a potential issue for discussion at the CEP XVII. In response, Belgium highlighted the "Bringing the Poles to Brussels" science fair that was taking place on 25 and 26 May 2013 at the Academy Palace, organised by the Association of Polar Early Career Scientists.

(234) Brazil acknowledged the importance of education and outreach within the CEP. Education and outreach activities of APECS Belgium on the weekend of 25 and 26 May 2013 are an example to follow. These activities will include scientific and educational talks by renowned scientists from Belgium, Portugal and Brazil promoting capacity building for early career scientists as well as other educational activities to the general public. Brazil noted that it aims to carry on these activities in the next CEP/ATCM in Brasilia and establish a platform for other countries in the coming years. Several Members suggested putting the education and outreach item on the agenda for CEP XVII.

(235) Other papers submitted under this agenda item were:

- IP 7 *State of Japanese Environmental Management in Antarctica, with reference to the practices of other National Antarctic Programmes* (Japan).

Item 14: Election Officers

(236) The Committee elected Dr Polly Penhale from the United States as Vice-chair and congratulated her on appointment to the role.

(237) The Committee warmly thanked Ms Verónica Vallejos from Chile for her term in serving as Vice-chair.

Item 15: Preparation for the Next Meeting

(238) The Committee adopted the Provisional Agenda for CEP XVII (Appendix 2).

Item 16: Adoption of the Report

(239) The Committee adopted its Report.

Item 17: Closing of the Meeting

(240) The Chair closed the Meeting on Friday 24th May 2013.

Annex 1

CEP XVI Agenda and Summary of Documents

1. OPENING OF THE MEETING	
2. ADOPTION OF THE AGENDA	
SP 1 rev. 2	*ATCM XXXVI AND CEP XVI AGENDA AND SCHEDULE*
SP 12	*CEP XVI SUMMARY OF PAPERS*
3. STRATEGIC DISCUSSION ON THE FUTURE WORK OF THE CEP	
WP 7 France	*CEP FIVE-YEAR WORK PLAN ADOPTED AT THE XVTH CEP MEETING AT HOBART.* This paper provides the CEP Five-Year Work Plan as adopted at CEP XV so that it may be considered and updated at CEP XVI.
WP 28 Australia, Belgium, New Zealand, Norway and SCAR	*ANTARCTIC ENVIRONMENTS PORTAL: PROGRESS REPORT.* At CEP XV, New Zealand, SCAR and Australia introduced the concept of an Antarctic Environments Portal. This paper provides an update on the development of the Portal, addresses issues raised during informal intersessional discussions, and outlines the next steps for the project.
WP 58 Argentina	*CONTRIBUTIONS TO DISCUSSIONS ON ACCESS TO ENVIRONMENT-RELATED INFORMATION AND ITS MANAGEMENT WITHIN THE FRAMEWORK OF THE ANTARCTIC TREATY SYSTEM.* Argentina maintains that any information that is communicated in relation to or linked with the Committee for Environmental Protection or the Antarctic Treaty, or the manner in which it is communicated, must preserve the spirit of consensus in which these fora are handled, especially if the ultimate purpose of the information is to assist in decision-making processes.
IP 61 ASOC	*HUMAN IMPACTS IN THE ARCTIC AND ANTARCTIC: KEY FINDINGS RELEVANT TO THE ATCM AND CEP.* This paper informs on the two projects launched at the IPY Oslo Science Conference, 2010, exploring the subject of human impacts and future scenarios for the Antarctic environment. ASOC informs that the vast majority of future scenarios concur that existing environmental management practices and the current system of governance are insufficient to meet the obligations of the Environmental Protocol to protect the Antarctic environment.
4. OPERATION OF THE CEP	

5. COOPERATION WITH OTHER ORGANISATIONS	
WP 49 Belgium, Germany & Netherlands	THE ANTARCTIC TREATY SYSTEM ROLE REGARDING THE DEVELOPMENT OF A COMPREHENSIVE SYSTEM OF MARINE PROTECTED AREAS. This paper discusses the responsibility of Parties to environmental protection and the conservation of marine living resources under the international agreements that comprise the Antarctic Treaty system, and the connection between both. The Working Paper notes the work carried out so far towards the establishment of a representative system of marine protected areas in the CCAMLR Convention area, and invites the CEP to acknowledge this work and encourage its prompt and positive conclusion.
IP 3 COMNAP	THE ANNUAL REPORT FOR 2012 OF THE COUNCIL OF MANAGERS OF NATIONAL ANTARCTIC PROGRAMS (COMNAP). This document presents COMNAP highlights and achievements as well as products and tools developed in 2012.
IP 4 SCAR	THE SCIENTIFIC COMMITTEE ON ANTARCTIC RESEARCH (SCAR) ANNUAL REPORT 2012/13. This paper informs on the new Scientific Research Programs approved by the Meeting of Delegates of SCAR held in 2012 and on several major SCAR meetings to be held during the coming year.
IP 6 CCAMLR	REPORT BY THE SC-CAMLR OBSERVER TO THE SIXTEENTH MEETING OF THE COMMITTEE FOR ENVIRONMENTAL PROTECTION. This report focuses on the five issues of common interest to the CEP and SC-CAMLR: Climate change and the Antarctic marine environment; Biodiversity and non-native species in the Antarctic marine environment; Antarctic species requiring special protection; Spatial marine management and protected areas; and Ecosystem and environmental monitoring.
IP 15 Belgium	CCAMLR MPA TECHNICAL WORKSHOP. This paper informs on the workshop held in September 2012 aimed to provide a start to the process of the MPA planning of domains 3 (Weddell Sea), 4 (Bouvet-Maud) and 9 (Amundsen-Bellingshausen) for which there had been no active work towards the development of MPAs.
IP 52 SCAR	OCEAN ACIDIFICATION: SCAR FUTURE PLANS. This paper informs on the future work plan of the SCAR international ocean acidification Action Group, whose final report will be launched at the SCAR Open Science Conference in August 2014.
IP 105 Chile	REPORT OF THE CEP OBSERVER TO THE XXXII SCAR DELEGATES' MEETING. In 2012, SCAR invited the Environmental Protection Committee to attend as an observer the meeting that would be held in the United States that year. This paper presents the most relevant aspects of the meeting, to inform the CEP.
BP 20 SCAR	THE SCIENTIFIC COMMITTEE ON ANTARCTIC RESEARCH (SCAR) SELECTED SCIENCE HIGHLIGHTS 2012/13. This Background Paper highlights some recent key science papers published since the last Treaty meeting and should be read in conjunction with IP 4.

BP 21 SCAR	*ANTARCTIC CLIMATE CHANGE AND THE ENVIRONMENT: AN UPDATE.* This paper is the full "Antarctic climate change and the environment: an update" paper recently published in the journal Polar Record. It should be read in conjunction with WP 38 that summarises the key highlights.

6. REPAIR AND REMEDIATION OF ENVIRONMENTAL DAMAGE

WP 27 New Zealand	*REPAIR OR REMEDIATION OF ENVIRONMENTAL DAMAGE: REPORT OF THE CEP INTERSESSIONAL CONTACT GROUP.* This paper reports on the discussions of the ICG which considered environmental issues related to the practicality of repair or remediation of environmental damage in the circumstances of Antarctica, in order to assist the ATCM in adopting an informed decision in 2015 related to the resumption of negotiations on liability.
WP 32 Australia and United Kingdom	*AN ANTARCTIC CLEAN-UP MANUAL: REPORT OF INFORMAL INTERSESSIONAL DISCUSSION.* This paper informs on the intersessional informal discussions on the proposal originally made at CEP XV on an Antarctic Clean-Up Manual. Australia and the United Kingdom recommend that the CEP endorse the revised manual, encourage Members and Observers to develop practical guidelines and supporting resources for inclusion in the manual, and forward the attached draft Resolution and manual to the ATCM for approval.
WP 42 France & Italy	*THE NEED TO TAKE INTO ACCOUNT THE DISMANTLING COSTS OF STATIONS IN COMPREHENSIVE ENVIRONMENTAL EVALUATIONS (CEE) RELATING TO THEIR CONSTRUCTION.* This paper informs on a theoretical estimation of cost and duration that are necessary for the dismantling of Concordia Station. The paper suggests that the results would be also applicable to coastal stations, and that an estimate of decommissioning costs be most systematically taken into account when a CEE is prepared for the construction of a new station.
IP 36 France	*CLEAN-UP OF THE CONSTRUCTION SITE OF UNUSED AIRSTRIP "PISTE DU LION", TERRE ADÉLIE, ANTARCTICA.* This paper informs on the procedure put in place to remove the unused airstrip facilities at Ile du Lion, describing the planning process, clean-up activities and monitoring, as well as lessons learned from the activity.
IP 68 ASOC	*REUSE OF A SITE AFTER REMEDIATION. A CASE STUDY FROM CAPE EVANS, ROSS ISLAND.* Using a case study from a small site at Cape Evans, this paper examines the use of a remediated site by an operator different to the one which conducted the remediation activity, and makes a number of suggestions relevant to assessing cumulative impacts, assessing the effectiveness of remediation, and managing remediated sites.

IP 70 Brazil	*ENVIRONMENTAL DAMAGE REPAIR: DISASSEMBLING OF FERRAZ STATION, ADMIRALTY BAY, ANTARCTICA.* In this paper Brazil presents the structure of the Environmental Management Plan that guided the disassembling of Comandante Ferraz station, destroyed by a fire in February 2012.

7. CLIMATE CHANGE IMPLICATIONS FOR THE ENVIRONMENT: STRATEGIC APPROACH

WP 38 SCAR	*THE ANTARCTIC CLIMATE CHANGE AND THE ENVIRONMENT REPORT (ACCE): A KEY UPDATE.* This paper represents a major update of the original SCAR ACCE report. It summarises subsequent advances in knowledge concerning how the climates of the Antarctic and Southern Ocean have changed in the past and how they might change in the future, and examines the associated impacts on the marine and terrestrial biota.
SP 7 Secretariat	*ACTIONS TAKEN BY THE CEP AND THE ATCM ON THE ATME RECOMMENDATIONS ON CLIMATE CHANGE.* This paper presents an update of actions taken by the ATCM and the CEP on the 30 recommendations on climate change agreed at the ATME on Climate Change in 2009.
IP 32 COMNAP	*COST/ENERGY ANALYSIS OF NATIONAL ANTARCTIC PROGRAM TRANSPORTATION.* This paper presents the results of a transportation cost and energy analysis that was recently undertaken on behalf of the Alfred Wegener Institute–Helmholtz Center for Polar and Marine Research. It focuses on the analysis of transportation of people and cargo via both maritime and air transportation methods.
IP 34 COMNAP	*BEST PRACTICE FOR ENERGY MANAGEMENT – GUIDANCE AND RECOMMENDATIONS.* Considering ATME Recommendation 4, this paper presents an update to the information presented last year, and includes the updated results of the survey of COMNAP Members and a report on progress on the voluntary implementation of the guidance and recommendations developed by COMNAP in 2007 based on the survey replies.
IP 62 ASOC	*AN ANTARCTIC CLIMATE CHANGE REPORT CARD.* This paper summarizes the recent results of research in the areas of environmental and ecosystem changes, and finds that changes are occurring in a variety of areas, from the pH level of seawater to the stability of the West Antarctic Ice Sheet.
IP 65 ASOC	*BLACK CARBON AND OTHER SHORT-LIVED CLIMATE POLLUTANTS: IMPACTS ON ANTARCTICA.* In this paper ASOC proposes that the analysis of the extent of black carbon and other short-lived climate pollutants emissions, especially from local sources, should be a priority for ongoing research, and included in the Strategic Work Plan.

IP 69 ASOC	*UPDATE: THE FUTURE OF THE WEST ANTARCTIC ICE SHEET.* This paper provides significant updates from *The Future of the West Antarctic Ice Sheet: Observed and Predicted Changes, Tipping Points, and Policy Considerations* (IP07 at ATME on Climate Change 2010).
IP 101 IAATO	*IAATO's CLIMATE CHANGE WORKING GROUP: REPORT OF PROGRESS.* This paper informs on the developments of the IAATO's Climate Change Working Group, including additional efforts towards raising awareness of climate change in the Antarctic resulting from human activities worldwide and a list of ways in which IAATO member operators manage their carbon emissions.
BP 21	*ANTARCTIC CLIMATE CHANGE AND THE ENVIRONMENT:* an *UPDATE.* This paper is the full "Antarctic climate change and the environment: an update" paper recently published in the journal *Polar Record*. It should be read in conjunction with WP 38.

8. ENVIRONMENTAL IMPACT ASSESSMENT

a) Draft Comprehensive Environmental Evaluations

b) Other EIA Matters

WP 24 Russian Federation	*APPROACHES TO STUDY OF THE WATER LAYER OF SUBGLACIAL LAKES IN THE ANTARCTIC.* This paper informs on the technologies being used in the drilling activities at Lake Vostok and on the future activities to be developed. The Russian Federation informs that the work undertaken has proved the validity of proposed measures and proposes to use this principle in future studies of the lake water layer.
IP 49 Russian Federation	*RESULTS OF STUDIES OF SUBGLACIAL LAKE VOSTOK AND DRILLING OPERATIONS IN DEEP ICE BOREHOLE OF VOSTOK STATION IN THE SEASON 2012-2013.* This paper presents additional information on the technical procedures and preliminary results of scientific activities conducted at Lake Vostok during the past summer season.
SP 5 Secretariat	*ANNUAL LIST OF INITIAL ENVIRONMENTAL EVALUATIONS (IEE) AND COMPREHENSIVE ENVIRONMENTAL EVALUATIONS (CEE) PREPARED BETWEEN APRIL 1ST 2012 AND MARCH 31ST 2013.* This paper informs on the Environmental Impact Assessments prepared during the most recent reporting period.

IP 24 Republic of Korea	PROGRESS OF THE JANG BOGO STATION DURING THE FIRST CONSTRUCTION SEASON, *2012/13.* This paper informs on the Jang Bogo Station construction activities, which started in December 2012 and will continue for two Antarctic summer seasons. The paper reports on material transportation, construction activities, waste management and environmental monitoring as well as on accidents and incidents that have occurred. The paper also informs on the activities to be undertaken in the 2013/14 season.
IP 25 Republic of Korea	MITIGATION MEASURES OF ENVIRONMENTAL IMPACTS CAUSED BY JANG BOGO CONSTRUCTION DURING *2012/2013* SEASON. This paper informs on the implementation of the mitigation measures proposed in the CEE presented in 2011 and suggested by the Parties, to reduce the environmental impacts caused by the construction activity of Jang Bogo Station.
IP 42 Russian Federation	TO DISCOVERY OF UNKNOWN BACTERIA IN LAKE VOSTOK. This paper describes the technical and scientific procedures put in place which allowed, in late February 2013, the discovery of previously unknown bacteria in the subglacial Lake Vostok.
IP 48 Russian Federation	PERMIT FOR THE ACTIVITY OF THE RUSSIAN ANTARCTIC EXPEDITION IN *2013-17.* This paper informs on the legal requirements and permits granted by the Russian Federation, namely on the Environmental Impact Assessments for the declared activities. The paper describes in particular the IEE prepared for the activities planned in the five-year expedition from 1 January 2013 to 31 December 2017.
IP 58 Brazil	TERMS OF REFERENCE OF THE INITIAL ENVIRONMENTAL EVALUATION *(IEE): PROJECT OF THE NEW FERRAZ STATION (ADMIRALTY BAY, ANTARCTICA).* This paper informs on the process for the reconstruction of Comandante Ferraz Station. The paper presents information on the procedures undertaken, including the selection of the conceptual project for the future station and the terms of reference for the preparation of the IEE.
IP 75 India	INITIAL ENVIRONMENTAL EVALUATION FOR ESTABLISHMENT OF THE GROUND STATION FOR EARTH OBSERVATION SATELLITES AT THE INDIAN RESEARCH STATION BHARATI AT LARSEMANN HILLS, EAST ANTARCTICA. This document presents the IEE related to the proposed activities for installing a ground station for earth observing satellites. India concludes that the adverse impacts on the environment at the site are of a low category and that the IEE is sufficient to address the issue.
IP 80 Italy	FIRST STEPS TOWARDS THE REALIZATION OF A GRAVEL RUNWAY NEAR MARIO ZUCCHELLI STATION: INITIAL CONSIDERATIONS AND POSSIBLE BENEFITS FOR THE TERRA NOVA BAY AREA. In this paper Italy informs on the first results of surveys and studies on the technical, economical and environmental feasibility of a gravel runway in the vicinity of Mario Zucchelli Station.

BP 2 New Zealand	*ASSESSING THE VULNERABILITY OF ANTARCTIC SOILS TO TRAMPLING.* This paper provides information on the specific objectives of management in the Area, proposed as ASMA 2 in 2004.

9. AREA PROTECTION AND MANAGEMENT

a) Management Plans

i.	*Draft management plans which had been reviewed by the Subsidiary Group on Management Plans*
WP 56 Norway	*SUBSIDIARY GROUP ON MANAGEMENT PLANS – REPORT ON 2012/13 INTERSESSIONAL WORK.* During the 2012/13 intersessional period the Subsidiary Group on Management Plans reviewed eight draft ASPA management plans. The SGMP recommends that the Committee approve three revised management plans: ASPA 132, ASPA 151 and a New ASPA: *Cape Washington and Silverfish Bay, Terra Nova Bay, Ross Sea.* The SGMP also advises the CEP that further intersessional work will be conducted with regards to five management plans submitted for intersessional review: ASPA 128, ASPA 144, ASPA 145, ASPA 146 and a New ASPA: *High altitude geothermal sites of the Ross Sea region.*

ii.	*Draft revised management plans which had not been reviewed by the Subsidiary Group on Management Plans*
WP 2 United States	*REVISED MANAGEMENT PLAN FOR ANTARCTIC SPECIALLY PROTECTED AREA No 137 NORTHWEST WHITE ISLAND, McMURDO SOUND.* Since the revisions were minor and focused on bringing the plan formatting in line with the Guide to the Preparation of Management Plans for Antarctic Specially Protected Areas adopted in Resolution 2 (2011), the United States recommends that the CEP adopt the revised Management Plan for ASPA 137.
WP 3 United States	*REVISED MANAGEMENT PLAN FOR ANTARCTIC SPECIALLY PROTECTED AREA No 123 BARWICK AND BALHAM VALLEYS, SOUTHERN VICTORIA LAND.* Since the revisions were minor and focused on bringing the plan formatting in line with the Guide to the Preparation of Management Plans for Antarctic Specially Protected Areas adopted in Resolution 2 (2011), the United States recommends that the CEP adopt the revised Management Plan for ASPA 123.
WP 5 United States	*REVISED MANAGEMENT PLAN FOR ANTARCTIC SPECIALLY PROTECTED AREA No 138 LINNAEUS TERRACE, ASGARD RANGE, VICTORIA LAND.* Since the revisions were minor and focused on bringing the plan formatting in line with the Guide to the Preparation of Management Plans for Antarctic Specially Protected Areas adopted in Resolution 2 (2011), the United States recommends that the CEP adopt the revised Management Plan for ASPA 138.

WP 6 Japan	REVISION OF THE MANAGEMENT PLAN FOR ANTARCTIC SPECIALLY PROTECTED AREA NO 141 YUKIDORI VALLEY, LANGHOVDE, LÜTZOW-HOLM BAY. Given that this Management Plan has been amended, Japan recommends that the CEP ask the Subsidiary Group on Management Plans to undertake a more detailed intersessional review of the revised Management Plan and report back to CEP XVII.
WP 11 United Kingdom	REVISED MANAGEMENT PLAN FOR ANTARCTIC SPECIALLY PROTECTED AREA NO 108, GREEN ISLAND, BERTHELOT ISLANDS, ANTARCTIC PENINSULA. Since there are no major changes to the Area description or management measures, the United Kingdom proposes that the CEP approve the revised Management Plan for ASPA 108.
WP 12 United Kingdom	REVISED MANAGEMENT PLAN FOR ANTARCTIC SPECIALLY PROTECTED AREA NO 117, AVIAN ISLAND, MARGUERITE BAY, ANTARCTIC PENINSULA. Since only minor amendments are required, the United Kingdom proposes that the CEP approve the revised Management Plan for ASPA 117.
WP 13 United Kingdom	REVISED MANAGEMENT PLAN FOR ANTARCTIC SPECIALLY PROTECTED AREA NO 147, ABLATION VALLEY AND GANYMEDE HEIGHTS, ALEXANDER ISLAND. Since only minor amendments are required, the United Kingdom proposes that the CEP approve the revised Management Plan for ASPA 147.
WP 14 United Kingdom	REVISED MANAGEMENT PLAN FOR ANTARCTIC SPECIALLY PROTECTED AREA NO 170, MARION NUNATAKS, CHARCOT ISLAND, ANTARCTIC PENINSULA. Since only minor amendments are required, the United Kingdom proposes that the CEP approve the revised Management Plan for ASPA 170.
WP 29 New Zealand	REVISION OF MANAGEMENT PLAN FOR ANTARCTIC SPECIALLY PROTECTED AREA NO 154: BOTANY BAY, CAPE GEOLOGY, VICTORIA LAND. New Zealand informs that all revisions made in the management plan of ASPA 154 are minor with standard wording applied where applicable, and therefore recommends that the CEP approve the revised management plan.
WP 30 New Zealand	REVISION OF MANAGEMENT PLAN FOR ANTARCTIC SPECIALLY PROTECTED AREA NO 156: LEWIS BAY, MOUNT EREBUS, ROSS ISLAND. New Zealand informs that all revisions made in the management plan of ASPA 156 are minor with standard wording applied where applicable, and therefore recommends that the CEP approve the revised management plan.
WP 36 Australia	REVIEW OF MANAGEMENT PLANS FOR ANTARCTIC SPECIALLY PROTECTED AREAS (ASPAS) 135, 143 AND 160. Australia informs that only minor amendments are required in the management plans of ASPA 135 North-East Bailey Peninsula, ASPA 143 Marine Plain, and ASPA 160 Frazier Islands, and recommends that the CEP approve the revised Management Plans for these ASPAs.

WP 54 rev. 1 Brazil, Ecuador, Perú & Poland	REVIEW OF THE MANAGEMENT PLAN FOR ASMA NO 1: KING GEORGE ISLAND, SOUTH SHETLAND ISLANDS. The Admiralty Bay Management Group has conducted its first five-yearly review of the Management Plan for ASMA 1, and recommends that the CEP ask the Subsidiary Group on Management Plans to undertake an intersessional review and report back to CEP XVI.
WP 59 Argentina	REVISED MANAGEMENT PLAN FOR ASPA 134 (CIERVA POINT AND OFFSHORE ISLANDS, DANCO COAST, ANTARCTIC PENINSULA). Argentina has carried out the review of the Management Plan for ASPA 134 and requests the CEP to assess the need to refer the SGMP for intersessional consideration, or, if not deemed necessary, to proceed with the adoption of this revised Management Plan.
WP 60 Italy	REVISION OF MANAGEMENT PLAN FOR ANTARCTIC SPECIALLY PROTECTED AREA N° 161 TERRA NOVA BAY, ROSS SEA. Italy informs that there have been no substantial changes made to the provisions of the existing Management Plan. The boundaries, map and descriptions of the area remain the same, without changes. Italy recommends that the CEP approve the revised Management Plan for ASPA 161.

iii.	*New draft management plans for protected/managed areas*
WP 8 China	PROPOSAL FOR A NEW ANTARCTIC SPECIALLY MANAGED AREA AT CHINESE ANTARCTIC KUNLUN STATION, DOME A. This paper presents an initial draft management plan for Kunlun Station Dome A aimed to protect the environment of the Dome A area. China proposes that the draft management plan be considered intersessionally by the SGMP.
WP 63 Australia, China, India & Russian Federation	DRAFT ANTARCTIC SPECIALLY PROTECTED AREA (ASPA) MANAGEMENT PLAN FOR STORNES, LARSEMANN HILLS, PRINCESS ELIZABETH LAND. This paper proposes the adoption of a new ASPA aimed to protect the geological features of the area that are unique to Antarctica, specifically the rare mineral occurrences and the highly unusual host rocks in which they occur. The paper recommends that the CEP, as appropriate, refer the draft Management Plan to ATCM XXXVI for adoption or to the SGMP for intersessional review.

iv.	*Other matters relating to management plans for protected/managed areas*
SP 6 Secretariat	STATUS OF ANTARCTIC SPECIALLY PROTECTED AREA AND ANTARCTIC SPECIALLY MANAGED AREA MANAGEMENT PLANS. This paper presents information on the status of ASPA and ASMA management plans according to the review requirements of Annex V to the Protocol.

IP 26 rev. 1 Republic of Korea	*MANAGEMENT REPORT OF NARĘBSKI POINT (ASPA NO 171) DURING THE 2012/2013 PERIOD.* This paper informs on the activities undertaken in accordance with the provisions of the Management Plan for ASPA 171. The paper describes scientific studies carried out as well as management activities, lessons learned and recommendations.
IP 74 Argentina, Chile, Norway, Spain UK & USA	*DECEPTION ISLAND SPECIALLY MANAGED AREA (ASMA) MANAGEMENT GROUP REPORT.* This paper summarizes the activities undertaken within ASMA 4, and the work of the Management Group to fulfill the objectives and principles of the Management Plan during the intersessional period.

b) Historic Sites and Monuments

WP 18 rev. 1 Germany	*PROPOSAL TO ADD THE SITE COMMEMORATING THE LOCATION OF THE FORMER GERMAN ANTARCTIC RESEARCH STATION "GEORG FORSTER" TO THE LIST OF HISTORIC SITES AND MONUMENTS.* Germany proposes that the historic site of the German Georg Forster Station marked by a commemorative plaque at the Schirmacher Oasis in Dronning Maud Land be added to the list of Historic Sites and Monuments approved by the ATCM. The plaque commemorates the first permanently used German research base in Antarctica.
WP 23 Russian Federation	*PROPOSED ADDITION OF THE PROFESSOR KUDRYASHOV'S DRILLING COMPLEX BUILDING AT THE RUSSIAN ANTARCTIC VOSTOK STATION TO THE LIST OF HISTORIC SITES AND MONUMENTS.* This paper proposes to add to the List of HSMs the Professor Kudryashov's drilling complex building at the Russian Antarctic Vostok station. This proposal is connected with the need to commemorate the unique achievement of the Russian drillers and glaciologists in the field of drilling deep ice boreholes, reconstruction of paleoclimatic changes based on ice core data, microbiological studies of these ice cores, and ecologically clean unsealing of the subglacial Lake Vostok.
WP 62 United Kingdom, New Zealand & United States	*NEW HISTORIC SITES AND MONUMENTS: MOUNT EREBUS CAMP SITES USED BY A CONTINGENT OF THE TERRA NOVA EXPEDITION IN DECEMBER 1912.* This paper proposes two new HSMs in the locations of camp sites on Mount Erebus, used between 8 and 13 December 1912 by a team of scientists who were in Antarctica as part of Captain Scott's Terra Nova expedition 1910-1912. The sites were located in December 2012. The locations of the camps are of significant interest to Antarctic historians, and uncontrolled access to the sites, which might disturb any additional historic remains, would be of concern. The United Kingdom, New Zealand and the United States are therefore of the view that these sites should be afforded protection under Annex V of the Protocol.

BP 1 New Zealand	*ANTARCTIC HERITAGE TRUST CONSERVATION UPDATE 2013.* This paper forms an update to the paper provided to the CEP XV/ATCM XXXV of the restoration project being undertaken at ASPAs 155,157,158 at Ross Island, and ASPA 159 at Cape Adare.

c) Site Guidelines

WP 15 UK, Argentina, Australia & USA	*POLICY ISSUES ARISING FROM THE 2013 ON-SITE REVIEW OF GUIDELINES FOR VISITOR SITES IN THE ANTARCTIC PENINSULA.* This paper reports on an On-Site Review of Site Guidelines during January 2013 by the United Kingdom, Argentina, Australia, the United States and IAATO. The paper discusses those issues in light of the CEP's recent considerations and the developments in visitor use and makes recommendations for consideration by the Committee.
WP 16 UK, Argentina, Australia & USA	*SITE GUIDELINES FOR I) ORNE HARBOUR AND II) ORNE ISLANDS.* Further to the review reported in WP 15, new site guidelines have been prepared for i) Orne Harbour and ii) Orne Islands. The proponents recommend that the CEP submit both Site Guidelines for adoption by the ATCM.
WP 20 UK, Argentina, Australia & USA	*ON-SITE REVIEW OF GUIDELINES FOR VISITOR SITES IN THE ANTARCTIC PENINSULA: SUMMARY OF PROGRAMME AND SUGGESTED AMENDMENT OF ELEVEN GUIDELINES.* Further to WP 15, this paper provides an overview of the work of the United Kingdom, Argentina, Australia, the United States and IAATO, and proposes the amendment of 11 Site Guidelines to ensure that they are brought up to date and can continue to be an effective tool for visitor management.
WP 26 United States	*PROPOSED AMENDMENT FOR ANTARCTIC TREATY SITE GUIDELINES FOR VISITORS TORGERSEN ISLAND.* This paper proposes, as a precautionary measure in light of changes in the penguin population on the island, an amendment to the Site Guidelines to strongly discourage visits during the early breeding season when the birds are most sensitive to brown skua predation and potential human disturbance.
WP 46 United States, Argentina, Chile, Norway, Spain, United Kingdom, ASOC & IAATO.	*PROPOSED AMENDMENT FOR ANTARCTIC TREATY SITE GUIDELINES FOR VISITORS BAILY HEAD, DECEPTION ISLAND.* This paper informs on a review of the Site Guidelines by the Deception Island Management Group, following a report of a significant decline in the chinstrap penguins breeding at Baily Head. Although the decrease is most likely related to numerous and complex effects of climate change, the Group used the review as an opportunity to decrease redundancy between these site specific Site Guidelines for Visitors and the General Guidelines for Visitors to the Antarctic.

WP 64 Ecuador	*UPDATED MAP OF BARRIENTOS ISLAND.* This paper presents for consideration of the Committee and the Parties an updated map of the Barrientos island to contribute to compliance with Resolution 5 (2012) and facilitate tourism and research activities that are performed at this site.
IP 20 United States	*ANTARCTIC SITE INVENTORY: 1994-2013.* This paper provides an update on results of the Antarctic Site Inventory project through February 2013, which has collected biological data and site-descriptive information in the Antarctic Peninsula since 1994.
IP 97 IAATO	*REPORT ON IAATO OPERATOR USE OF ANTARCTIC PENINSULA LANDING SITES AND ATCM VISITOR SITE GUIDELINES, 2012-13 SEASON.* This paper presents the data collected by IAATO covering the landing sites and site guidelines use for the 2012-13 season.
IP 102 IAATO	*BARRIENTOS ISLAND FOOTPATH EROSION.* This paper informs on the IAATO internal investigation of a footpath erosion in vegetation at Barrientos Island presented at the CEP XV meeting by Ecuador and Spain.

d) Human footprint and wilderness values	
WP 35 New Zealand	*POSSIBLE GUIDANCE MATERIAL TO ASSIST PARTIES TO TAKE ACCOUNT OF WILDERNESS VALUES WHEN UNDERTAKING ENVIRONMENTAL IMPACT ASSESSMENTS.* This paper provides a report developed from intersessional discussions on the issue of wilderness management in Antarctica. The paper suggests an option for further developing the EIA guidelines so as to provide a structured means of taking account of wilderness values when preparing environmental impact assessments of proposed activities.
IP 39 New Zealand	*INTERSESSIONAL REPORT ON THE PROVISION OF GUIDANCE MATERIAL TO ASSIST PARTIES TO TAKE ACCOUNT OF WILDERNESS VALUES WHEN UNDERTAKING ENVIRONMENTAL IMPACT ASSESSMENTS.* This report, connected to WP 35, suggests guidance material that will assist Parties to take account of wilderness values when undertaking environmental impact assessments of proposed activities.
IP 33 COMNAP	*ANALYSIS OF NATIONAL ANTARCTIC PROGRAM INCREASED DELIVERY OF SCIENCE.* This paper presents the results of an analysis that was recently undertaken by the Chilean National Antarctic Program, Instituto Antartico Chileno (INACH) which looked at reducing the environmental impact while doing more science. This analysis allowed it to then set procedures and strategies to continue to deliver more science while reducing its programs' Antarctic footprint.

IP 60 ASOC	MAPPING AND MODELLING WILDERNESS VALUES IN ANTARCTICA: CONTRIBUTION TO CEP'S WORK IN DEVELOPING GUIDANCE MATERIAL ON WILDERNESS PROTECTION USING PROTOCOL TOOLS. This paper summarizes the recommendations of the report "Mapping and modelling wilderness values in Antarctica" produced by the Wildland Research Institute, as a contribution to the CEP's work in developing guidance material on wilderness protection using Protocol tools.

e) Marine Spatial Protection and Management

BP 17 ASOC	ANTARCTIC OCEAN LEGACY UPDATE 1 – SECURING ENDURING PROTECTION FOR THE ROSS SEA REGION. This paper summarizes the Antarctic Ocean Legacy Update Report, reviewing why the region should be protected, updating on the latest developments and calling for the Ross Sea marine reserve to be designated as one of the keystones of a Southern Ocean system of marine protected areas and marine reserves.

f) Other Annex V Matters

WP 10 United Kingdom	IDENTIFICATION OF POTENTIAL CLIMATE CHANGE REFUGIA FOR EMPEROR PENGUINS: A SCIENCE-BASED APPROACH. Over the coming century, climate change will probably impact upon emperor penguin distribution range and breeding success in the Antarctic Peninsula region and wider Antarctica. The United Kingdom therefore recommends that the CEP endorse the monitoring of emperor penguin colonies using remote sensing techniques to identify potential climate change *refugia*, and encourages other Parties to undertake similar work in other regions of Antarctica.
WP 21 Russian Federation	ANALYSIS OF THE ASPA AND ASMA WILDLIFE VALUES. Noting Resolution 2 (2011) on the Revised Guide to the Preparation of Management Plans, the Russian Federation recommends the adoption of a Measure on the need of conducting monitoring programs in reviewing ASPA and ASMA management plans in which representatives of living Antarctic nature are designated as the main values to be protected .
WP 22 Russian Federation	RUSSIAN ANTARCTIC BIOGEOGRAPHIC REGIONING AS COMPARED WITH THE NEW ZEALAND CLASSIFICATION. In this paper, taking into account Resolution 6 (2012) on Antarctic Conservation Biogeographic Regions, the Russian Federation proposes to consider further developments of biogeographic regioning related to landscape science of Antarctica.

WP 39 Belgium, South Africa, United Kingdom & SCAR	*HUMAN FOOTPRINT IN ANTARCTICA AND THE LONG-TERM CONSERVATION AND STUDY OF TERRESTRIAL MICROBIAL HABITATS.* Recent advances in molecular biology techniques have shown the presence of diverse microbial communities and the existence of species endemic to Antarctica. The purpose of this paper is to highlight potential threats both to the conservation of terrestrial microbial ecosystems in Antarctica and to future scientific research requiring study of these ecosystems.
WP 55 Spain	*RECOVERY OF MOSS COMMUNITIES ON THE PATHS OF BARRIENTOS ISLAND AND A PROPOSAL FOR TOURISM MANAGEMENT.* This paper reports on the results of a monitoring program of visits to the island, an assessment of the vegetation cover and as a result, a management proposal for visitors.
IP 35 Argentina, Spain & United Kingdom	*THE NON-NATIVE GRASS POA PRATENSIS AT CIERVA POINT, DANCO COAST, ANTARCTIC PENINSULA – ON-GOING INVESTIGATIONS AND FUTURE ERADICATION PLANS.* This paper describes the research undertaken by Argentina, Spain and the UK during the season 2012/13 at Cierva Point in order to eradicate the non-native grass *Poa pratensis*.
IP 46 Australia, China, India & Russian Federation	*REPORT OF THE ANTARCTIC SPECIALLY MANAGED AREA NO 6 LARSEMANN HILLS MANAGEMENT GROUP.* This paper gives a brief report on the Management Group's activities during 2012-13. The paper informs that the Management Group aims to finalise the review of the management plan at its next meeting in July 2013, and to submit a revised management plan for consideration at CEP XVII.
IP 73 United Kingdom & Norway	*ANTARCTIC TRIAL OF WWF's RAPID ASSESSMENT OF CIRCUM-ARCTIC ECOSYSTEM RESILIENCE (RACER) TOOL: INITIAL FINDINGS.* This paper provides a brief update on the progress of the trial of the RACER, a tool from the Arctic to assess ecosystem resilience and areas of conservation importance, and the possible application of RACER to Antarctica.
IP 111 United Kingdom & Spain	*MANAGEMENT OF ANTARCTIC SPECIALLY PROTECTED AREAS: PERMITTING, VISITATION AND INFORMATION EXCHANGE PRACTICES.* This paper presents research into Parties' information exchange practices associated with the visitation of ASPAs. Improved provision and formal interpretation of ASPA visitation data are recommended to enable more co-ordinated and effective management of activities within ASPAs.
BP 10 United States & New Zealand	*UPDATE ON DEVELOPING PROTECTION FOR A GEOTHERMAL AREA: VOLCANIC ICE CAVES AT MOUNT EREBUS, ROSS ISLAND.* This paper presents an update on the progress of the development of protection for the geothermal ice caves on the summit of Mount Erebus, and informs on plans for the 2013-14 intersessional period.

10. CONSERVATION OF ANTARCTIC FLORA AND FAUNA	
a) Quarantine and Non-native Species	
WP 19 Germany	REPORT ON THE RESEARCH PROJECT "THE IMPACT OF HUMAN ACTIVITIES ON SOIL ORGANISMS OF THE MARITIME ANTARCTIC AND THE INTRODUCTION OF NON-NATIVE SPECIES IN ANTARCTICA". Germany presents the results of the research project, and invites Parties and the CEP to consider the results of the project and the recommendations which concern biosecurity measures against the transfer and introduction of non-native soil organisms, and decide as appropriate.
IP 55 Germany	FINAL REPORT ON THE RESEARCH PROJECT "THE IMPACT OF HUMAN ACTIVITIES ON SOIL ORGANISMS OF THE MARITIME ANTARCTIC AND THE INTRODUCTION OF NON-NATIVE SPECIES IN ANTARCTICA". This paper presents the final report of the Project.
IP 28 United Kingdom	COLONISATION STATUS OF KNOWN NON-NATIVE SPECIES IN THE ANTARCTIC TERRESTRIAL ENVIRONMENT (UPDATED 2013). This paper is an update on the information presented during the past three years. The United Kingdom informs that during the last year there has been further development in the understanding of the colonisation potential and biology of some of the non-native species described previously, and evidence of a possible new non-native species within ASPA 128.
IP 35 Argentina, Spain & United Kingdom	THE NON-NATIVE GRASS POA PRATENSIS AT CIERVA POINT, DANCO COAST, ANTARCTIC PENINSULA – ON-GOING INVESTIGATIONS AND FUTURE ERADICATION PLANS. This paper describes the research undertaken by Argentina, Spain and the UK during the season 2012/13 at Cierva Point in order to eradicate the non-native grass *Poa pratensis*.
BP 9 Australia	AUSTRALIA'S NEW ANTARCTIC CARGO AND BIOSECURITY OPERATIONS FACILITY. This paper informs on the new cargo and biosecurity operations facility established in Hobart by the Australian Antarctic Division to support its Antarctic operations.
b) Specially Protected Species	
c) Other Annex II Matters	
WP 10 United Kingdom	IDENTIFICATION OF POTENTIAL CLIMATE CHANGE REFUGIA FOR EMPEROR PENGUINS: A SCIENCE-BASED APPROACH. Over the coming century, climate change will probably impact upon emperor penguin distribution range and breeding success in the Antarctic Peninsula region and wider Antarctica. The United Kingdom therefore recommends that the CEP endorse the monitoring of emperor penguin colonies using remote sensing techniques to identify potential climate change *refugia*, and encourages other Parties to undertake similar work in other regions of Antarctica.

IP 31 COMNAP	*USE OF HYDROPONICS BY NATIONAL ANTARCTIC PROGRAMS.* The national Antarctic programs of Australia, New Zealand and the United States operate hydroponic facilities in Antarctica. Each program has reviewed the potential environmental impacts of hydroponics and has risk-based management measures in place.

11. ENVIRONMENTAL MONITORING AND REPORTING

WP 37 Belgium & SCAR	*WWW.BIODIVERSITY.AQ: THE NEW ANTARCTIC BIODIVERSITY INFORMATION NETWORK.* This paper informs on the renewed international Antarctic Biodiversity portal, which builds on the legacy of the SCAR Marine Biodiversity Information Network and the Antarctic Biodiversity Information Facility, providing access to both marine and terrestrial Antarctic biodiversity data.
IP 5 SCAR	*THE SOUTHERN OCEAN OBSERVING SYSTEM (SOOS) 2012 REPORT.* This report highlights SOOS achievements in 2012, and planned activities for 2013.
IP 19 SCAR	*1ST SCAR ANTARCTIC AND SOUTHERN OCEAN SCIENCE HORIZON SCAN.* The SCAR 2011-2016 Strategic Plan calls for instituting a "Horizon Scanning" activity, to be held every 4 or 5 years, to support SCAR's vision of leadership and international cooperation in Antarctic and Southern Ocean science and assist in achieving its mission of excellence in science and scientific advice to policy makers. The Scan will assemble 50 of the world's leading Antarctic scientists, policy makers, leaders, and visionaries to identify the most important scientific questions that will or should be addressed by research in and from the southern Polar Regions over the next two decades.
IP 27 Rep. of Korea & Germany	*KOREAN/GERMAN WORKSHOP ABOUT ENVIRONMENTAL MONITORING ON KING GEORGE ISLAND.* This paper informs on the joint Workshop held in April 2012. The paper reports that there was a very fruitful exchange of information on the previous and ongoing monitoring and research activities in the Maxwell Bay area, and that the participants reached an agreement that the successful dialog between Korea and Germany should be carried out on a regular basis e.g. by annual meetings.
IP 29 United Kingdom	*REMOTE SENSING FOR MONITORING ANTARCTIC SPECIALLY PROTECTED AREAS: PROGRESS ON USE OF MULTISPECTRAL AND HYPERSPECTRAL DATA FOR MONITORING ANTARCTIC VEGETATION.* This paper provides an update on the development and application of new remote sensing techniques to monitor vegetation within Antarctic Specially Protected Areas and the wider Antarctic environment.

IP 59 ASOC	*UPDATE TO VESSEL INCIDENTS IN ANTARCTIC WATERS.* This paper provides additional information and analysis of vessel incidents in Antarctic waters, including a map of vessel incidents and case studies of several recent incidents in the context of the evolving Polar Code which point to a number of inadequacies in the current draft Polar Code.
IP 66 ASOC	*DISCHARGE OF SEWAGE AND GREY WATER FROM VESSELS IN ANTARCTIC TREATY WATERS.* This paper provides information on discharges of black (sewage) and grey water from vessels, expresses concerns that the current system for the management of sewage and grey water waste streams may not be sufficient to provide adequate protection for Antarctic ecosystems and wildlife, and summarises the current regulation.
IP 67 ASOC	*MANAGEMENT IMPLICATIONS OF TOURIST BEHAVIOUR.* This paper examines aspects of Antarctic tourist behaviour in the context of current tourism trends, and discusses the implications for tourism regulation and management.
IP 76 Italy	*REPORT ON THE ACCIDENT OCCURRED TO AN EXCAVATOR VEHICLE AT MARIO ZUCCHELLI STATION, ROSS SEA, ANTARCTICA.* This paper informs on an excavator that fell into the sea in front of Mario Zucchelli Station in December 2012.
IP 107 Chile	*ANTARCTIC CENTER FOR RESEARCH AND ENVIRONMENTAL MONITORING, CIMAA: ADVANCES IN WATER QUALITY MONITORING AND OPPORTUNITIES FOR COOPERATION.* This paper presents the results obtained by the Antarctic Center for Research and Environmental Monitoring, CIMAA, in the Chilean Bernardo O'Higgins Base during the 2012-2013 season. In addition, reports on new international collaborative activities to verify the operation of sewage treatment plants.

12. INSPECTION REPORTS	
WP 4 Germany & South Africa	*INSPECTION BY GERMANY AND SOUTH AFRICA IN ACCORDANCE WITH ARTICLE VII OF THE ANTARCTIC TREATY AND ARTICLE 14 OF THE PROTOCOL ON ENVIRONMENTAL PROTECTION: JANUARY 2013.* In this paper Germany and South Africa report on the inspections conducted of four stations in Dronning Maud Land from 9 to 29 January 2013 under the applicable provisions of the Antarctic Treaty and Madrid Protocol.
IP 53 Germany & South Africa	*INSPECTION BY GERMANY AND SOUTH AFRICA IN ACCORDANCE WITH ARTICLE VII OF THE ANTARCTIC TREATY AND ARTICLE 14 OF THE PROTOCOL ON ENVIRONMENTAL PROTECTION: JANUARY 2013.* This paper presents the full inspection report describing the observations and conclusions of the 2013 German-South African Joint Antarctic Inspection Team.

WP 9 United Kingdom, the Netherlands & Spain	*GENERAL RECOMMENDATIONS FROM THE JOINT INSPECTIONS UNDERTAKEN BY THE UNITED KINGDOM, THE NETHERLANDS AND SPAIN UNDER ARTICLE VII OF THE ANTARCTIC TREATY AND ARTICLE 14 OF THE ENVIRONMENTAL PROTOCOL.* This paper informs that inspections were conducted jointly by the United Kingdom, the Netherlands and Spain in the Antarctic Peninsula region in December 2012. The Observers identified a series of general recommendations arising from their Inspection which have potential relevance beyond just those bases, stations, sites and vessels inspected.
IP 38 United Kingdom, the Netherlands & Spain	*REPORT OF THE JOINT INSPECTIONS UNDERTAKEN BY THE UNITED KINGDOM, THE NETHERLANDS AND SPAIN UNDER ARTICLE VII OF THE ANTARCTIC TREATY AND ARTICLE 14 OF THE ENVIRONMENTAL PROTOCOL.* Full Report of the joint Inspection described in WP 9.
WP 51 rev. 1 Uruguay & Argentina	*ADDITIONAL AVAILABILITY OF INFORMATION ON LISTS OF OBSERVERS OF THE CONSULTATIVE PARTIES THROUGH THE ANTARCTIC TREATY SECRETARIAT*. This paper suggests that the Antarctic Treaty Secretariat could provide a complementary source of information for the Parties on the appointment of Observers in accordance with Article 7 of the Antarctic Treaty and Article 14 of the Protocol. This information could be available through restricted access, in the Pre-season Information section of the EIES.
IP 16 France & Italy	*STATUS OF THE FLUID IN THE EPICA BOREHOLE AT CONCORDIA STATION: AN ANSWER TO THE US / RUSSIAN INSPECTION IN 2012.* At CEP XV, the US and the Russian Federation reported the results of their joint inspection at Concordia station in January 2012. Among the comments, a doubt was raised about a possible leakage of the drilling fluid of the EPICA borehole and inaccurate information was provided on the nature of this drilling fluid. The aim of this Information Paper is to answer to these remarks.
IP 45 Russian Federation & United States	*REPORT OF RUSSIA – US JOINT ANTARCTIC INSPECTION, NOVEMBER 29 – DECEMBER 6, 2012.* This paper informs on the second phase of the joint inspection of seven Antarctic stations. The paper also informs on the main conclusions of this second phase.
IP 77 Italy	*ITALY ANSWER TO THE US / RUSSIAN INSPECTION AT MARIO ZUCCHELLI STATION IN 2012.* This paper presents more detailed information about the ability of Italy to fully implement legal standards related to the Environmental Protocol, in answer to concerns expressed in the report of the 2012 inspection.

13. GENERAL MATTERS	
IP 7 Japan	*STATE OF JAPANESE ENVIRONMENTAL MANAGEMENT IN ANTARCTICA, WITH REFERENCE TO THE PRACTICES OF OTHER NATIONAL ANTARCTIC PROGRAMMES.* This paper informs that the Ministry of Environment of Japan decided to investigate the status of environmental conservation in Antarctic stations of each country as a reference to identify potential future improvements in environmental conservation.
IP 83 SCAR	*THE INTERNATIONAL BATHYMETRIC CHART OF THE SOUTHERN OCEAN (IBCSO): FIRST RELEASE.* This paper informs on the project initiated in 2006, in particular on the data repository and the map released by the Alfred-Wegener-Institute in Germany.
IP 104 Colombia	*IP 104. COLOMBIA IN ANTARCTICA.* This paper informs on a decision by Colombia of undertaking a more active role in Antarctica through a more active participation on Antarctic science, exchange of information, international cooperation and exchange of information. Colombia announced that is planning and Antarctic expedition for the 2014 or 2015 summer season and that it has initiated the process to ratify the Environmental Protocol.

14. ELECTION OF OFFICERS

15. PREPARATION FOR NEXT MEETING

16. ADOPTION OF THE REPORT

17. CLOSING OF THE MEETING

Appendix 1

CEP Five-Year Work Plan

Issue / Environmental Pressure Actions	CEP Priority	Intersessional Period	CEP XVII 2014	Intersessional Period	CEP XVIII 2015	Intersessional Period	CEP XIX 2016	Intersessional Period	CEP XX 2017
Introduction of non-native species **Actions:** 1. Continue developing practical guidelines & resources for all Antarctic operators. 2. Continue advancing recommendations from climate change ATME. 3. Consider the spatially explicit +A10	1	Informal intersessional discussions (Germany) Interested members, experts, NAPs work on response measures and eradication.	Discuss further monitoring measures for inclusion in NSS manual, including a surveillance strategy for areas at high risk of establishment. Discuss further response measures for inclusion in NNS manual	Prepare for review of manual-consider informal discussion group	Review non-native species manual		2016		*Period*	
Tourism and NGO activities **Actions:** 1. Provide advice to ATCM as requested 2. Advance recommendations from ship-borne tourism ATME.	1	Parties to cooperate to prepare material in response to recommendations 3 and 6 of the tourism study	Provide interim response to ATCM on tourism study recommendations 3 and 6 Consider format of site guidelines in response to recommendation 8 of WP15 (2013)						
Global Pressure: Climate Change **Actions:** 1. Consider implications of climate change for management of Antarctic environment. 2. Advance recommendations from climate change ATME.	1	ICG to advance recommendations from ATME	Interim report from the ICG Standing agenda item SCAR provides update	ICG continues to advance recommendations from ATME	ICG report Standing agenda item SCAR provides update	Continue to advance recommendations from ATME	Standing agenda item SCAR provides update	Continue to advance recommendations from ATME	Standing agenda item SCAR provides update

Issue / Environmental Pressure Actions	CEP Priority	*Intersessional Period*	CEP XVII 2014	*Intersessional Period*	CEP XVIII 2015	*Intersessional Period*	CEP XIX	*Intersessional*	CEP XX 2017
Processing new and revised protected / managed area management plans	1	SGMP / conducts work as per agreed work plan	Consideration of SGMP / report	SGMP / conducts work as per agreed work plan	Consideration of SGMP / report	SGMP / conducts work as per agreed work plan	Consideration of SGMP / report		
Actions: 1. Refine the process for reviewing new and revised management plans. 2. Update existing guidelines. 3. Advance recommendations from climate change ATME. 4. Develop guidelines to ASMAs preparation. 5. Consider the need to enhance the process for designation of new ASPAs and ASMAs.				Develop guidelines to ASMAs preparation.					
Marine spatial protection and management	1								
Actions: 1. Cooperate with CCAMLR on Southern Ocean bioregionalisation and other common interests and agreed principles. 2. Identify and apply processes for spatial marine protection. Advance recommendations from climate change ATME.									
Operation of the CEP and Strategic Planning	1		Standing item Review and revise work plan as appropriate		Preparations for the 25th anniversary Standing item Review and revise work plan as appropriate		25th anniversary of Protocol. Review and revise work plan as appropriate		
Actions: 1. Keep the 5 year plan up to date based on changing circumstances and ATCM requirements. 2. Identify opportunities for improving the effectiveness of the CEP. 3. Consider long-term objectives for Antarctica (50-100 years time).									

Issue / Environmental Pressure Actions	CEP Priority	*Intersessional Period*	CEP XVII 2014	*Intersessional Period*	CEP XVIII 2015	*Intersessional Period*	CEP XIX	*Intersessional*	CEP XX 2017
Repair or Remediation of Environmental Damage	1		Consider updating Clean-up Manual, as appropriate Consider further request by the ATCM		Secretariat requested to develop and maintain an inventory Consider further request by the ATCM for final advice				
Actions: 1. Respond to further request from the ATCM related to Decision 4 (2010), as appropriate 2. Establish Antarctic-wide inventory of sites of past activity. 3. Consider guidelines for repair and remediation. 4. Members develop practical guidelines and supporting resources for inclusion in the clean-up manual									
Human footprint / wilderness management	2	Continue informal intersessional discussions, including on microbiological issues							
Actions: 1. Develop an agreed understanding of the terms "footprint" and "wilderness". 2. Develop methods for improved protection of wilderness under Annexes I and V.									
Monitoring and state of the environment reporting	2		Report to the CEP as appropriate						
Actions: 1. Identify key environmental indicators and tools. 2. Establish a process for reporting to the ATCM. 3. SCAR to support information to COMNAP and CEP.									
Biodiversity knowledge	2				Discussion of SCAR update on underwater noise.				
Actions: 1. Maintain awareness of threats to existing biodiversity. 2. Advance recommendations from climate change ATME									

163

Issue / Environmental Pressure Actions	CEP Priority	Intersessional Period	CEP XVII 2014	Intersessional Period	CEP XVIII 2015	Intersessional Period	CEP XIX	Intersessional	CEP XX 2017
Site specific guidelines for tourist-visited sites	2	UK to coordinate an informal process to seek and collate information on National Operator's use of site guidelines	Standing agenda item; Parties to report on their reviews of site guidelines		Standing agenda item; Parties to report on their reviews of site guidelines		Standing agenda item; Parties to report on their reviews of site guidelines		Standing agenda item; Parties to report on their reviews of site guidelines
Actions: 1. Review site specific guidelines as required 2. Provide advice to ATCM as required 3. Review the format of the site guidelines			Report to the CEP with Barrientos Island, Aitcho Islands, monitoring results.						
Overview of the protected areas system	2		Discuss possible implications of an updated gap analysis based on EDA and ACBR.						
Actions: 1. Apply the Environmental Domains Analysis (EDA) and Antarctic Conservation Biogeographic Regions (ACBR) to enhance the protected areas system 2. Advance recommendations from climate change ATME. 3. Maintain and develop Protected Area database.									
Outreach and education	2								
Actions: 1. Review current examples and identify opportunities for greater education and outreach. 2. Encourage Members to exchange information regarding their experiences in this area. 3. Establish a strategy and guidelines for exchanging information between Members on Education and Outreach for long term perspective.									
Maintain the list of Historic Sites and Monuments	3	Secretariat update list of HSMs	Standing item	Secretariat update list of HSMs	Standing item	Secretariat update list of HSMs	Standing item	Secretariat update list of HSMs	Standing item
Actions: 1. Maintain the list and consider new proposals as they arise. 2. Consider strategic issues as necessary, including issues relating to designation of buildings as HSM versus clean-up provisions of the Protocol									

Issue / Environmental Pressure Actions	CEP Priority	Intersessional Period	CEP XVII 2014	Intersessional Period	CEP XVIII 2015	Intersessional Period	CEP XIX	Intersessional	CEP XX 2017
Exchange of Information	3		Secretariat Report		Secretariat Report		Secretariat Report		Secretariat Report
Actions: 1. Assign to the Secretariat. 2. Monitor and facilitate easy use of the EIES.									
Implementing and improving the EIA provisions of Annex I	3	Establish ICG to review draft CEEs as required	Consideration of ICG reports on draft CEE, as required	Start a revision of the EIA Guidelines, including human footprint, wilderness, decommissioning of stations, etc. Establish ICG to review draft CEEs as required	Consideration of ICG reports on draft CEE, as required	Establish ICG to review draft CEEs as required	Consideration of ICG reports on draft CEE, as required	Establish ICG to review draft CEEs as required	Consideration of ICG reports on draft CEE, as required
Actions: 1 Refine the process for considering CEEs and advising the ATCM accordingly. 2 Develop guidelines for assessing cumulative impacts. 3 Keep the EIA Guidelines under review. 4 Consider application of strategic environmental assessment in Antarctica 5 Advance recommendations from climate change ATME									
Specially protected species	3		Consider proposal as required						
Actions: 1 Consider proposals related to specially protected species.									
Emergency response action and contingency planning	3	Discussion		Discussion					
Actions: 1 Advance recommendations from ship-borne tourism ATME.									
Updating the Protocol and reviewing Annexes	3								
Actions: 1 Consider the need and aim to reviewing Protocol Annexes.									
Inspections (Article 14 of the Protocol)	3		Standing item		Standing item		Standing item		Standing item
Actions: 1 Review inspection reports as required.									

165

Issue / Environmental Pressure Actions	CEP Priority	Intersessional Period	CEP XVII 2014	Intersessional Period	CEP XVIII 2015	Intersessional Period	CEP XIX	Intersessional	CEP XX 2017
Waste	3								
Actions: 1. Develop guidelines for best practice disposal of waste including human waste.		COMNAP reviews information from 2006 waste management workshop							
Energy management	4								
Actions: 1. Develop best-practice guidelines for energy management at stations and bases.									
Outreach and education	2								
Actions: 1. Review current examples and identify opportunities for greater education and outreach. 2. Encourage Members to exchange information regarding their experiences in this area 3. Establish a strategy and guidelines for exchanging information between Members on Education and Outreach for long term perspective.									

Appendix 2

Provisional Agenda for CEP XVII

1. Opening of the Meeting
2. Adoption of the Agenda
3. Strategic Discussions on the Future Work of the CEP
4. Operation of the CEP
5. Cooperation with other Organisations
6. Repair and Remediation of Environment Damage
7. Climate Change Implications for the Environment: Strategic approach
8. Environmental Impact Assessment (EIA)
     a. Draft Comprehensive Environmental Evaluations
     b. Other EIA Matters
9. Area Protection and Management Plans
     a. Management Plans
     b. Historic Sites and Monuments
     c. Site Guidelines
     d. Human footprint and wilderness values
     e. Marine Spatial Protection and Management
     f. Other Annex V Matters
10. Conservation of Antarctic Flora and Fauna
     a. Quarantine and Non-native Species
     b. Specially Protected Species
     c. Other Annex II Matters
11. Environmental Monitoring and Reporting
12. Inspection Reports
13. General Matters
14. Election of Officers
15. Preparation for Next Meeting
16. Adoption of the Report
17. Closing of the Meeting

3. Appendices

ATCM XXXVI Communique

From 20 to 29 May 2013, Belgium hosted the XXXVI Antarctic Treaty Consultative Meeting and the XVI meeting of the Committee for Environmental Protection (CEP). The meetings were jointly organized by the Federal Departments of Foreign Affairs, Environment and Science Policy. The Parties welcomed the Czech Republic as the 29th Consultative Party.

Since 1959, the Antarctic Treaty has been the centrepiece of international cooperation to preserve the unique character of Antarctica as a natural reserve devoted to peace and science through exchange of information, consultation and formulation of Measures, Decisions and Resolutions.

More than 450 delegates representing the 50 Parties, including officials, renowned scientists, experts and international observers attended this yearly meeting with a common goal: to promote effective international cooperation on challenges and emerging threats facing Antarctica.

Science has remained at the center of the discussions. The Parties highlighted the strategic role of science in policy making on the study of the effects of climate change and other threats to the environment.

International cooperation is at the core of the Treaty and was again the key phrase in official statements and in discussions among delegates.

One of the key achievements of this year's ATCM was the adoption of a strategic work plan which identifies priorities to be pursued under 3 key areas in order to reinforce cooperation in ensuring a robust and effective Antarctic Treaty System, in strengthening the protection of the Antarctic environment and in the effective management and regulation of human activities in Antarctica.

In order to address potential environmental damage, the CEP identified a series of critical policy issues and endorsed a site clean-up manual. Following the report of the Scientific Committee on Antarctic Research (SCAR) on Climate change and impacts on the environment, the CEP decided to develop a prioritized climate change response work plan. The ATCM adopted, on the CEP's advice, 17 managements plans for Antarctic protected areas and 16 Site Guidelines for visitors.

Parties supported further international cooperation on Antarctic science and logistics. The Meeting held a full day special session on Search and Rescue in Antarctica and Parties decided to continue to collaborate actively, to share best practices, to cooperate with the International Maritime Organisation (IMO) and the International Civil Aviation Organisation (ICAO) and to encourage the five Rescue Coordination Centers in the Antarctic region to conduct exercises with each other and other relevant entities.

Tourism remains a point of attention. In response, Parties adopted a Decision on exchange of information and decided to focus in particular on land based and adventure tourism at the next meeting.

The participants expressed their appreciation for the hospitality provided by Belgium, one of the twelve founding Parties of the Antarctic Treaty and congratulated the Belgian government for an excellent organization and a smooth conduct of the meetings. Brazil will host the next ATCM in Brasilia, tentatively from 12 to 21 May 2014.

Brussels, 29 May 2013

Preliminary Agenda for ATCM XXXVII

1. Opening of the Meeting

2. Election of Officers and Creation of Working Groups

3. Adoption of the Agenda and Allocation of Items

4. Operation of the Antarctic Treaty System: Reports by Parties, Observers and Experts

5. Operation of the Antarctic Treaty System: General Matters

6. Operation of the Antarctic Treaty System: Matters related to the Secretariat

7. Multi-Year Strategic Work Plan

8. Report of the Committee for Environmental Protection

9. Liability: Implementation of Decision 4 (2010)

10. Safety and Operations in Antarctica

11. Tourism and Non-Governmental Activities in the Antarctic Treaty Area

12. Inspections under the Antarctic Treaty and the Environment Protocol

13. Science Issues, Scientific Cooperation and Facilitation

14. Implications of Climate Change for Management of the Antarctic Treaty Area

15. Education Issues

16. Exchange of Information

17. Biological Prospecting in Antarctica

18. Preparation of the 38th Meeting

19. Any Other Business

20. Adoption of the Final Report

21. Close of the meeting

PART II
Measures, Decisions and Resolutions

1. Measures

Antarctic Specially Protected Area No 108
(Green Island, Berthelot Islands, Antarctic Peninsula): Revised Management Plan

The Representatives,

Recalling Articles 3, 5 and 6 of Annex V to the Protocol on Environmental Protection to the Antarctic Treaty, providing for the designation of Antarctic Specially Protected Areas ("ASPA") and approval of Management Plans for those Areas;

Recalling

- Recommendation IV-9 (1966), which designated Green Island, Berthelot Islands, Antarctic Peninsula as Specially Protected Area ("SPA") 9;

- Recommendation XVI-6 (1991), which annexed a Management Plan for the Area;

- Decision 1 (2002), which renamed and renumbered SPA 9 as ASPA 108;

- Measure 1 (2002), which adopted a revised Management Plan for ASPA 108;

Recalling that Recommendation IV-9 (1966) was designated as no longer current by Decision 1 (2011);

Recalling that Recommendation XVI-6 (1991) has not become effective;

Noting that the Committee for Environmental Protection has endorsed a revised Management Plan for ASPA 108;

Desiring to replace the existing Management Plan for ASPA 108 with the revised Management Plan;

Recommend to their Governments the following Measure for approval in accordance with Paragraph 1 of Article 6 of Annex V to the Protocol on Environmental Protection to the Antarctic Treaty:

That:

1. the revised Management Plan for Antarctic Specially Protected Area No 108 (Green Island, Berthelot Islands, Antarctic Peninsula), which is annexed to this Measure, be approved; and

2. the Management Plan for ASPA 108 annexed to Measure 1 (2002) cease to be effective.

Antarctic Specially Protected Area No 117
(Avian Island, Marguerite Bay, Antarctic Peninsula): Revised Management Plan

The Representatives,

Recalling Articles 3, 5 and 6 of Annex V to the Protocol on Environmental Protection to the Antarctic Treaty, providing for the designation of Antarctic Specially Protected Areas ("ASPA") and approval of Management Plans for those Areas;

Recalling

- Recommendation XV-6 (1989), which designated as Site of Special Scientific Interest ("SSSI") No 30 and annexed a Management Plan for the site;

- Recommendation XVI-4 (1991), which redesignated SSSI 30 as Specially Protected Area ("SPA") No 21 and annexed a revised Management Plan for the Area;

- Decision 1 (2002), which renamed and renumbered SPA 21 as ASPA 117;

- Measure 1 (2002), which adopted a revised Management Plan;

Recalling that Recommendation XV-6 (1989) and Recommendation XVI -4 (1991) have not become effective and were designated as no longer current by Decision 1 (2011);

Noting that the Committee for Environmental Protection has endorsed a revised Management Plan for ASPA 117;

Desiring to replace the existing Management Plan for ASPA 117 with the revised Management Plan;

Recommend to their Governments the following Measure for approval in accordance with paragraph 1 of Article 6 of Annex V to the Protocol on Environmental Protection to the Antarctic Treaty:

That:

1. the revised Management Plan for Antarctic Specially Protected Area No 117 (Avian Island, Marguerite Bay, Antarctic Peninsula), which is annexed to this Measure, be approved; and

2. the Management Plan for ASPA 117 annexed to Measure 1 (2002) shall cease to be effective.

Antarctic Specially Protected Area No 123
(Barwick and Balham Valleys, Southern Victoria Land): Revised Management Plan

The Representatives,

Recalling Articles 3, 5 and 6 of Annex V to the Protocol on Environmental Protection to the Antarctic Treaty, providing for the designation of Antarctic Specially Protected Areas ("ASPA") and approval of Management Plans for those Areas;

Recalling

- Recommendation VIII-4 (1975), which designated Barwick Valley, Victoria Land as Site of Special Scientific Interest ("SSSI") No 3 and annexed a Management Plan for the site;

- Recommendation X-6 (1979), Recommendation XII-5 (1983), Recommendation XIII-7 (1985), Resolution 7 (1995) and Measure 2 (2000), which extended the expiry date of SSSI 3;

- Decision 1 (2002), which renamed and renumbered SSSI 3 as ASPA 123;

- Measure 1 (2002) and Measure 6 (2008), which adopted revised Management Plans for ASPA 123;

Recalling that Recommendation VIII-4 (1975), Recommendation X-6 (1979), Recommendation XII-5 (1983), Recommendation XIII-7 (1985) and Resolution 7 (1995) were designated as no longer current by Decision 1 (2011);

Recalling that Measure 2 (2000) has not become effective and was withdrawn by Measure 5 (2009);

Noting that the Committee for Environmental Protection has endorsed a revised Management Plan for ASPA 123;

Desiring to replace the existing Management Plan for ASPA 123 with the revised Management Plan;

Recommend to their Governments the following Measure for approval in accordance with paragraph 1 of Article 6 of Annex V to the Protocol on Environmental Protection to the Antarctic Treaty:

That:

1. the revised Management Plan for Antarctic Specially Protected Area No 123 (Barwick and Balham Valleys, South Victoria Land), which is annexed to this Measure, be approved; and

2. the Management Plan for ASPA 123 annexed to Measure 6 (2008) shall cease to be effective.

Antarctic Specially Protected Area No 132
(Potter Peninsula, King George Island (Isla 25 de Mayo), South Shetland Islands): Revised Management Plan

The Representatives,

Recalling Articles 3, 5 and 6 of Annex V to the Protocol on Environmental Protection to the Antarctic Treaty, providing for the designation of Antarctic Specially Protected Areas ("ASPA") and approval of Management Plans for those Areas;

Recalling

- Recommendation XIII-8 (1985), which designated Potter Peninsula, King George Island, (Isla 25 de Mayo), South Shetland Islands as Site of Special Scientific Interest ("SSSI") No 13 and annexed a Management Plan for the site;

- Measure 3 (1997), which annexed a revised Management Plan for SSSI 13;

- Decision 1 (2002), which renamed and renumbered SSSI 13 as ASPA 132;

- Measure 2 (2005), which adopted a revised Management Plan for ASPA 132;

Recalling that Measure 3 (1997) has not become effective yet;

Noting that the Committee for Environmental Protection has endorsed a revised Management Plan for ASPA 132;

Desiring to replace the existing Management Plan for ASPA 132 with the revised Management Plan;

Recommend to their Governments the following Measure for approval in accordance with Paragraph 1 of Article 6 of Annex V to the Protocol on Environmental Protection to the Antarctic Treaty:

That:

1. the revised Management Plan for Antarctic Specially Protected Area No 132 (Potter Peninsula, King George Island (Isla 25 de Mayo), South Shetland Islands), which is annexed to this Measure, be approved; and

2. the Management Plan for the ASPA 132 annexed to Measure 2 (2005) shall cease to be effective.

Antarctic Specially Protected Area No 134
(Cierva Point and offshore islands, Danco Coast, Antarctic Peninsula): Revised Management Plan

The Representatives,

Recalling Articles 3, 5 and 6 of Annex V to the Protocol on Environmental Protection to the Antarctic Treaty, providing for the designation of Antarctic Specially Protected Areas ("ASPA") and approval of Management Plans for those Areas;

Recalling

- Recommendation XIII-8 (1985), which designated Cierva Point and offshore islands, Danco Coast, Antarctic Peninsula as Site of Special Scientific Interest ("SSSI") No 15 and annexed a Management Plan for the Site;

- Resolution 7 (1995), which extended the expiry date of SSSI 15;

- Measure 3 (1997), which annexed a revised Management Plan for SSSI 15;

- Decision 1 (2002), which renamed and renumbered SSSI 15 as ASPA 134;

- Measure 1 (2006), which adopted a revised Management Plan for ASPA 134;

Recalling that Resolution 7 (1995) was designated as no longer current by Decision 1 (2011);

Recalling that Measure 3 (1997) has not become effective yet;

Noting that the Committee for Environmental Protection has endorsed a revised Management Plan for ASPA 134;

Desiring to replace the existing Management Plan for ASPA 134 with the revised Management Plan;

Recommend to their Governments the following Measure for approval in accordance with paragraph 1 of Article 6 of Annex V to the Protocol on Environmental Protection to the Antarctic Treaty:

That:

1. the revised Management Plan for Antarctic Specially Protected Area No 134 (Cierva Point and offshore islands, Danco Coast, Antarctic Peninsula), which is annexed to this Measure, be approved; and

2. the Management Plan for the ASPA 134 annexed to Measure 1 (2006) shall cease to be effective.

Antarctic Specially Protected Area No 135
(North-east Bailey Peninsula, Budd Coast, Wilkes Land): Revised Management Plan

The Representatives,

Recalling Articles 3, 5 and 6 of Annex V to the Protocol on Environmental Protection to the Antarctic Treaty, providing for the designation of Antarctic Specially Protected Areas ("ASPA") and approval of Management Plans for those Areas;

Recalling

- Recommendation XIII-8 (1985), which designated North-east Bailey Peninsula, Budd Coast, Wilkes Land as Site of Special Scientific Interest ("SSSI") No 16 and annexed a Management Plan for the site;

- Resolution 7 (1995) and Measure 2 (2000), which extended the expiry date of SSSI 16;

- Decision 1 (2002), which renamed and renumbered SSSI 16 as ASPA 135;

- Measure 2 (2003) and Measure 8 (2008), which adopted revised Management Plans for ASPA 135;

Recalling that Resolution 7 (1995) was designated as no longer current by Decision 1 (2011);

Recalling that Measure 2 (2000) has not become effective and was withdrawn by Measure 5 (2009);

Noting that the Committee for Environmental Protection has endorsed a revised Management Plan for ASPA 135;

Desiring to replace the existing Management Plan for ASPA 135 with the revised Management Plan;

Recommend to their Governments the following Measure for approval in accordance with Paragraph 1 of Article 6 of Annex V to the Protocol on Environmental Protection to the Antarctic Treaty:

That:

1. the revised Management Plan for Antarctic Specially Protected Area No 135 (North-east Bailey Peninsula, Budd Coast, Wilkes Land), which is annexed to this Measure, be approved; and

2. the Management Plan for ASPA 135 annexed to Measure 8 (2008) shall cease to be effective.

Antarctic Specially Protected Area No 137
(Northwest White Island, McMurdo Sound):
Revised Management Plan

The Representatives,

Recalling Articles 3, 5 and 6 of Annex V to the Protocol on Environmental Protection to the Antarctic Treaty providing for the designation of Antarctic Specially Protected Areas ("ASPA") and approval of Management Plans for those Areas;

Recalling

- Recommendation XIII-8 (1985), which designated Northwest White Island, McMurdo Sound as Site of Special Scientific Interest ("SSSI") No 18 and annexed a Management Plan for the site;

- Recommendation XVI-7 (1991) and Measure 3 (2001), which extended the expiry date of SSSI 18;

- Decision 1 (2002), which renamed and renumbered SSSI 18 as ASPA 137;

- Measure 1 (2002), which adopted a revised Management Plan for ASPA 137;

Recalling that Measure 3 (2001) and Recommendation XVI-7 (1991) have not become effective, and that Recommendation XVI-7 (1991) was designated as no longer current by Decision 1 (2011);

Noting that the Committee for Environmental Protection has endorsed a revised Management Plan for ASPA 137;

Desiring to replace the existing Management Plan for ASPA 137 with the revised Management Plan;

Recommend to their Governments the following Measure for approval in accordance with Paragraph 1 of Article 6 of Annex V to the Protocol on Environmental Protection to the Antarctic Treaty:

That:

1. the revised Management Plan for Antarctic Specially Protected Area No 137 (Northwest White Island, McMurdo Sound), which is annexed to this Measure, be approved; and

2. the Management Plan for ASPA 137 annexed to Measure 1 (2002) shall cease to be effective.

Antarctic Specially Protected Area No 138
(Linnaeus Terrace, Asgard Range, Victoria Land): Revised Management Plan

The Representatives,

Recalling Articles 3, 5 and 6 of Annex V to the Protocol on Environmental Protection to the Antarctic Treaty, providing for the designation of Antarctic Specially Protected Areas ("ASPA") and approval of Management Plans for those Areas;

Recalling

- Recommendation XIII-8 (1985), which designated Linnaeus Terrace, Asgard Range, Victoria Land as Site of Special Scientific Interest ("SSSI") No 19 and annexed a Management Plan for the site;

- Resolution 7 (1995), which extended the expiry date of SSSI;

- Measure 1 (1996), which annexed a revised Management Plan for SSSI 19;

- Decision 1 (2002), which renamed and renumbered SSSI 19 as Antarctic Specially Protected Area No 138;

- Measure 10 (2008), which adopted a revised Management Plan for ASPA 138;

Recalling that Resolution 7 (1995) was designated as no longer current by Decision 1 (2011);

Recalling that Measure 1 (1996) has not become effective and was withdrawn by Measure 10 (2008);

Noting that the Committee for Environmental Protection has endorsed a revised Management Plan for ASPA 138;

Desiring to replace the existing Management Plan for ASPA 138 with the revised Management Plan;

Recommend to their Governments the following Measure for approval in accordance with paragraph 1 of Article 6 of Annex V to the Protocol on Environmental Protection to the Antarctic Treaty:

That:

1. the revised Management Plan for Antarctic Specially Protected Area No 138 (Linneaus Terrace, Asgard Range, Victoria Land), which is annexed to this Measure, be approved;

2. the Management Plan for ASPA 138 annexed to Measure 10 (2008) shall cease to be effective.

Antarctic Specially Protected Area No 143
(Marine Plain, Mule Peninsula, Vestfold Hills, Princess Elizabeth Land): Revised Management Plan

The Representatives,

Recalling Articles 3, 5 and 6 of Annex V to the Protocol on Environmental Protection to the Antarctic Treaty, providing for the designation of Antarctic Specially Protected Areas ("ASPA") and approval of Management Plans for those Areas;

Recalling

- Recommendation XIV-5 (1987), which designated Marine Plain, Mule Peninsula, Vestfold Hills, Princess Elizabeth Land as Site of Special Scientific Interest ("SSSI") No 25 and annexed a Management Plan for the site;

- Resolution 3 (1996), which extended the expiry date for SSSI;

- Measure 2 (2000), which extended the expiry date of the Management Plan for SSSI;

- Decision 1 (2002), which renamed and renumbered SSSI 25 as ASPA 143;

- Measure 2 (2003), which adopted a revised Management Plan for ASPA 143;

Recalling that Resolution 3 (1996) was designated as no longer current by Decision 1 (2011);

Recalling that Measure 2 (2000) has not become effective and was withdrawn by Measure 5 (2009);

Noting that the Committee for Environmental Protection has endorsed a revised Management Plan for ASPA 143;

Desiring to replace the existing Management Plan for ASPA 143 with the revised Management Plan;

Recommend to their Governments the following Measure for approval in accordance with Paragraph 1 of Article 6 of Annex V to the Protocol on Environmental Protection to the Antarctic Treaty:

That:

1. the revised Management Plan for Antarctic Specially Protected Area No 143 (Marine Plain, Mule Peninsula, Vestfold Hills, Princess Elizabeth Land), which is annexed to this Measure, be approved; and

2. the Management Plan for ASPA 143 annexed to Measure 2 (2003) shall cease to be effective.

Antarctic Specially Protected Area No 147
(Ablation Valley and Ganymede Heights, Alexander Island): Revised Management Plan

The Representatives,

Recalling Articles 3, 5 and 6 of Annex V to the Protocol on Environmental Protection to the Antarctic Treaty, providing for the designation of Antarctic Specially Protected Areas ("ASPA") and approval of Management Plans for those Areas;

Recalling

- Recommendation XV-6 (1989), which designated Ablation Valley and Ganymede Heights, Alexander Island as Site of Special Scientific Interest ("SSSI") No 29 and annexed a Management Plan for the site;

- Resolution 3 (1996), which extended the expiry date for SSSI 29;

- Measure 2 (2000), which extended the expiry date for the Management Plan for SSSI 29;

- Decision 1 (2002), which renamed and renumbered SSSI 29 as ASPA 147;

Recalling that Recommendation XV-6 (1989) and Resolution 3 (1996) were designated as no longer current by Decision 1 (2011);

Recalling that Measure 2 (2000) has not become effective and was withdrawn by Measure 5 (2009);

Noting that the Committee for Environmental Protection has endorsed a revised Management Plan for ASPA 147;

Desiring to replace the existing Management Plan for ASPA 147 with the revised Management Plan;

Recommend to their Governments the following Measure for approval in accordance with Paragraph 1 of Article 6 of Annex V to the Protocol on Environmental Protection to the Antarctic Treaty:

That:

1. the revised Management Plan for Antarctic Specially Protected Area No 147 (Ablation Valley and Ganymede Heights, Alexander Island), which is annexed to this Measure, be approved; and

2. the Management Plan for ASPA 147 annexed to Measure 1 (2002) shall cease to be effective.

Antarctic Specially Protected Area No 151
(Lions Rump, King George Island (Isla 25 de Mayo), South Shetland Islands): Revised Management Plan

The Representatives,

Recalling Articles 3, 5 and 6 of Annex V to the Protocol on Environmental Protection to the Antarctic Treaty, providing for the designation of Antarctic Specially Protected Areas ("ASPA") and approval of Management Plans for those Areas;

Recalling

- Recommendation XVI-2 (1991), which designated Lions Rump, King George Island, South Shetland Islands as Site of Special Interest ("SSSI") No 34 and annexed a Management Plan for the site;

- Measure 1 (2000), which annexed a revised Management Plan for SSSI 34;

- Decision 1 (2002), which renamed and renumbered SSSI 23 as ASPA 151;

Recalling that Recommendation XVI-2 (1991) and Measure 1 (2000) have not become effective;

Noting that the Committee for Environmental Protection has endorsed a revised Management Plan for ASPA 151;

Desiring to replace the existing Management Plan for ASPA 151 with the revised Management Plan;

Recommend to their Governments the following Measure for approval in accordance with Paragraph 1 of Article 6 of Annex V to the Protocol on Environmental Protection to the Antarctic Treaty:

That:

1. the revised Management Plan for Antarctic Specially Protected Area No 151 (Lions Rump, King George Island (isla 25 de Mayo), South Shetland Islands), which is annexed to this Measure, be approved; and

2. the Management Plan for the ASPA 151 annexed to Measure 1 (2000), which has not become effective, shall be withdrawn.

Antarctic Specially Protected Area No 154
(Botany Bay, Cape Geology, Victoria Land): Revised Management Plan

The Representatives,

Recalling Articles 3, 5 and 6 of Annex V to the Protocol on Environmental Protection to the Antarctic Treaty, providing for the designation of Antarctic Specially Protected Areas ("ASPA") and approval of Management Plans for those Areas;

Recalling

- Measure 3 (1997), which designated Botany Bay, Cape Geology, Victoria Land, as Site of Special Scientific Interest ("SSSI") No 37 and adopted a Management Plan for the site;

- Decision 1 (2002), which renamed and renumbered SSSI 37 as ASPA 154;

- Measure 2 (2003) and Measure 11 (2008), which adopted revised Management Plans for ASPA 154

Recalling that Measure 3 (1997) has not become effective;

Noting that the Committee for Environmental Protection has endorsed a revised Management Plan for ASPA 154;

Desiring to replace the existing Management Plan for ASPA 154 with the revised Management Plan;

Recommend to their Governments the following Measure for approval in accordance with Paragraph 1 of Article 6 of Annex V to the Protocol on Environmental Protection to the Antarctic Treaty:

That:

1. the revised Management Plan for Antarctic Specially Protected Area No 154 (Botany Bay, Cape Geology, Victoria Land), which is annexed to this Measure, be approved; and

2. the Management Plan for ASPA 154 annexed to Measure 11 (2008) shall cease to be effective.

Antarctic Specially Protected Area No 156
(Lewis Bay, Mount Erebus, Ross Island): Revised Management Plan

The Representatives,

Recalling Articles 3, 5 and 6 of Annex V to the Protocol on Environmental Protection to the Antarctic Treaty, providing for the designation of Antarctic Specially Protected Areas ("ASPA") and approval of Management Plans for those Areas;

Recalling

- Measure 2 (1997), which designated Lewis Bay, Mount Erebus, Ross Island as Specially Protected Area ("SPA") No 26 and adopted a Management Plan for the Area;

- Decision 1 (2002), which renamed and renumbered SPA 26 as ASPA 156;

- Measure 2 (2003), which adopted a revised Management Plan for ASPA 156;

Recalling that the Committee for Environmental Protection ("CEP") XI (2008) reviewed and continued without changes the Management Plan for ASPA 156, which is attached to Measure 2 (2003);

Recalling that Measure 2 (1997) has not become effective and was withdrawn by Measure 8 (2010);

Noting that the CEP has endorsed a revised Management Plan for ASPA 156;

Desiring to replace the existing Management Plan for ASPA 156 with the revised Management Plan;

Recommend to their Governments the following Measure for approval in accordance with Paragraph 1 of Article 6 of Annex V to the Protocol on Environmental Protection to the Antarctic Treaty:

That:

1. the revised Management Plan for Antarctic Specially Protected Area No 156 (Lewis Bay, Mount Erebus, Ross Island), which is annexed to this Measure, be approved; and

2. the Management Plan for ASPA 156 annexed to Measure 2 (2003) shall cease to be effective.

Antarctic Specially Protected Area No 160
(Frazier Islands, Windmill Islands, Wilkes Land, East Antarctica): Revised Management Plan

The Representatives,

Recalling Articles 3, 5 and 6 of Annex V to the Protocol on Environmental Protection to the Antarctic Treaty, providing for the designation of Antarctic Specially Protected Areas ("ASPA") and approval of Management Plans for those Areas;

Recalling

- Measure 2 (2003), which designated Frazier Islands, Windmill Islands, Wilkes Land, East Antarctica as ASPA 160 and adopted a Management Plan for the Area;

- Measure 13 (2008), which adopted a revised Management Plan for ASPA 160;

Noting that the Committee for Environmental Protection has endorsed a revised Management Plan for ASPA 160;

Desiring to replace the existing Management Plan for ASPA 160 with the revised Management Plan;

Recommend to their Governments the following Measure for approval in accordance with Paragraph 1 of Article 6 of Annex V to the Protocol on Environmental Protection to the Antarctic Treaty:

That:

1. the revised Management Plan for Antarctic Specially Protected Area No 160 (Frazier Islands, Windmill Islands, Wilkes Land, East Antarctica), which is annexed to this Measure, be approved; and

2. the Management Plan for the ASPA 160 annexed to Measure 13 (2008) shall cease to be effective.

Antarctic Specially Protected Area No 161
(Terra Nova Bay, Ross Sea): Revised Management Plan

The Representatives,

Recalling Articles 3, 5 and 6 of Annex V to the Protocol on Environmental Protection to the Antarctic Treaty, providing for the designation of Antarctic Specially Protected Areas ("ASPA") and approval of Management Plans for those Areas;

Recalling

- Measure 2 (2003), which designated Terra Nova Bay as ASPA 161 and adopted a Management Plan for the Area;

- Measure 14 (2008), which adopted a revised Management Plan for ASPA 161;

Noting that the Committee for Environmental Protection has endorsed a revised Management Plan for ASPA 161;

Desiring to replace the existing Management Plan for ASPA 161 with the revised Management Plan;

Recommend to their Governments the following Measure for approval in accordance with Paragraph 1 of Article 6 of Annex V to the Protocol on Environmental Protection to the Antarctic Treaty:

That:

1. the revised Management Plan for Antarctic Specially Protected Area No 161 (Terra Nova Bay, Ross Sea), which is annexed to this Measure, be approved; and

2. the Management Plan for the ASPA 161 annexed to Measure 14 (2008) shall cease to be effective.

Antarctic Specially Protected Area No 170
(Marion Nunataks, Charcot Island, Antarctic Peninsula): Revised Management Plan

The Representatives,

Recalling Articles 3, 5 and 6 of Annex V to the Protocol on Environmental Protection to the Antarctic Treaty, providing for the designation of Antarctic Specially Protected Areas ("ASPA") and approval of Management Plans for those Areas;

Recalling Measure 4 (2008) which designated Marion Nunataks, Charcot Island, Antarctic Peninsula as ASPA 170 and adopted a Management Plan for the Area;

Noting that the Committee for Environmental Protection has endorsed a revised Management Plan for ASPA 170;

Desiring to replace the existing Management Plan for ASPA 170 with the revised Management Plan;

Recommend to their Governments the following Measure for approval in accordance with Paragraph 1 of Article 6 of Annex V to the Protocol on Environmental Protection to the Antarctic Treaty:

That:

1. the revised Management Plan for Antarctic Specially Protected Area No 170 (Marion Nunataks, Charcot Island, Antarctic Peninsula), which is annexed to this Measure, be approved; and

2. the Management Plan for ASPA 170 annexed to Measure 4 (2008) shall cease to be effective.

Antarctic Specially Protected Area No 173
(Cape Washington and Silverfish Bay, Terra Nova Bay, Ross Sea): Management Plan

The Representatives,

Recalling Articles 3, 5 and 6 of Annex V to the Protocol on Environmental Protection to the Antarctic Treaty providing for the designation of Antarctic Specially Protected Areas ("ASPA") and approval of Management Plans for those Areas;

Noting that the Committee for Environmental Protection has endorsed a Proposal for a new ASPA at Cape Washington and Silverfish Bay, Terra Nova Bay, Ross Sea and endorsed the Management Plan annexed to this Measure;

Noting further the approval of the Commission for the Conservation of Antarctic Marine Living Resources, at its thirty-first meeting, of the draft Management Plan for a new ASPA at Cape Washington and Silverfish Bay, Terra Nova Bay, Ross Sea.

Recognising that this area supports outstanding environmental, scientific, historic, aesthetic or wilderness values, or ongoing or planned scientific research, and would benefit from special protection;

Desiring to designate Cape Washington and Silverfish Bay, Terra Nova Bay, Ross Sea as an ASPA and to approve the Management Plan for this Area;

Recommend to their Governments the following Measure for approval in accordance with Paragraph 1 of Article 6 of Annex V to the Protocol on Environmental Protection to the Antarctic Treaty:

That:

1. Cape Washington and Silverfish Bay, Terra Nova Bay, Ross Sea be designated as Antarctic Specially Protected Area No 173; and

2. the Management Plan, which is annexed to this Measure, be approved.

Antarctic Historic Sites and Monuments:
Location of the first permanently occupied German Antarctic research station "Georg Forster" at the Schirmacher Oasis, Dronning Maud Land

The Representatives,

Recalling the requirements of Article 8 of Annex V to the Protocol on Environmental Protection to the Antarctic Treaty to maintain a list of current Historic Sites and Monuments, and that such sites shall not be damaged, removed or destroyed;

Recalling Measure 3 (2003), which revised and updated the "List of Historic Sites and Monuments";

Desiring to add a further Historic Site to the "List of Historic Sites and Monuments";

Recommend to their Governments the following Measure for approval in accordance with Paragraph 2 of Article 8 of Annex V to the Protocol on Environmental Protection to the Antarctic Treaty:

That the following Historic Site be added to the "List of Historic Sites and Monuments" annexed to Measure 3 (2003):

"No 87: Location of the first permanently occupied German Antarctic research station "Georg Forster" at the Schirmacher Oasis, Dronning Maud Land

The original site is situated by the Schirmacher Oasis and marked by a commemorative bronze plaque with the label in German language:

Antarktisstation
Georg Forster
70° 46' 39" S
11° 51' 03" E
von 1976 bis 1996

The plaque is well preserved and affixed to a rock wall at the southern edge of the location. This Antarctic research station was opened on 21 April 1976 and closed down in 1993. The entire site has been completely cleaned up after the dismantling of the station was successfully terminated on 12 February 1996. The site is located about 1.5 km east of the current Russian Antarctic research station Novolazarevskaya."

Location: 70° 46' 39" S, 11° 51' 03" E; Elevation: 141 meters above sea level

Original proposing Party: Germany

Party undertaking management: Germany

Antarctic Historic Sites and Monuments:
Professor Kudryashov's Drilling Complex Building, Vostok Station

The Representatives,

Recalling the requirements of Article 8 of Annex V to the Protocol on Environmental Protection to the Antarctic Treaty to maintain a list of current Historic Sites and Monuments, and that such sites shall not be damaged, removed or destroyed;

Recalling Measure 3 (2003), which revised and updated the "List of Historic Sites and Monuments";

Desiring to add a further Historic Monument to the "List of Historic Sites and Monuments";

Recommend to their Governments the following Measure for approval in accordance with Paragraph 2 of Article 8 of Annex V to the Protocol on Environmental Protection to the Antarctic Treaty:

That the following Historic Monument be added to the "List of Historic Sites and Monuments" annexed to Measure 3 (2003):

"No 88: Professor Kudryashov's Drilling Complex Building

The drilling complex building was constructed in the summer season of 1983-84. Under the leadership of Professor Boris Kudryashov, ancient mainland ice samples were obtained."

Location: 78°28' S, 106° 48' E, and height above sea level - 3488 m.

Original proposing Party: Russian Federation

Party undertaking management: Russian Federation

Antarctic Historic Sites and Monuments:
Upper "Summit Camp", Mount Erebus

The Representatives,

Recalling the requirements of Article 8 of Annex V to the Protocol on Environmental Protection to the Antarctic Treaty to maintain a list of current Historic Sites and Monuments, and that such sites shall not be damaged, removed or destroyed;

Recalling Measure 3 (2003), which revised and updated the "List of Historic Sites and Monuments";

Desiring to add a further Historic Site to the "List of Historic Sites and Monuments";

Recommend to their Governments the following Measure for approval in accordance with Paragraph 2 of Article 8 of Annex V to the Protocol on Environmental Protection to the Antarctic Treaty:

That the following Historic Site be added to the "List of Historic Sites and Monuments" annexed to Measure 3 (2003):

> "No 89: Terra Nova Expedition 1910-12, Upper "Summit Camp" used during survey of Mount Erebus in December 1912
>
> Camp Site location includes part of a circle of rocks, which were likely used to weight the tent valences. The camp site was used by a science party on Captain Scott's Terra Nova Expedition, who undertook mapping and collected geological specimens on Mount Erebus in December 1912."
>
> Location: 77° 30.348' S, 167° 10.223'E (circa 3,410m above sea level)
>
> Original proposing Parties: United Kingdom, New Zealand and United States
>
> Parties undertaking management: United Kingdom, New Zealand and United States

Antarctic Historic Sites and Monuments:
Lower "Camp E", Mount Erebus

The Representatives,

Recalling the requirements of Article 8 of Annex V to the Protocol on Environmental Protection to the Antarctic Treaty to maintain a list of current Historic Sites and Monuments, and that such sites shall not be damaged, removed or destroyed;

Recalling Measure 3 (2003), which revised and updated the "List of Historic Sites and Monuments";

Desiring to add a further Historic Site to the List of Historic Sites and Monuments;

Recommend to their Governments the following Measure for approval in accordance with Paragraph 2 of Article 8 of Annex V to the Protocol on Environmental Protection to the Antarctic Treaty:

That the following Historic Site be added to the "List of Historic Sites and Monuments" annexed to Measure 3 (2003):

"No 90: Terra Nova Expedition 1910-12, Lower "Camp E" Site used during survey of Mount Erebus in December 1912

Camp Site location consists of a slightly elevated area of gravel and includes some aligned rocks, which may have been used to weight the tent valences. The camp site was used by a science party on Captain Scott's Terra Nova Expedition, who undertook mapping and collected geological specimens on Mount Erebus in December 1912."

Location: 77° 30.348' S, 167° 9.246'E (circa 3,410 m above sea level)

Original proposing Parties: United Kingdom, New Zealand and United States

Parties undertaking management: United Kingdom, New Zealand and United States

2. Decisions

Recognition of the Czech Republic as a Consultative Party

The Representatives,

Recalling Decision 4 (2005);

Recalling that the Czech Republic succeeded to the Antarctic Treaty on 1 January 1993 in accordance with Article XIII;

Recalling that the Czech Republic deposited its instrument of accession to the Protocol on Environmental Protection to the Antarctic Treaty ("the Protocol") on 25 August 2004, and that the Protocol entered into force for the Czech Republic on 24 September 2004;

Noting that the Czech Republic thus fulfills the requirement of Article 22.4 of the Protocol;

Noting that the Czech Republic notified the Depository Government on 18 April 2013 of its view that it had met the requirements of Article IX(2) of the Antarctic Treaty by conducting substantial scientific research in Antarctica;

Noting that the Czech Republic notified the Depository Government on 10 May 2013 of its intention to approve the Recommendations and Measures adopted at the Antarctic Treaty Consultative Meetings ("the ATCM") in pursuance of the Treaty and subsequently approved by all the Contracting Parties whose Representatives were entitled to participate in those Meetings, and to consider approval of the other Recommendations and Measures;

Decide:

1. that the Czech Republic has fulfilled the requirements established in Article IX(2) of the Antarctic Treaty;

2. that the Czech Republic shall be entitled as of 1 April 2014, and during such time as it continues in accordance with Article IX(2) of the Antarctic Treaty to demonstrate its interest in Antarctica by conducting substantial scientific research there, to appoint representatives in order to participate in the Antarctic Treaty Consultative Meeting provided for in Article IX(1) of the Antarctic Treaty;

3. to invite the Czech Republic to furnish information to ATCM XXXVII on the progress made in its approval of Recommendations and Measures adopted at the ATCMs; and

4. to warmly welcome the Czech Republic as a Consultative Party in the ATCMs.

Re-appointment of the Executive Secretary

The Representatives,

Recalling Article 3 of Measure 1 (2003) regarding the appointment of an Executive Secretary to head the Secretariat of the Antarctic Treaty;

Recalling Decision 5 (2009), which appointed Dr Manfred Reinke as Executive Secretary of the Secretariat of the Antarctic Treaty for a term of four years from 1 September 2009;

Recalling Regulation 6.1 of the Staff Regulations for the Secretariat of the Antarctic Treaty;

Decide:

1. to re-appoint Dr. Manfred Reinke as Executive Secretary of the Secretariat of the Antarctic Treaty for an additional term of four years, pursuant to the terms and conditions set forth in the letter of the Chair of Antarctic Treaty Consultative Meeting XXXVI annexed to this Decision; and

2. that this re-appointment shall commence on 1 September 2013.

Dr. Manfred Reinke
Executive Secretary
Antarctic Treaty Secretariat

Dear Dr. Reinke,

Re-appointment to position of Executive Secretary

As Chair of the XXXVI Antarctic Treaty Consultative Meeting (ATCM) and in accordance with Decision x (2013) of the XXXVI ATCM, I am pleased to offer to you re-appointment to the position of Executive Secretary of the Secretariat of the Antarctic Treaty (the Secretariat).

The terms and conditions of your re-appointment are set out below. If you accept this offer, kindly sign your acceptance on the attached copy of this letter and return it to me.

Terms and Conditions of Appointment

1. By your acceptance of the re-appointment you shall pledge yourself to discharge your duties faithfully and to conduct yourself solely with the interests of the ATCM in mind. Your acceptance of the position of Executive Secretary includes a written statement of your familiarity with and acceptance of the conditions set out in the attached Staff Regulations as well as any changes which may be made to the Staff Regulations from time to time.

2. The duties of the Executive Secretary are to appoint, direct and supervise other staff members and to ensure that the Secretariat fulfills the functions identified in Article 2 of Measure 1 (2003).

3. In accordance with Decision 2 (2013), your re-appointment shall commence on September 1, 2013.

4. Your term of office shall be for four years.

5. The re-appointment is to the executive staff category. Your salary shall be at Level 1B, Step 5, as detailed in Schedule A to the Staff Regulations annexed to Decision 3 (2003), as amended.

6. The above salary includes the base salary (Level 1A, Step 5, Schedule A) with an additional 25% for salary on-costs (retirement fund and insurance premiums, installation and repatriation grants, education allowances, etc.) and is the total salary entitlement in accordance with Regulation 5.1 of the Staff Regulations. In addition, you will be entitled to travel allowances and relocation expenses in accordance with Regulation 9 of the Staff Regulations.

7. The ATCM may terminate this re-appointment by prior written notice at least three months in advance in accordance with Regulation 10.3 of the Staff Regulations. You may resign at any time upon giving three months written notice or such lesser period as may be approved by the ATCM.

Yours sincerely

{signed}

Ambassador Marc Otte

Chairman XXXVI Antarctic Treaty Consultative Meeting

I hereby accept the appointment described in this letter subject to the conditions therein specified and state that I am familiar with and accept the conditions set out in the Staff Regulations and any changes which may be made to the Staff Regulations from time to time.

———

29 May 2013

{signed}
Dr. Manfred Reinke

Mr. Héctor Timerman
Minister of Foreign Affairs and Worship
Argentine Republic
Buenos Aires

Dear Minister Timerman:

I address you in my capacity as Chair of the XXXVI Antarctic Treaty Consultative (ATCM) with reference to Article 21 of the Headquarters Agreement for the Secretariat of the Antarctic Treaty, attached to Measure 1 (2003), the letter of the Argentine Republic to the Chairman of ATCM XXVI of 16 June 2003, and the notification of the Argentine Republic to the Depositary Government of 19 May 2004.

In accordance with the requirements of Article 21, I hereby notify the Government of the Argentine Republic of the re-appointment by the XXXVI ATCM of Dr. Manfred Reinke to the position of Executive Secretary for one additional term of four years, effective on 1 September 2013.

I avail myself of this opportunity to express the assurances of my highest consideration.

Yours sincerely,

{signed}
Ambassador Marc Otte
Chair XXXVI Antarctic Treaty Consultative Meeting

Renewal of the Contract of the Secretariat's External Auditor

The Representatives,

Recalling the Financial Regulations for the Secretariat of the Antarctic Treaty ("the Secretariat") annexed to Decision 4 (2003), and specifically Regulation 11 (External Audit);

Conscious that the Secretariat conducts the majority of its financial transactions in Argentina, and that the detailed rules of book-keeping and accounting are country-specific;

Noting Argentina's proposal to designate the Sindicatura General de la Nación as the external auditor of the Secretariat;

Decide:

1. to designate the Sindicatura General de la Nación ("SIGEN") as the external auditor of the Secretariat of the Antarctic Treaty ("the Secretariat") for the Financial Years ending in 2014 to 2017, in accordance with Regulation 11.1 of the Financial Regulations for the Secretariat; and

2. to authorise the Executive Secretary to negotiate a contract with SIGEN to carry out annual external audits for the above-mentioned years in accordance with Regulation 11.3, the Annex to this Decision and the budgetary limits set by the Antarctic Treaty Consultative Meeting ("ATCM").

Tasks to be carried out by the external auditor

To provide external audit reports covering the financial years ending in 2014, 2015, 2016 and 2017 in accordance with Regulation 11.3 of the Financial Regulations annexed to Decision 4 (2003).

The audit report shall address:

– Implementation of regulations adopted by the Antarctic Treaty Consultative Meeting ("ATCM");

– Internal controls - Regulations and Procedures;

– Internal oversight of administrative processes, payments, custody of funds, and assets;

– Budgeting;

– Comparative budget reports;

– Expenditure efficiency analysis;

– Budget execution oversight;

– Analysis of the establishment of new area units;

– Control and reporting of contributions;

– Establishment and oversight of the General Fund, the Working Capital Fund, the Future Meeting Fund, the Staff Replacement Fund, the Staff Termination Fund and any other Funds held by the Secretariat of the Antarctic Treaty ("the Secretariat");

– Income and expense accounts;

– Trust funds;

– Custody of funds - Investments;

– Accounting oversight in accordance with Regulation 10 of Decision 4 (2003);

– Drafting an external auditor report;

– Other matters which may be necessary to ensure sound financial management of the Secretariat.

The provisional financial report for each Financial Year should be submitted by the Executive Secretary to the Sindicatura General de la Nación ("SIGEN") no later than 1 June of the year in which the Financial Year concludes and the final audited report should be submitted by SIGEN to the Executive Secretary no later than 1 September of the year in which the Financial Year concludes.

Secretariat Report, Programme and Budget

The Representatives,

Recalling Measure 1 (2003) on the establishment of the Secretariat of the Antarctic Treaty ("the Secretariat");

Recalling Decision 2 (2012) on the establishment of the open-ended Intersessional Contact Group on financial issues to be convened by the host country of the next Antarctic Treaty Consultative Meeting;

Bearing in mind the Financial Regulations for the Secretariat annexed to Decision 4 (2003);

Decide:

1. to approve the audited Financial Report for 2011/12, annexed to this Decision (Annex 1);

2. to take note of the Secretariat Report 2012/13 (SP 2), which includes the Provisional Financial Report (2012/13), annexed to this Decision (Annex 2);

3. to approve the Secretariat Programme (SP3 rev.1), including the Budget for 2013/14 and the Forecast Budget for 2014/15, annexed to this Decision (Annex 3); and

4. to invite the host country for the next Antarctic Treaty Consultative Meeting ("ATCM") to request the Executive Secretary to open the ATCM forum for the Intersessional Contact Group ("ICG") and to provide assistance to the ICG.

Audited Financial Report 2011/12

Presidencia de la ~ Nación
Sindicatura General de la ~ Nación

Annex I

AUDITOR'S REPORT

XXXVI Antarctic Treaty Consultative Meeting 2013, Brussels, Belgium

1. Report on Financial Statements

We have audited the attached Financial Statements of the Antarctic Treaty Secretariat, which include the following: Statement of Income and Expenditure, Statement of Financial Situation, Statement of Trend of Net Assets, Statement on Flow of Funds and Notes on Financial Statements for the period commencing 1st April 2011 and ending 31st March 2012.

2. Management Responsibility for Financial Statements

The Antarctic Treaty Secretariat is responsible for the preparation and reasonable presentation of these Financial Statements according to International Accounting Standards and the specific Rules of the Antarctic Treaty Consultative Meetings. Such responsibility includes: the design, implementation and maintenance of internal controls for the preparation and presentation of the Financial Statements, such that they are free of misstatements due to error or fraud; the selection and implementation of appropriate accounting policies, and the preparation of accounting estimates which are reasonable under the circumstances.

3. AUDITOR'S RESPONSIBILITY

Our responsibility is to express an opinion on these Financial Statements based on the audit conducted.

The audit was conducted in accordance with International Auditing Standards and the Annex to Decision 3 (2008) of the XXXI Antarctic Treaty Consultative Meeting, in which the tasks to be carried out by the external audit are described.

These rules require compliance with ethical requirements, and planning and execution of the audit so as to provide reasonable assurance that the Financial Statements are free of misstatements.

An audit includes the implementation of procedures in order to obtain evidence on the amounts and the exposure in the Financial Statements. Relevant procedures are selected based on the auditor's judgement, including an assessment of the risks of material misstatement in the Financial Statements, either by fraud or error.

On conducting such assessment of risks, the auditor considers the internal control relevant to the preparation and reasonable presentation of the financial statements by

Presidencia de la Nación

Sindicatura General de la Nación

the organisation, in order to design suitable procedures that are appropriate to the circumstances.

An audit also includes an assessment of appropriateness, of the accounting principles used, an opinion on whether the accounting estimates made by management are reasonable, as well as an assessment of the general presentation of the Financial Statements.

We believe that the audited evidence we have obtained is sufficient and appropriate to provide a basis for our opinion as auditors.

4. *Opinion*

In our opinion, the Financial Statements audited present fairly, in all material aspects, the Financial Position of the Antarctic Treaty Secretariat as at 31st March 2012 and its Financial performance for the period ending on the above date in accordance with International Accounting Standards and the specific rules of the Antarctic Treaty Consultative Meetings.

Dr. Edgardo de Rose
Public Accountant
Registered with the Professional Councilof Economic Science for the City of BuenosAires (CPCECABA) in Book No. 182, Page No. 195

Buenos Aires, 10 April 2013

Sindicatura General de la Nación
Av. Corrientes 389, Buenos Aires
Argentine Republic

1. **Statement of Income and Expenditure for all Funds for the Period 1st April 2011 31st March 2012.**

		Budget	
Income	**31/03/2011**	**31/03/2012**	**31/03/2012**
Contributions (Note 10)	899.942	1.339.600	1.339.600
Other income (Note 2)	528	70	1.623
Total income	900.470	1.339.670	1.341.223

EXPENDITURE

Salaries and remuneration	469.948	578.100	577.637
Translation and interpreting services	159.270	365.825	367.846
Travel and accommodation	61.325	52.815	56.022
IT	37.615	42.500	39.147
Printing, editing and copying	15.964	14.000	27.025
General services	38.886	44.060	47.547
Communications	12.207	13.368	14.580
Office expenses	8.217	11.984	14.060
Administration	4.582	4.698	11.580
Representation expenses	3.143	4.500	6.676
Moving expenses (Note 9)	0	50.000	24.803
Financing	8.477	0	7.326
Total expenditure	819.635	1.181.850	1.194.250

FUND APPROPRIATION

Staff termination fund	25.974	42.502	54.332
Staff replacement fund	8.333	18.246	23.490
Working capital fund	62.260	67.072	31.615
Contingency fund	0	30.000	30.000
Total fund appropriation	96.567	157.820	139.436
Total expenses and appropriations	916.202	1.339.670	1.333.686
(Deficit) / Surplus for period	-15.732	0	7.537

This statement should be read in conjunction with Notes 1 to 10 attached

2. **Statement of Financial Position as at 31 March 2012, and comparison with previous financial year**

ASSETS

	31/03/2011	31/03/2012
Current Assets		
Cash and cash equivalent (Note 3)	818.991	798.946
Contributions owed (Note 10)	23.257	89.457
Other debtors (Note 4)	23.606	47.893
Other current assets (Note 5)	26.658	59.644
Total current assets	892.512	995.940
Non-current assets		
Fixed assets (Note 1.3 and 6)	68.727	73.506
Total non-current assets	68.727	73.506
Total Assets	961.239	1.069.446

LIABILITIES

	31/03/2011	31/03/2012
Current liabilities		
Payables (Note 7)	26.345	40.659
Contributions received in advance (Note 10)	618.929	549.493
Remuneration and contributions payable (Note 8)	11.298	22.873
Total current liabilities	656.572	613.026
Non-current liabilities		
Staff termination fund (Note 1.4)	64.755	119.087
Staff replacement fund (Note 1.5)	26.510	50.000
Contingency fund (Note 1.7)	0	30.000
Fixed asset replacement fund (Note 1.8)	2.430	7.210
Total non-current liabilities	93.696	206.296
Total Liabilities	750.268	819.322
NET ASSETS	210.971	250.123

This statement should be read in conjunction with Notes 1 to 10 attached

3. **Statement of changes in Net Assets as at 31 March 2012 and 2011**

Represented by:	Net assets 31/03/2011	Income	Expenditure and appropriations	Earned interests	Net assets 31/03/2012
General Fund	19.319	1.339.600	-1.332.295	232	26.856
Working capital fund (Note 1.6)	191.652		31.615		223.267
Net assets	210.971				250.123

This statement should be read in conjunction with Notes 1 to 10 attached

4. Cash flow statement for the period 1st April 2011 to 31st March 2012

Variations in cash and cash equivalents

Cash and cash equivalent at beginning of the year	818.991	
Cash and cash equivalent at year end	798.946	
Net Decrease in cash and cash equivalents		-20.044

Causes for the variations in cash and cash equivalent

Operational activities

Contributions received	654.477	
Payment of salaries	-569.637	
Payment of translation services	-367.846	
Payment of travel, accommodation, etc.	-46.484	
Payment of printing, editing and copying	-27.025	
Payment of office relocation	-78.634	
Other payments	-106.891	
Net flow of cash and cash equivalents from operational activities		-542.042

Investment Activities

Purchase of fixed assets	-18.164	
Specific contribution Argentina (Note 9)	53.800	
Net flow of cash and cash equivalents from investment activities		35.636

Financing Activities

Contributions received in advance	549.493	
Collection pt. 5.6 of Staff Regulations	95.736	
Payment pt. 5.6 of Staff Regulations	-119.574	
Pre paid expenses ATCM XXXV	-31.968	
Net flow of cash and cash equivalents from financing activities		493.687

Foreign currency activities

Net Loss	-7.326	
Net flow of cash and cash equivalents from foreign currency activities		-7.326
Net Decrease in cash and cash equivalents		-20.044

This statement should be read in conjunction with Notes 1 to 10 attached

NOTES to the FINANCIAL STATEMENTS as at 31st March 2012

1 BASIS FOR PREPARATION OF THE FINANCIAL STATEMENTS

These financial statements are expressed in US dollars, in accordance with the guidelines set in the Financial Regulations, in Annex to Decision 4 (2003). These statements were prepared in accordance with International Financial Reporting Standards (IFRS) of the International Accounting Standards Board (IASB).

1,1 Historical Cost
The accounts are drawn up in accordance with the convention of historical cost, except where otherwise indicated.

1,2 Premises
The Secretariat Offices are provided by the Ministry of Foreign Affairs, International Trade and Cult of the Argentine Republic. Premises are free of rent and common expenses.

1,3 Fixed Asset
All items are valued at historical cost, less accumulated depreciation. Depreciation is calculated on a straight-line basis at annual rates appropriate to their estimated useful life. The aggregate residual value of fixed assets does not exceed their use value.

1,4 Executive staff termination fund
Pursuant to Section 10.4 of the Staff Regulations, this fund shall be sufficiently funded to compensate executive staff members at a rate of one month base pay for each year of service.

1,5 Staff replacement fund
This fund is used to cover Secretariat executive staff relocation expenses to and from the Secretariat Head Office.

1,6 Working capital fund
Pursuant to Financial Regulations 6.2 (a), the fund shall not exceed one-sixth (1/6) of the budget for the current financial year.

1,7 Contingency fund
Pursuant to Decision 4 (2009), the Fund was created to cover the translation costs, which can be caused by the unexpected increase in the volume of documents submitted to the ATCM for translation.

1,8 Fixed asset replacement fund
Pursuant to IAS, assets with a useful life beyond the current financial year shall be reflected as an asset in the Statement of Financial Position. Until March 2010, the offsetting entry was an adjustment to the General Fund. From April 2010 the offsetting entry of these assets shall be reflected as a liability under this heading.

NOTES to the FINANCIAL STATEMENTS as at 31st March 2012

		31/03/2011	31/03/2012
2 Other Income			
	Earned interest	255	232
	Discounts obtained	273	1.391
	Total	528	1.623
3 Cash and banks			
	Cash US dollars	1.338	1.638
	Cash Argentine pesos	544	46
	BNA US dollar special account	755.882	756.983
	BNA Argentine peso account	61.227	40.279
	Total	818.991	798.946
4 Other debtors			
	Staff Regulations pt. 5.6	23.606	47.893
5 Other current assets			
	Advance payments	13.675	38.296
	VAT receivable	12.726	20.912
	Other recoverable expenses	256	435
	Total	26.658	59.644
6 Fixed Asset			
	Books and subscriptions	4.515	4.515
	Office equipment	30.787	6.592
	Furniture	23.092	45.466
	IT equipment and software	54.164	66.744
	Total original cost	112.558	123.318
	Accumulated Depreciation	-43.831	-49.812
	Total	68.727	73.506
7 Payables			
	Business	7.700	2.272
	Accrued Expenses	17.978	37.229
	Other	667	1.158
	Total	26.345	40.659
8 Remuneration and contributions payable (Note 8)			
	Remuneration	0	8.000
	Contributions	11.298	14.873
	Total	11.298	22.873

9 Relocation

The government of the Argentine Republic made a specific contribution of $ 53.800 to compensate for the expenses incurred by the relocation of the Secretariat offices. The total disbursement of the relocation and arrangements was $53.831. The balance along with disbursements for equipping the new office are outlined in this section.

NOTES to the FINANCIAL STATEMENTS as at 31st March 2012

10 Contributions owed, pledged, received, received in advance.

Contributions Parties	Owed 31/03/2011	Pledged	Received $	Owed 31/03/2012	In advance 31/03/2013
Argentina		60.346	60.346	0	0
Australia		60.346	60.346	0	60.346
Belgium	36	40.110	40.129	18	0
Brazil	12	40.110	40.090	32	0
Bulgaria		34.039	34.028	11	0
Chile		46.181	31.024	15.157	31.024
China		46.181	46.181	0	0
Ecuador		34.039	34.039	0	0
Finland		40.110	40.110	0	40.110
France		60.346	60.346	0	0
Germany	62	52.251	52.302	11	52.251
India	124	46.181	46.293	12	0
Italy		52.251	52.251	0	0
Japan	-1	60.346	60.345	0	0
Korea		40.110	40.110	0	0
Netherlands		46.181	46.181	0	46.181
New Zealand		60.346	60.320	26	60.346
Norway	30	60.346	60.346	30	0
Peru	22.867	34.039	22.868	34.038	0
Poland		40.110	40.110	0	0
Russia		46.181	46.181	0	46.181
South Africa		46.181	46.181	0	46.181
Spain	115	46.181	46.296	0	0
Sweden		46.181	46.181	0	46.181
Ukraine	12	40.110	0	40.122	0
United Kingdom		60.346	60.346	0	60.346
United States		60.346	60.346	0	60.346
Uruguay		40.110	40.110	0	0
Total	23.257	1.339.605	1.273.406	89.457	549.493

Dr Manfred Reinke
Executive Secretary

Roberto A. Fennell
Finance Officer

Estimate of Income and Expenditures 2012/2013

Estimate of Income and Expenditure for all Funds
for the Period 1 April 2012 to 31 March 2013

APPROPRIATION LINES	Statement 2011/12	Budget 2012/13	Prov, Statement 2012/13
INCOME			
CONTRIBUTIONS pledged	$ -1,339,600	$ -1,339,600	$ -1,339,600
Interest Investments	$ -1,623	$ -1,000	$ -1,801
Total Income	**$ -1,341,223**	**$ -1,340,600**	**$ -1,341,401**
EXPENDITURE			
SALARIES			
Executive	$ 305,654	$ 311,323	$ 311,323
General Staff	$ 241,159	$ 294,966	$ 291,527
ATCM Support Staff	$ 11,561	$ 12,750	$ 12,810
Trainee	$ 4,800	$ 4,800	$ 4,000
Overtime	$ 14,926	$ 10,000	$ 8,443
	$ 577,637	**$ 633,839**	**$ 628,103**
TRANSLATION AND INTERPRETATION			
Translation and Interpretation	**$ 367,846**	**$ 361,000**	**$ 291,052**
TRAVEL			
Travel	**$ 56,022**	**$ 90,000**	**$ 91,766**
INFORMATION TECHNOLOGY			
Hardware	$ 8,211	$ 8,500	$ 8,807
Software	$ 5,344	$ 3,000	$ 2,251
Development	$ 16,420	$ 16,500	$ 14,233
Support	$ 7,746	$ 13,000	$ 12,264
	$ 39,147	**$ 42,500**	**$ 37,555**
PRINTING, EDITING & COPYING			
Final report	$ 27,025	$ 16,500	$ 12,765
Site guidelines	$ 0	$ 2,500	$ 0
	$ 27,025	**$ 19,000**	**$ 12,765**

APPROPRIATION LINES	Statement 2011/12	Budget 2012/13	Prov, Statement 2012/13
GENERAL SERVICES			
Legal advice	$ 9,000	$ 4,000	$ 1,374
External audit	$ 9,304	$ 10,764	$ 10,127
Cleaning, maintenance & security	$ 16,118	$ 25,093	$ 26,860
Training	$ 4,758	$ 6,000	$ 5,377
Banking	$ 5,665	$ 5,624	$ 4,226
Rental of equipment	$ 2,702	$ 4,752	$ 2,674
	$ 47,547	**$ 56,232**	**$ 50,638**

COMMUNICATION			
Telephone	$ 4,381	$ 3,864	$ 4,289
Internet	$ 1,380	$ 2,161	$ 2,063
Web hosting	$ 6,089	$ 6,894	$ 9,305
Postage	$ 2,730	$ 2,471	$ 1,230
	$ 14,580	**$ 15,390**	**$ 16,887**

OFFICE			
Stationery & supplies	$ 3,753	$ 2,200	$ 2,754
Books & subscriptions	$ 1,403	$ 5,898	$ 2,750
Insurance	$ 1,739	$ 1,958	$ 2,058
Furniture	$ 1,373	$ 800	$ 35
Office equipment	$ 4,192	$ 4,000	$ 1,397
Maintenance	$ 1,600	$ 2,000	$ 4,595
	$ 14,060	**$ 16,856**	**$ 13,589**

ADMINISTRATIVE			
Supplies	$ 2,386	$ 2,000	$ 1,662
Local transport	$ 808	$ 1,000	$ 654
Miscellaneous	$ 4,373	$ 2,500	$ 4,019
Utilities (Energy)	$ 4,012	$ 8,000	$ 5,218
	$ 11,580	**$ 13,500**	**$ 11,552**

REPRESENTATION			
Representation	**$ 6,676**	**$ 3,000**	**$ 3,096**

RELOCATION			
Relocation Av, Leandro Alem 884 - Maipú 757	**$ 24,803**		

APPROPRIATION LINES	Statement 2011/12	Budget 2012/13	Prov. Statement 2012/13
FINANCING			
Exchange loss	$ 7,326	$ 5,000	$ 5,840
SUBTOTAL APPROPRIATIONS	$ 1,194,250	$ 1,256,318	$ 1,162,845
ALLOCATION TO FUNDS			
Translation Contingency Fund	$ 30,000	$ 0	$ 0
Staff Replacement Fund	$ 23,490	$ 0	$ 0
Staff Termination Fund	$ 54,332	$ 28,403	$ 28,424
Working Capital Fund	$ 31,615	$ 0	$ 0
	$ 139,437	$ 28,403	$ 28,424
TOTAL APPROPRIATIONS	$ 1,333,687	$ 1,284,721	$ 1,191,269
BALANCE	$ 7,537	$ 55,879	$ 150,132
TOTAL EXPENDITURES	$ 1,341,224	$ 1,340,600	$ 1,341,401
Summary of Funds			
Translation Contingency Fund	$ 30,000	$ 30,000	$ 30,000
Staff Replacement Fund	$ 50,000	$ 50,000	$ 50,000
Staff Termination Fund	$ 119,087	$ 147,490	$ 147,511
Working Capital Fund	$ 223,267	$ 223,267	$ 223,267
General Fund	$ 26,856	$ 82,735	$ 176,988
Maximum Required Amount Working Capital Fund (Fin, Reg, 6,2)	$ 223,267	$ 223,267	$ 223,267

247

Secretariat Programme 2013/14

Introduction

This work programme outlines the activities proposed for the Secretariat in the Financial Year 2013/14 (1 April 2013 to 31 March 2014). The main areas of activity of the Secretariat are treated in the first three chapters, which are followed by a section on management and a forecast of the programme for the Financial Year 2013/14.

The Budget for the Financial Year 2013/14, the Forecast Budget for the Financial Year 2014/15, and the accompanying contribution and salary scales are included in the appendices.

The programme and the accompanying budget figures for 2013/14 are based on the Forecast Budget for the Financial Year 2013/14 (Decision 2 (2012), Annex 3, Appendix 1).

The programme focuses on the regular activities, such as the preparation of the ATCM XXXVI and ATCM XXXVII, the publication of Final Reports, and the various specific tasks assigned to the Secretariat under Measure 1 (2003).

Contents:

1. ATCM/CEP support
2. Information Exchange
3. Documentation
4. Public Information
5. Management
6. Forecast Programme for the Financial Year 2013/14

   Appendix 1: Provisional Report for the Financial Year 2012/13, Budget for the Financial Year 2013/14, Forecast Budget for the Financial Year 2014/15

   Appendix 2: Contribution Scale for th Financial Year 2014/15

   Appendix 3: Salaries Scale

1. ATCM/CEP Support

ATCM XXXVI

The Secretariat will support the ATCM XXXVI by gathering and collating the documents for the meeting and publishing them in a restricted section of the Secretariat website. The Delegates section will also provide online registration for delegates and a downloadable, up-to-date list of delegates.

The Secretariat will support the functioning of the ATCM through the production of Secretariat Papers, a Manual for Delegates, and summaries of papers for the ATCM, the CEP, and the ATCM Working Groups.

The Secretariat will organise the services for translation and interpretation. It is responsible for pre- and post-sessional translation and for the translation services during the ATCM. It maintains contact with the provider of interpretation services.

The Secretariat will organise the rapporteur services in cooperation with the secretariat of the host country and is responsible for the compilation and editing of the Reports of the CEP and ATCM for adoption during the final plenary of the Meeting.

Coordination and contact

Aside from maintaining constant contact via email, telephone and other means with the Parties and international institutions of the Antarctic Treaty System, attendance at meetings is an important tool to maintain coordination and communication.

The travelling to be undertaken is as follows:

-   COMNAP Annual General Meeting (AGM), Seoul, Republic of Korea, 8 July to 10 July 2013. Attending the meeting will provide an opportunity to further strengthen the connections and interaction with COMNAP and SCAR.
-   CCAMLR, Hobart, Australia, 23 October to 1 November 2013. The CCAMLR meeting, which takes place roughly halfway between succeeding ATCMs, provides an opportunity for the Secretariat to brief the ATCM Representatives, many of whom attend the CCAMLR meeting, on developments in the Secretariat's work. Liaison with the CCAMLR Secretariat is also important for the Antarctic Treaty Secretariat, as many of its regulations are modelled after those of the CCAMLR Secretariat.

Development of the Secretariat website

The website will continue to be improved to make it more concise and easier to use, and to increase the visibility of the most relevant sections and information. The searching facilities of the website databases, especially the Meeting Document database and the Electronic Information Exchange System (EIES), will be further developed.

Support of intersessional activities

During recent years both the CEP and the ATCM have produced an important amount of intersessional work, mainly through Intersessional Contact Groups (ICG). The Secretariat will provide technical support for the online establishment of the ICGs agreed at the ATCM XXXVI and CEP XVI, and will produce specific documents if required by the ATCM or the CEP.

The Secretariat will update the website with the measures adopted by the ATCM and with the information produced by the CEP and the ATCM.

Printing

The Secretariat will translate, publish and distribute the Final Report and its Annexes of the ATCM XXXVI in the four Treaty languages. The text of the Final Report will be published on the website of the Secretariat and will be printed in book form with the annexes published as a CD attached to the printed report. The full text of the Final Report will be available in book form (two volumes) through online retailers and also in electronic book form.

2. Information Exchange

General

The Secretariat will continue to assist Parties in posting their information exchange materials, as well as integrating information on Environmental Impact Assessments (EIAs) in the EIA database.

Electronic Information Exchange System

During the next operational season and depending on the decisions of the ATCM XXXVI, the Secretariat will continue to make the adjustments necessary to facilitate the use of the electronic system for the Parties, as well as develop tools to compile and present summarised reports.

3. Records and Documents

Documents of the ATCM

The Secretariat will continue its efforts to complete its archive of the Final Reports and other records of the ATCM and other meetings of the Antarctic Treaty System in the four Treaty languages. Assistance from Parties in searching their files will be essential in order to achieve a complete archive at the Secretariat. The Secretariat received a set of Working Papers from ATCMs between 1961 and 1998 from a joint project with the Scott Polar Research Institute (Cambridge, UK) and incorporated them into the Antarctic Treaty Database. The project will continue in the Financial Year 2013/14.

Antarctic Treaty database

The database of the Recommendations, Measures, Decisions and Resolutions of the ATCM is at present complete in English and almost complete in Spanish and French, although the Secretariat still lacks various Final Report copies in those languages. In Russian more Final Reports are lacking.

4. Public Information

The Secretariat and its website will continue to function as a clearinghouse for information on the Parties' activities and relevant developments in Antarctica.

5. Management

Personnel

On 1 April 2013 the Secretariat staff consisted of the following personnel:

Executive staff

Name	Position	Since	Rank	Term
Manfred Reinke	Executive Secretary	1-09-2009	E1	31-08-2013
José María Acero	Assistant Executive Secretary	1-01-2005	E3	31-12-2014

General staff

Name	Position	Since	Rank
José Luis Agraz	Information Officer	1-11-2004	G1
Diego Wydler	Information Technology Officer	1-02-2006	G1
Roberto Alan Fennell	Finance Officer (part time)	1-12-2008	G2
Pablo Wainschenker	Editor	1-02-2006	G3
Ms. Violeta Antinarelli	Librarian (part time)	1-04-2007	G3
Ms. Anna Balok	Data Entry Assistant (part time)	1-10-2010	G5
Ms. Viviana Collado	Office Manager	15-11-12	G5

ATCM XXXVI decided to reappoint the Executive Secretary for a term of four years starting on 1 September 2013 (see Decision 2 (2013)). To arrange for the timely appointment of a successor upon completion of this term, the ATCM may wish to commence consideration of this matter no later than ATCM XXXIX.

Financial Matters

The Budget for the Financial Year 2013/14 and the Forecast Budget for the Financial Year 2014/15 are shown in Appendix 1.

Translation and Interpretation

In August 2012 the Secretariat issued an international request for proposals (RfP) for translation and interpretation services for the 36th ATCM. The Maltese company "International Translation Agency Ltd (ITA)" won the competition. The full text of the evaluation of the RfP is available on the ATS Forum of the "Intersessional Contact Group on Financial Issues".

The costs of translation and interpretation are budgeted for the ATCM XXXVI at 284,961 US$.

Under European tax law no Belgian Value Added Tax (VAT) will be levied on any of the services as ITA Ltd is a company established in Malta, which is an EU Member State. Under the "Value Added Tax Act of Malta" the Secretariat will not be charged this tax, as the services will be provided:

a.   to an intergovernmental organization,

b.   whose offices/headquarters are based outside the territory of the Republic of Malta.

Salaries and Travel Costs

Costs of living continued to rise considerably in Argentina in the year 2012. To compare the development with previous years, the Secretariat calculated the increase of the IVS (Salary Variation Index provided by the Argentine National Office of Statistics and Census) adjusted for the devaluation of the Argentine Peso against the US$ during the same period. This method was explained by the Executive Secretary in 2009 at ATCM XXXII (Final Report p. 238).

In 2012 the IVS rose by 24.5%. The devaluation of the Argentine Peso against the US$ resulted in a calculated rise of cost of living of 9.2% in US$.

In former years, the IVS rose in 2011 by 29.4%, in 2010 by 26.3% and in 2009 by 16.7%. This caused a calculated rise in the cost of living in 2011 of 19.5% in US$, in 2010 of 19.9% in US$ and in 2009 of 7.9 % in US$.

The Executive Secretary proposes to not compensate for the rise in the cost of living, neither to the General Staff nor to the Executive Staff.

Regulation 5.10 of the Staff Regulations requires the compensation of General Staff members when they have to work more than 40 hours during on week. Overtime is requested during the ATCM Meetings.

To compensate for the rise in travel costs, the Secretariat has reduced the daily subsistence allowance (DSA) rates for the staff of the Secretariat to 80% of the DSA rates from the International Civil Service.

Funds

Working Capital Fund

According to Financial Regulation 6.2 (a), the Working Capital Fund has to be maintained at 1/6 of the Secretariat's budget of 223,267 US$ in the upcoming years. The contributions of the Parties form the basis of the calculation of the level of the Working Capital Fund.

Further Details of the Draft Budget for the Financial Year 2013/14

The allocation to the appropriation lines follows the proposal from last year. Some smaller adjustments have been implemented according to the foreseen expenses of the Financial Year 2013/2014.

- *Software* Development: From discussions in the ICG on "Information Exchange and the Environmental Aspects and Impacts of Tourism and Non-Governmental Activities in Antarctica" some changes in the EIES are expected.

- *Printing, Editing & Copying:* After the inspection of tourist sites in Antarctica, 11 revised Site Guidelines are expected.

- *General Services:* Some further maintenance tasks are foreseen concerning the repair of the climate control system of the office.

- *Administrative, Utilities:* Significant rises in energy costs are expected.

Appendix 1 shows the Budget for the Financial Year 2013/2014 and the Forecast Budget for the Financial Year 2014/2015. The salary scale is given in Appendix 3.

Contributions for the Financial Year 2014/15

The contributions for the Financial Year 2014/15 will not rise.

Appendix 2 shows the contributions of the Parties for the Financial Year 2014/15.

6. Forecast Programme for the Financial Year 2014/15 and the Financial Year 2015/16

It is expected that most of the ongoing activities of the Secretariat will be continued in the Financial Year 2014/15 and the Financial Year 2015/2016, and therefore, unless the programme undergoes major changes, no change in staff positions is foreseen for the following years.

Provisional Report 2012/13, Budget 2013/14 and Forecast 2015/16

APPROPRIATION LINES	Prov. Statement 2012/13*	Forecast 2013/14	Budget 2013/14	Forecast 2014/15
INCOME				
CONTRIBUTIONS pledged	$ -1,339,600	$ -1,339,600	$ -1,339,600	$ -1,339,600
Special Fund				
Workshop Interpretation (pledged)	$ 0	$ 0	$ -13,860	$ 0
Interest Investments	$ -1,801	$ -1,000	$ -1,000	$ -1,000
Total Income	**$ -1,341,401**	**$ -1,340,600**	**$ -1,354,460**	**$ -1,340,600**

EXPENDITURE				
SALARIES				
Executive Staff	$ 311,323	$ 317,001	$ 317,001	$ 322,658
General Staff	$ 291,527	$ 306,860	$ 303,929	$ 317,013
ATCM Support Staff	$ 12,810	$ 12,750	$ 14,850	$ 15,147
Trainee	$ 4,000	$ 4,800	$ 4,800	$ 4,800
Overtime	$ 8,443	$ 10,000	$ 10,000	$ 10,000
	$ 628,103	**$ 651,411**	**$ 650,580**	**$ 669,618**

TRANSLATION AND INTERPRETATION				
Translation and Interpretation	$ 291,052	$ 333,333	$ 272,101	$ 321,214
Interpretation Workshop	$ 0	$ 0	$ 13,860	$ 0
VAT / GST	$ 0	$ 66,667	$ 0	$ 32,121
Translation and Interpretation	**$ 291,052**	**$ 400,000**	**$ 285,961**	**$ 353,335**

TRAVEL				
Travel	**$ 91,766**	**$ 80,000**	**$ 96,000**	**$ 90,000**

INFORMATION TECHNOLOGY				
Hardware	$ 8,807	$ 10,000	$ 10,000	$ 10,500
Software	$ 2,251	$ 3,000	$ 3,000	$ 3,150
Development	$ 14,233	$ 16,500	$ 18,500	$ 17,325
Support	$ 12,264	$ 13,000	$ 13,000	$ 13,650
	$ 37,555	**$ 42,500**	**$ 44,500**	**$ 44,625**

APPROPRIATION LINES	Prov. Statement 2012/13*	Forecast 2013/14	Budget 2013/14	Forecast 2014/15
PRINTING, EDITING & COPYING				
Final report	$ 12,765	$ 18,975	$ 18,975	$ 20,721
Site guidelines	$ 0	$ 2,875	$ 2,875	$ 3,140
	$ 12,765	**$ 21,850**	**$ 21,850**	**$ 23,860**
GENERAL SERVICES				
Legal advice	$ 1,374	$ 4,600	$ 4,600	$ 5,023
External audit	$ 10,127	$ 12,379	$ 12,379	$ 13,518
Cleaning, maintenance & security	$ 26,860	$ 16,207	$ 25,207	$ 17,698
Training	$ 5,377	$ 6,000	$ 6,000	$ 6,552
Banking	$ 4,226	$ 6,467	$ 6,467	$ 7,062
Rental of equipment	$ 2,674	$ 5,465	$ 5,465	$ 5,968
	$ 50,638	**$ 51,118**	**$ 60,118**	**$ 55,821**
COMMUNICATION				
Telephone	$ 4,289	$ 4,444	$ 4,444	$ 4,853
Internet	$ 2,063	$ 2,485	$ 2,485	$ 2,714
Web hosting	$ 9,305	$ 7,928	$ 7,928	$ 8,657
Postage	$ 1,230	$ 2,842	$ 2,842	$ 3,103
	$ 16,887	**$ 17,699**	**$ 17,699**	**$ 19,327**
OFFICE				
Stationery & supplies	$ 2,754	$ 2,530	$ 2,530	$ 2,763
Books & subscriptions	$ 2,750	$ 6,782	$ 6,782	$ 7,406
Insurance	$ 2,058	$ 2,252	$ 2,252	$ 2,459
Furniture	$ 35	$ 800	$ 800	$ 874
Office equipment	$ 1,397	$ 4,600	$ 4,600	$ 5,023
Maintenance	$ 4,595	$ 2,300	$ 2,300	$ 2,512
	$ 13,589	**$ 19,264**	**$ 19,264**	**$ 21,036**
ADMINISTRATIVE				
Supplies	$ 1,662	$ 2,300	$ 2,300	$ 2,512
Local transport	$ 654	$ 1,150	$ 1,150	$ 1,256
Miscellaneous	$ 4,019	$ 2,875	$ 2,875	$ 3,140
Utilities (Energy)	$ 5,218	$ 10,400	$ 10,400	$ 11,357
	$ 11,552	**$ 16,725**	**$ 16,725**	**$ 18,264**
REPRESENTATION				
Representation	**$ 3,096**	**$ 3,000**	**$ 3,000**	**$ 3,000**

APPROPRIATION LINES	Prov. Statement 2012/13*	Forecast 2013/14	Budget 2013/14	Forecast 2014/15
FINANCING				
Exchange loss	$ 5,840	$ 5,000	$ 5,000	$ 5,460
SUBTOTAL APPROPRIATIONS	$ 1,162,845	$ 1,308,566	$ 1,220,697	$ 1,304,347
ALLOCATION TO FUNDS				
Translation Contingency Fund	$ 0	$ 0	$ 0	$ 0
Staff Replacement Fund	$ 0	$ 0	$ 0	$ 0
Staff Termination Fund	$ 28,424	$ 28,880	$ 29,368	$ 29,820
Working Capital Fund	$ 0	$ 0	$ 0	$ 0
	$ 28,424	$ 28,880	$ 29,368	$ 29,820
TOTAL APPROPRIATIONS	$ 1,191,269	$ 1,337,446	$ 1,250,065	$ 1,334,167
BALANCE	$ 150,132	$ 3,154	$ 104,395	$ 6,433
TOTAL EXPENDITURES	$ 1,341,401	$ 1,340,600	$ 1,354,460	$ 1,340,600

Summary of Funds

	Prov. Statement 2012/13*	Forecast 2013/14	Budget 2013/14	Forecast 2014/15
Translation Contingency Fund	$ 30,000	$ 30,000	$ 30,000	$ 30,000
Staff Replacement Fund	$ 50,000	$ 50,000	$ 50,000	$ 50,000
Staff Termination Fund	$ 147,511	$ 175,914	$ 176,879	$ 204,794
** Working Capital Fund	$ 223,267	$ 223,267	$ 223,267	$ 223,267
General Fund	$ 176,988	$ 91,447	$ 281,382	$ 287,815

* Provisonal Statement
  as of 1 Apr 2013

Maximum Required Amount ** Working Capital Fund (Fin, Reg, 6,2)	$ 223,267	$ 223,267	$ 223,267	$ 223,267

Appendix 2

Contribution Scale 2014/15

2013/14	Cat.	Mult.	Variable	Fixed	Total
Argentina	A	3.6	$ 36,424.17	$ 23,921.43	$60,346
Australia	A	3.6	$ 36,424.17	$ 23,921.43	$60,346
Belgium	D	1.6	$ 16,188.52	$ 23,921.43	$40,110
Brazil	D	1.6	$ 16,188.52	$ 23,921.43	$40,110
Bulgaria	E	1.0	$ 10,117.82	$ 23,921.43	$34,039
Chile	C	2.2	$ 22,259.21	$ 23,921.43	$46,181
China	C	2.2	$ 22,259.21	$ 23,921.43	$46,181
Ecuador	E	1.0	$ 10,117.82	$ 23,921.43	$34,039
Finland	D	1.6	$ 16,188.52	$ 23,921.43	$40,110
France	A	3.6	$ 36,424.17	$ 23,921.43	$60,346
Germany	B	2.8	$ 28,329.91	$ 23,921.43	$52,251
India	C	2.2	$ 22,259.21	$ 23,921.43	$46,181
Italy	B	2.8	$ 28,329.91	$ 23,921.43	$52,251
Japan	A	3.6	$ 36,424.17	$ 23,921.43	$60,346
Korea	D	1.6	$ 16,188.52	$ 23,921.43	$40,110
Netherlands	C	2.2	$ 22,259.21	$ 23,921.43	$46,181
New Zealand	A	3.6	$ 36,424.17	$ 23,921.43	$60,346
Norway	A	3.6	$ 36,424.17	$ 23,921.43	$60,346
Peru	E	1.0	$ 10,117.82	$ 23,921.43	$34,039
Poland	D	1.6	$ 16,188.52	$ 23,921.43	$40,110
Russia	C	2.2	$ 22,259.21	$ 23,921.43	$46,181
South Africa	C	2.2	$ 22,259.21	$ 23,921.43	$46,181
Spain	C	2.2	$ 22,259.21	$ 23,921.43	$46,181
Sweden	C	2.2	$ 22,259.21	$ 23,921.43	$46,181
Ukraine	D	1.6	$ 16,188.52	$ 23,921.43	$40,110
United Kingdom	A	3.6	$ 36,424.17	$ 23,921.43	$60,346
United States	A	3.6	$ 36,424.17	$ 23,921.43	$60,346
Uruguay	D	1.6	$ 16,188.52	$ 23,921.43	$40,110
		66.2	$ 669,800.00	$ 669,800.00	**$1,339,600**

Budget amount	$1,339,600
Base rate	$10,118

Appendix 3

Salary Scale 2013/14

Schedule A
SALARY SCALE FOR THE EXECUTIVE STAFF CATEGORY
(United States dollars)

2013/14 Level		I	II	III	IV	V	VI	VII	VIII	IX	X	XI	XII	XIII	XIV	XV
E1	A	$133,830	$136,320	$138,810	$141,301	$143,791	$146,281	$148,771	$151,262							
E1	B	$167,287	$170,400	$173,512	$176,626	$179,739	$182,851	$185,964	$189,078							
E2	A	$112,692	$114,812	$116,931	$119,050	$121,168	$123,286	$125,404	$127,524	$129,643	$131,761	$133,880	$134,120	$136,210		
E2	B	$140,865	$143,515	$146,164	$148,812	$151,460	$154,107	$156,755	$159,405	$162,054	$164,702	$167,349	$167,650	$170,263		
E3	A	$93,973	$96,016	$98,061	$100,106	$102,151	$104,195	$106,240	$108,285	$110,328	$112,372	$114,417	$115,643	$116,869	$118,886	$120,901
E3	B	$117,466	$120,020	$122,577	$125,133	$127,689	$130,243	$132,800	$135,356	$137,910	$140,465	$143,021	$144,553	$146,086	$148,607	$151,126
E4	A	$77,922	$79,815	$81,710	$83,599	$85,494	$87,386	$89,275	$91,171	$93,065	$94,955	$96,849	$97,377	$99,244	$101,110	$102,977
E4	B	$97,403	$99,768	$102,138	$104,498	$106,868	$109,232	$111,594	$113,964	$116,332	$118,694	$121,062	$121,722	$124,055	$126,388	$128,721
E5	A	$64,604	$66,299	$67,992	$69,685	$71,377	$73,070	$74,763	$76,452	$78,147	$79,841	$81,530	$82,078			
E5	B	$80,755	$82,874	$84,989	$87,106	$89,222	$91,337	$93,454	$95,565	$97,684	$99,801	$101,913	$102,597			
E6	A	$51,143	$52,771	$54,396	$56,025	$57,650	$59,276	$60,905	$62,531	$64,156	$65,146	$65,784				
E6	B	$63,929	$65,963	$67,994	$70,031	$72,062	$74,095	$76,131	$78,164	$80,195	$81,432	$82,230				

Note: Row B is the base salary (shown in Row A) with an additional 25% for salary on-costs (retirement fund and insurance premiums, installation and repatriation grants, education allowances etc.) and is the total salary entitlement for executive staff in accordance with regulation 5.1

Schedule B
SALARY SCALE FOR THE GENERAL STAFF
(United States dollars)

Level	I	II	III	IV	V	VI	VII	VIII	IX	X	XI	XII	XIII	XIV	XV
G1	$60,439	$63,258	$66,079	$68,897	$71,836	$74,901									
G2	$50,366	$52,715	$55,066	$57,415	$59,864	$62,417									
G3	$41,970	$43,928	$45,887	$47,845	$49,887	$52,016									
G4	$34,976	$36,608	$38,240	$39,871	$41,573	$43,346									
G5	$28,893	$30,242	$31,590	$32,939	$34,346	$35,814									
G6	$23,684	$24,787	$25,893	$26,998	$28,151	$29,353									

Decide

Multi-Year Strategic Work Plan
for the Antarctic Treaty Consultative Meeting

The Representatives,

Reafirming the values, objectives and principles contained in the Antarctic Treaty and its Protocol on Environmental Protection;

Considering that a Multi-Year Strategic Work Plan ("Plan") may contribute positively to the Antarctic Treaty Consultative Meeting ("ATCM"), so that the ATCM focuses on matters of priority and timely importance, operates more effectively and efficiently and schedules its work appropriately;

Recalling ATCM XXXII in Baltimore (2009), where Antarctic Treaty Parties ("Parties") expressed support for the development of a Plan;

Recalling Decision 3 (2012), which agreed to develop a Plan for the ATCM and which adopted Principles for the completion and development of the Plan;

Bearing in mind that the Plan is complementary to the ATCM agenda and that the Parties and other ATCM participants are encouraged to contribute as usual to other matters on the ATCM agenda;

Decide:

1. that the following Principles will guide implementation and further development of the Plan;

    a. the Plan will reflect the objectives and principles of the Antarctic Treaty and its Protocol on Environmental Protection;

    b. consistent with the operation of the ATCM, adoption of the Plan, inclusion of items on the Plan and decisions regarding the Plan, will be made by consensus;

c. the purpose of the Plan is to complement the agenda by assisting the ATCM to identify a limited number of priority issues and to operate more effectively and efficiently;

d. the Parties and other ATCM participants are encouraged to contribute as usual to other matters on the ATCM agenda;

e. the Plan will cover a rolling multi-year period, and should be reviewed at each ATCM and updated as necessary to reflect work still to be completed, new issues and changing priorities;

f. the Plan will be dynamic and flexible and will incorporate emerging issues as they arise;

g. the Plan will identify issues that require the collective attention of the ATCM, and that require discussion and/or decisions by the ATCM; and

h. the Plan should not interfere with the regular development of the ATCM agenda;.

2. to adopt the Plan annexed to this Decision, taking into account the need for further development of the multi-year concept of the Plan;

3. to designate Decision 3 (2012) as no longer current.

ATCM Multi-Year Strategic Work Plan

The Multi Year Strategic Work Plan has been prepared in accordance with Decision 3 (2012) and the Principles adopted at ATCM XXXV

Decision 3 (2012) - ATCM XXXV - CEP XV, Hobart - The Development of a Multi-Year Strategic Work Plan for the Antarctic Treaty Consultative Meeting

The Representatives,

Reaffirming the values, objectives and principles contained in the Antarctic Treaty and its Protocol on Environmental Protection;

Considering that a Multi-Year Strategic Work Plan (Plan) may contribute positively to the Antarctic Treaty Consultative Meeting ("ATCM"), so that the ATCM focuses on matters of priority and timely importance, operates more effectively and efficiently and schedules its work appropriately;

Bearing in mind that the Plan is complementary to the ATCM agenda and that the Antarctic Treaty Parties and other ATCM participants are encouraged to contribute as usual to other matters on the ATCM agenda;

Recalling ATCM XXXII in Baltimore (2009), where Parties expressed support for a Plan;

Decide:

1. to develop a Multi-Year Strategic Work Plan within existing resources;
2. to adopt the principles annexed to this Decision (Annex 1) to guide the completion of the Plan;
3. to establish an open-ended Intersessional Contact Group, co-convened by Australia and Belgium, as the Chairs of Antarctic Treaty Consultative Meetings XXXV and XXXVI respectively, to coordinate the further development of the Plan; and
4. to hold a workshop immediately prior to ATCM XXXVI, with the following terms of reference:
   a. develop a draft Plan for consideration at ATCM XXXVI; and
   b. report to ATCM XXXVI on the outcomes of this workshop.

Principles

1. The Multi-Year Strategic Work Plan (Plan) will reflect the objectives and principles of the Antarctic Treaty and its Protocol on Environmental Protection.
2. Consistent with the operation of the Antarctic Treaty Consultative Meeting ("ATCM"), adoption of the Plan, inclusion of items on the Plan and decisions regarding the Plan, will be made by consensus.

3. The purpose of the Plan is to complement the agenda by assisting the ATCM to identify a limited number of priority issues and to operate more effectively and efficiently.

4. The Antarctic Treaty Parties and other ATCM participants are encouraged to contribute as usual to other matters on the ATCM agenda.

5. The Plan will cover a rolling multi-year period to be determined, and should be reviewed at each ATCM and updated as necessary to reflect work still to be completed, new issues and changing priorities.

6. The Plan will be dynamic and flexible and will incorporate emerging issues as they arise.

7. The Plan will identify issues that require the collective attention of the ATCM, and that require discussion and/or decisions by the ATCM.

8. The Plan should not interfere with the regular development of the ATCM agenda.

Work area	Priority	2013	Intersessional	2014	2015	2016	2017	2018
Ensuring a robust and effective ATS	Conduct a comprehensive review of existing requirements for information exchange and of the functioning of the Electronic Information Exchange System, and the identification of any additional requirements		Secretariat to prepare a summary including the outcome from informal CEP discussions on EIES Invite Parties, experts and observers to prepare working and other papers	Dedicated discussion of this topic in the Legal and Institutional Working Group including presentation by the Secretariat on Electronic Information Exchange System Consider updating Resolution 6 (2001) Establishment of an ICG, if required, to address any unresolved issues				
	Consider coordinated outreach to non-party states whose nationals or assets are active in Antarctica		*					
	Share and discuss strategic science priorities in order to identify and pursue opportunities for collaboration as well as capacity building in science, particularly in relation to climate change		*	Invite parties, experts and observers to provide information about their strategic science priorities				
Strengthening protection of the Antarctic environment	Consider the advice of the CEP on addressing repair and remediation of environmental damage and consider for example appropriate follow up actions with regard to liability		*					
	Assess the progress of the CEP on its ongoing work to reflect best practices and to improve existing tools and develop further tools for environmental protection, including environmental impact assessment procedures (and consider, if appropriate, further development of the tools)		*					

Work area	Priority	2013	Intersessional	2014	2015	2016	2017	2018
The effective management and regulation of human activities	Address the recommendations of the Antarctic Treaty Meeting of Experts on Implications of Climate Change for Antarctic Management and Governance (CEP-ICG)		*					
	Strengthen cooperation among Parties on current Antarctic specific air and marine operations and safety practices, and identify any issues that may be brought forward to the IMO and ICAO, as appropriate	Special Working Group on Search and Rescue	Secretariat to provide a compilation of existing ATCM Recommendations and Resolutions on safety issues Invite Parties, experts and observers to prepare working and other papers Invite the IMO to provide an update on the Polar Code negotiations at ATCM XXXVII Request ICAO and the IMO to present their views on air and maritime safety issues	Dedicated discussion of this topic in Operations Working Group COMNAP to present to the ATCM information on preparations for the triennial Search and Rescue Workshop.				
	Review and assess the need for additional actions regarding area management and permanent infrastructure related to tourism, as well as issues related to land based and adventure tourism and address the recommendations of the CEP tourism study	T o u r i s m W o r k i n g Group	Parties, Observers and Experts prepare and submit working and other papers on land-based and adventure tourism CEP Intersessional work on Recommendations 3 and 6 (on site sensitivity methodology and monitoring). The Secretariat to produce a digest of previous ATCM discussion and Measures and Resolutions relating to land based and adventure tourism.	Dedicated discussion on issues related to land-based and adventure tourism in the Tourism and Non-Governmental Activities Working Group taking into account issues raised in the papers submitted, as well as issues previously raised in the TWG and ICGs. Consideration of any interim report material received from the CEP.				

* The Parties, Experts and Observers are invited to consult among themselves in the ICG on Antarctic Cooperation on the elaboration of this priority in the Plan.

Information Exchange on Tourism and Non-Governmental Activities

The Representatives,

Recalling Article III(1)(a) and Article VII(5) of the Antarctic Treaty;

Conscious of the obligations within the Protocol on Environmental Protection to the Antarctic Treaty and its Annexes to exchange information;

Conscious also of Recommendation VIII-6 (1975) and other commitments that the Parties have made with respect to keeping each other informed by regular or occasional exchanges;

Desiring to ensure that the exchange of information between the Parties is conducted in the most efficient and timely manner;

Further desiring to respond to Recommendation 1 of the 2012 Committee on Environmental Protection study on the Environmental Aspects and Impacts of Tourism and Non-governmental Activities in Antarctica on the development of an Antarctic Treaty Consultative Meeting ("ATCM") centrally managed database of tourism activities;

Further recalling Resolution 6 (2005), which recommended the use of a revised standard Post Visit Site Report Form for Tourism and Non-Governmental Activities in Antarctica;

Reaffirming Decision 4 (2012), which made mandatory the use of the Electronic Information Exchange System ("EIES") for Parties to fulfil their information exchange obligations under the Antarctic Treaty and its Environmental Protocol and specified that Parties shall continue to work with the Antarctic Treaty Secretariat to refine and improve the EIES;

Desiring to supplement Appendix 4 of the ATCM XXIV Final Report on information exchange to ensure consistent reporting of types of tourist activity for both ship-based and land-based operations and to align that reporting with the information collected in the Post Visit Site Report Form endorsed in Resolution 6 (2005);

Decide:

1. to strengthen the exchange of information by supplementing Appendix 4 of the Antarctic Treaty Consultative Meeting XXIV Final Report to include:

   a) "type of activity" in Non-Governmental Expeditions – Ship-based Operations requirements;

   b) the number of visitors that participate in each of the specific activities;

   c) replace the heading of 1.1.2. A to 'vessel-based operations' as reflected in the Appendix to this Decision.

2. to revise the Electronic Information Exchange System ("EIES") to include:

   a) a list of non-governmental ship-based and land-based expedition activities from which Parties can select one or more for reporting in annual information, to be aligned with the activity fields in the Post Visit Site Report Form endorsed in Resolution 6 (2005), with the flexibility to enter additional activities; and

   b) the number of visitors that participate in each of the specific activities;

3. to provide this information to the EIES and as a general principle, make that information publicly available.

Information Exchange Requirements

1. Pre-season Information

The following information should be submitted as early as possible, preferably by 1 October, and in any event no later than the start of the activities being reported.

1.1 Operational information

1.1.1 National Expeditions

A. Stations

Names of wintering stations (giving region, latitude and longitude), maximum population and medical support available.

Names of summer stations/bases and field camps (giving region, latitude, longitude), operating period, maximum population and medical support available.

Names of refuges (region, latitude and longitude) medical facilities and accommodation capacity. Other major field activities, e.g. scientific traverse (giving locations)

B. Vessels

Name of vessels, country of registry of vessels, number of voyages, planned departure dates, areas of operation, ports of departure and arrival to and from Antarctica, and purpose of voyage (e.g. science deployment, resupply, change-over, oceanography, etc)

C. Aircraft

Type of aircraft, planned number of flights, period of flights or planned departure dates, routes and purpose.

D. Research Rockets

Coordinates of the place of launching, time and date/period, direction of launching, planned maximum altitude, impact area, type and specifications of rockets, purpose and title of research project.

E. Military

- Number of military personnel in expeditions, and rank of any officers
- Number and types of armaments possessed by personnel.

- Number and types of armaments of ships and aircraft and information on military equipment, if any, and its location in the Antarctic Treaty Area.

1.1.2 Non-governmental Expeditions

A. Vessel-based Operations

Name of operator, name of vessel, country of registry of vessel, number of voyages, planned departure dates, ports of departure and arrival to and from Antarctica, areas of operation including the names of proposed visited sites and the planned dates at which these visits will take place, type of activity, the number of visitors that participate in each of the specific activities.

B. Land-based Operations

Name of expedition, method of transportation to, from and within Antarctica, type of adventure/activity, location, dates of expedition, number of personnel involved, contact address, web-site address.

1.2 Visits to Protected Areas

Name and number of protected area, number of people permitted to visit, date/period and purpose.

2. Annual Report

The following information should be submitted as early as possible after the end of the austral summer season, but in all cases before 1 October, with a reporting period of 1 April to 30 March.

2.1 Scientific Information

2.1.1 Forward Plans

Details of strategic or multi-year science plans or contact point for printed version. List of planned participations in major, international, collaborative science programs/projects.

2.1.2 Science Activities in Previous Year

List of research projects undertaken in previous year under science discipline (giving location and principal investigator).

2.2 Operational information

2.2.1 National expeditions

Update of information given under 1.1.1.

2.2.2 Non-governmental expeditions

Update of information given under 1.1.2.

2.3 Permit Information

2.3.1 Visits to Protected Areas

Update of information provided under 1.2.

2.3.2 Taking and harmful interference with flora and fauna

Species, location, amount, sex, age and purpose.

2.3.3 Introduction of non-native species

Species, location, amount and purpose.

2.4 Environmental Information

2.4.1 Compliance with the Protocol

New measures adopted during past year in accordance with Article 13 of the Protocol on Environmental Protection to the Antarctic Treaty giving description of measure, date of effect.

2.4.2 List of IEEs and CEEs

List of IEEs/CEEs undertaken during year giving proposed activity, location, level of assessment and decision taken.

2.4.3 Monitoring activities report

Name of activity, location, procedures put in place, significant information obtained, action taken in consequence thereof.

2.4.4 Waste Management Plans

Waste management plans issued during the year giving title including name of station/vessel/location.

Report on implementation of waste management plans during the year.

2.5 Relevant National Legislation

Legislation adopted during the year to give effect to the Antarctic Treaty and to obligations arising from measures, decisions and resolutions of the Antarctic Treaty Consultative Meeting, giving description of measure and date of effect.

2.6 Other information

2.6.1 Inspection Reports

Report of any inspections conducted under Antarctic Treaty Article VII and Article 14 and Article 10 (Annex V) of the Environmental Protocol during the year giving date of inspection, person(s) conducting inspection, nationality of inspector(s), locations inspected, where inspection report located.

2.6.2 Notice of Activities Undertaken in Case of Emergencies

Description of emergency, location (latitude and longitude) and action undertaken.

3. Permanent Information

The following information should be submitted in accordance with the requirements of the Antarctic Treaty and Protocol on Environmental Protection to the Antarctic Treaty. The information can be updated at any time.

3.1. Science Facilities

3.1.1 Automatic Recording Stations/Observatories

Site name, co-ordinates (latitude and longitude), elevation (m), parameters recorded, observation frequency, reference number (e.g. WMO no.).

3.2 Operational Information

A. Stations

Name of wintering stations (giving region, latitude and longitude, and maximum population), date established and accommodation and medical facilities.

Name of summer stations/bases and field camps (giving region, latitude, longitude, operating period and maximum population)

Names of refuges (region, latitude and longitude) medical facilities and accommodation capacity.

B. Vessels

Name of vessels, Flag State, ice strength, length, beam and gross tonnage (a link may be provided to COMNAP data).

C. Aircraft

Number and type of aircraft operated.

D. Aircraft landing facilities

E. Communications facilities and frequencies

3.3 Waste Management Plans

Title of Plan, copy (PDF) or contact point for printed version and brief report on implementation.

3.4 Contingency Plans

Title of Contingency Plan(s) for Oil Spills and other emergencies, copies (PDFs) or contact point for printed versions. Brief report on implementation.

3.5 Inventory of Past Activities

Name of station/base/field camp/traverse/crashed aircraft/etc, co-ordinates (latitude and longitude) period during which activity undertaken; description/purpose of activities undertaken; description of equipment or facilities remaining.

3.6 Relevant National Legislation

Description of law, regulation, administrative action or other measure, date of effect/enacted, giving copy (PDF) or contact point for printed version.

Additional availability of information on lists of Observers of the Consultative Parties through the Secretariat of the Antarctic Treaty

The Representatives,

Welcoming the proposal to use the Secretariat of the Antarctic Treaty (the Secretariat) in the framework of its functions, as a complementary information tool for the Parties, in this case the Observers appointed by them;

Bearing in mind that since the entry into force of the Antarctic Treaty and the creation of the Secretariat, new ways of transmitting information have been developed, and that it is very useful to have a database of the appointed Observers on the Secretariat website, available for consultation;

Considering that dissemination of information through the Secretariat is defined as a function of the Secretariat;

Recognising that the delivery of this information to the Secretariat is complementary to notification to the Parties through diplomatic channels;

Recalling the provisions of Article VII of the Antarctic Treaty and Article 14 of the Protocol on Environmental Protection to the Antarctic Treaty, as well as Article 2 of Measure 1 (2003);

Decide:

1. that the Antarctic Treaty Consultative Parties (ATCPs) should inform the Secretariat of the Antarctic Treaty, in addition to notification through diplomatic channels, of the designation of Observers to carry out inspections, the date of designation, as well as termination of such designations; and that the Secretariat be required to notify all ATCP contacts, as notified under Recommendation XIII-1, Paragraph 6, by electronic mail; and

2. that the Secretariat is to include this information notified under paragraph 1 with restricted access in its Contacts database, and make it available to the Parties. The contacts database will only include those Observers notified through diplomatic channels, in accordance with Article VII of the Antarctic Treaty and Article 14 of the Protocol on Environmental Protection to the Antarctic Treaty.

3. Resolutions

Air Safety in Antarctica

The Representatives,

Recalling Recommendation XV-20 (1989);

Noting, with appreciation, the Report of the Meeting of Experts on Air Safety in Antarctica, held in Paris from 2 to 5 May 1989;

Recognising the importance of ensuring safe air operations in the Antarctic, and that the principal body of knowledge and experience of Antarctic air operations, and its current challenges, lies with the operators of national Antarctic programmes;

Desiring to contribute to air safety in Antarctica through updated recommendations;

Recommend that:

1. for the purpose of ensuring that measures for improved air safety apply to all flights in Antarctica, measures to improve air safety set out in paragraphs 2-8 below should be elaborated on the basis of ICAO criteria, taking due account of the specific features of Antarctica as well as of existing practices and services;

2. for the purpose of ensuring the safety of air operations in the Antarctic Treaty area, Parties should exchange, preferably by 1 September and no later than 15 November each year, information about their planned air operations in accordance with the standardized format of the Electronic Information Exchange System (EIES);

3. for the purpose of improving air safety in Antarctica, national Antarctic programmes operating aircraft in Antarctica and their aircrews should be provided with a continuously updated compendium produced by the Council of Managers of National Antarctic Programs (COMNAP) and now known as the COMNAP Antarctic Flight Information Manual (AFIM) describing

ground facilities, aircraft (including helicopters) and aircraft operating procedures and associated communications facilities operated by each national Antarctic programme (out of the use of which questions of liability will not arise) and, therefore, they should:

(a) facilitate the ongoing revision of AFIM by their national Antarctic programme operators by collective action through COMNAP;

(b) adopt a format in which information provided by each national operator is kept in a manner that facilitates updating of information; and

(c) request their national Antarctic operators to provide information for the purpose of maintaining the AFIM.

4. for the purpose of ensuring mutual awareness of current air operations and exchanging information about them, Parties should designate:

(a) Primary Air Information Stations (PAIS) which coordinate their own air information and information from their Secondary Air Information Stations (if any) for the purpose of notifying current air operations to other PAIS. These PAIS should have adequate communication facilities able to transmit "hard copy" information by appropriate and agreed means; and

(b) Secondary Air Information Stations (SAIS) which comprise stations/bases (including field bases and ships) which provide air information to their parent coordinating PAIS;

5. for the purpose of avoiding air incidents in areas beyond the range of VHF radio coverage of primary and secondary stations, aircraft outside the areas covered by primary and secondary stations should use a specific radio frequency to apply the "TIBA" procedure laid down in Annex 11 to the Convention on International Civil Aviation;

6. so as to ensure compliance with Article VII, paragraph 5 of the Antarctic Treaty and also Recommendation X-8, Part IV, Parties should keep one another informed about non-governmental flights and a reminder about the AFIM should be given to all pilots filing a flight plan for flights to Antarctica;

7. so as to provide for the improved collection from, and for the exchange within Antarctica of meteorological data and information of significance to the safety of Antarctic air operations, Parties should:

(a) encourage the World Meteorological Organisation in its work towards this end;

(b) take steps to improve meteorological services available in Antarctica, specifically to meet aviation requirements; and

(c) take account of The International Antarctic Weather Forecasting Handbook;

8. for the purpose of ensuring effective communications between PAIS, the Parties should ensure that their PAIS have adequate facilities for communicating with other PAIS; and

9. Parties consider Recommendation XV-20 (1989) as no longer current.

Antarctic Clean-Up Manual

The Representatives,

Reaffirming the commitment of Parties to the Protocol on Environmental Protection to the Antarctic Treaty (the Protocol) to reduce as far as practicable the amount of waste produced or disposed of in the Antarctic Treaty area, so as to minimise impact on the Antarctic environment and to minimise interference with the natural values of Antarctica, with scientific research and with other uses of Antarctica that are consistent with the Antarctic Treaty;

Recalling the requirement under Article 1(5) of Annex III to the Protocol that past and present waste disposal sites on land and abandoned work sites of Antarctic activities shall be cleaned up by the generator of such wastes and the user of such sites, provided that such actions shall not require the removal of any structure designated as a historic site or monument, or the removal of any structure or waste material in circumstances where the removal by any practical option would result in greater adverse environmental impact than leaving the structure or waste material in its existing location;

Recalling also the 2010 Antarctic Treaty Meeting of Experts on Implications of Climate Change for Antarctic Management and Governance, which noted that climate changes create the potential for localised release of contamination from past waste disposal sites and abandoned work sites through increased melting;

Noting the actions taken by Parties since the entry into force of the Protocol to effectively handle waste and to clean up past waste disposal sites on land and abandoned work sites;

Noting also the efforts of the Council of Managers of National Antarctic Programs to develop and formulate best practice procedures for waste management, including through the workshop on Waste Management in Antarctica held in Hobart in 2006;

Welcoming the development by the Committee for Environmental Protection of a Clean-Up Manual that Parties can apply and use, as appropriate, to assist with meeting their obligations under Article 1(5) of Annex III to the Protocol;

Recommend that Parties:

1. disseminate and encourage the use of the Clean-Up Manual annexed to this Resolution, as appropriate, to assist with addressing their obligations under Article 1(5) of Annex III to the Protocol on Environmental Protection to the Antarctic Treaty; and

2. encourage the Committee for Environmental Protection to continue to develop the Clean-Up Manual with the input of the Scientific Committee on Antarctic Research and the Council of Managers of National Antarctic Programs on scientific and practical matters, respectively.

Committee for Environmental Protection
Clean-Up Manual

1. Introduction

a)   Background

In 1975 the Antarctic Treaty Parties adopted Recommendation VIII-11, which contained the first agreed guidance for the appropriate management and disposal of waste generated by expeditions and stations, with a view to minimising impacts on the Antarctic environment. As awareness of the potential environmental impacts of the disposal of waste in the Antarctic region increased, in parallel with improvements in logistics and technology, the Parties identified a need for improved on-site treatment of wastes and for the removal of some wastes from the Antarctic Treaty area.

Through Recommendation XV-3 (1989) the Parties adopted more stringent waste disposal and management practices, based on recommendations from a SCAR Panel of Experts on Waste Disposal in the Antarctic, with the aim of minimising impact on the Antarctic environment and minimising interference with scientific research or other legitimate uses of the Antarctic. These practices not only addressed requirements for the management of wastes associated with present and future activities, but also called for programs to clean up existing waste disposal sites and abandoned work sites, and for an inventory of locations of past activities.

Many elements of Recommendation XV-3 are closely reflected in the current provisions for waste disposal and management, contained in Annex III to the Environmental Protocol, on Waste Disposal and Waste Management. The Environmental Protocol as a whole sets the context in which the provisions of Annex III should be implemented.

Among other requirements Annex III provides, in Article 1.5, that:

"Past and present waste disposal sites on land and abandoned work sites of Antarctic activities shall be cleaned up by the generator of such wastes and the user of such sites. This obligation shall not be interpreted as requiring:

a)   the removal of any structure designated as a historic site or monument; or

b)   the removal of any structure or waste material in circumstances where the removal by any practical option would result in greater adverse environmental impact than leaving the structure or waste material in its existing location."

Prior to these instruments, waste management at Antarctic facilities often involved the open burning and disposal of waste in tips. Similarly, it was commonplace to abandon disused facilities and leave them to deteriorate. Many past waste disposal sites and abandoned work sites require ongoing management today. Such sites are frequently characterised by a mix of physical debris (e.g. building materials, machinery, vehicles, general rubbish) plus chemical contaminants, some of which may be in containers (which are subject to deterioration) and some of which may have been released into the environment. In some instances waste disposal sites extend into the near shore marine environment. Seepage and runoff from abandoned sites, and from more recent spill sites, can result in contamination spreading to other parts of the environment. In general such contaminants degrade very slowly in Antarctic conditions.

Based on extrapolation from a few well documented sites, it has been estimated that the volume of abandoned, unconfined tip materials in Antarctica may be greater than 1 million m3 and that the volume of petroleum-contaminated sediment may be similar (Snape and others, 2001). Although this is a relatively small volume compared to the situation in other parts of the world, the significance of the associated environmental impacts is magnified due to the fact that many Antarctic contaminated sites are located in the relatively rare coastal ice-free areas that provide habitat for most of the terrestrial flora and fauna.

b)   Overall Clean-Up objective

The overall objective for Parties' actions to address environmental risks posed by past waste disposal sites on land, abandoned works sites of Antarctic activities, and sites contaminated by spills of fuel or other hazardous substances is:

To minimise adverse impact on the Antarctic environment, and to minimise interference with the natural values of Antarctica, with scientific research and with other uses of Antarctica which are consistent with the Antarctic Treaty, by cleaning up past waste disposal sites on land, abandoned work sites of Antarctic activities, and sites contaminated by spills of fuel or other hazardous substances. Such clean-up actions shall not require the removal of any: structure designated as a historic site or monument: pre-1958 historic artefacts / sites subject to the provisions of Resolution 5 (2001); or structure or waste material in circumstances where the removal by any practical option would result in greater adverse environmental impact than leaving the structure or waste material in its existing location.

This objective reflects requirements outlined in Annex III (Waste Disposal and Waste Management) to the Protocol on Environmental Protection to the Antarctic Treaty (the Environmental Protocol).

c)   Purpose of the Clean-Up Manual

The purpose of this manual is to provide guidance to Antarctic Treaty Parties in order to meet the objective above. The manual includes key guiding principles and links to practical guidelines and resources that operators can apply and use, as appropriate, to assist with addressing the requirements of the Environmental Protocol, in particular Annex III. The practical guidelines are recommendatory and not all guidelines will be appropriate to all operations, or to all sites. The manual is intended to be updated and added to as new work, research and best practice emerges.

The guidance provided here is focussed on the repair and remediation of past waste disposal sites on land, abandoned work sites of Antarctic activities, and sites contaminated by spills of fuel or other hazardous substances. Practical guidance for preventing, monitoring and responding to the introduction of non-native species is presented in the Committee for Environmental Protection (CEP) Non-Native Species Manual.

The Council of Managers of National Antarctic Programs (COMNAP) has developed a Fuel Manual, which outlines important measures for spill prevention and containment. This Clean-Up Manual complements the COMNAP Fuel Manual by providing guidance on appropriate clean-up and restoration actions, which the COMNAP Fuel Manual indicates should be addressed as part of the Operational Plans to be prepared for individual facilities or relevant geographic areas.

In practice, it will not be practicable to clean up all past waste disposal sites on land, abandoned work sites of Antarctic activities and contaminated sites immediately or concurrently, so the manual also aims to provide guidance on identifying priorities for clean-up activities, and on remediating or removing contaminated materials to a level where ongoing environmental risks are mitigated.

Reasons to undertake timely clean-up action, in accordance with the provisions of the Environmental Protocol, include:

- many abandoned waste disposal sites and abandoned work sites contain potential contaminants in containers (e.g. drums filled with fuel, oil, chemicals), and there is a limited time before they deteriorate, causing contamination and making clean-up much more difficult;
- as noted by the 2010 Antarctic Treaty Meeting of Experts on Climate Change and Implications for Antarctic Management and Governance, climate changes could accelerate localised release of contamination from past waste disposal sites and abandoned work sites through increased melting;
- the harmful effects of chemical contaminants on the environment and ecosystem can increase with increasing exposure time, and increase the chance of cumulative impacts from exposure to other environmental stressors;
- dispersion processes (e.g. entrainment with melt water) can cause the total area contaminated to increase with time, in some cases resulting in contamination of the marine environment;
- some sites may otherwise be lost to the ocean or covered by ice/snow where they may continue to have detrimental impacts but will be much more difficult and costly to manage; and
- possible risks to human health (e.g. hazardous chemicals or other substances, such as asbestos).

d)   Glossary

The practice of environmental clean-up uses some technical terminology. Additionally, some words that are commonly used in everyday language have a specific meaning when used in the context of environmental clean-up. To help ensure a common understanding, this glossary will be expanded as part of the development of the manual. Definitions generally applicable to assessing, mitigating and monitoring the environmental impacts of activities are presented in the *Guidelines for Environmental Impact Assessment in Antarctica.*

CLEAN-UP: the removal and/or on-site remediation of past waste disposal sites on land, abandoned work sites and sites contaminated by spills of fuel or other hazardous substances.

2. Key Guiding Principles

Information management

Record keeping is important throughout the clean-up process and should commence well before any clean-up activities occur on site.

1) Record keeping should be designed so that information on individual sites is easily accessible and so that information on actions and events at each site can be added over time.

2) The record of information should be kept up to date and should include the precise location and status of contaminated sites, the clean-up actions that have occurred, the reasons why key decisions were made and the lessons learned.

3) The type of information to be recorded should reflect its intended use, including:

- site assessment and prioritisation;

- supporting operational decisions;

- ensuring compliance to environmental impact assessment / permit conditions;

- monitoring and evaluating the effectiveness of a clean-up process; and

- facilitating the exchange of information between Parties and with other stakeholders.

4) Record keeping should be designed so that it can also be used as the foundation for the Antarctic-wide inventory of locations of past activity, in accordance with Article 8.3 of Annex III.

Site assessment / characterisation

An assessment of the features of the site that will influence how contaminants behave, and the environmental values that may be impacted, should be undertaken before considering how best to clean-up a site.

5) The site assessment should consider:

- the nature and extent of physical debris and/or chemical contamination, and the landscape (e.g. geology, geomorphology, glaciology) of the site and surrounding area, with particular emphasis on slope, aspect and water flows;

- potential challenges for clean-up actions presented by the location, landscape, and surrounding area (e.g. accessibility and susceptibility to damage from machinery or recovery equipment);

- the environmental values of the site and surrounding area, including the range of values protected under the Environmental Protocol; and

- likely changes at the site including deterioration of containers (such as rusting fuel drums), changes in chemical compositions (e.g. through natural weathering processes) and transport of the contaminants (e.g. from wind or water flow).

6) All available information should be used to assess the current impact and potential future threat to the environment from the contamination.

Environmental risk assessment

Environmental risk assessment is the process of determining the inherent risks posed by the site to the environmental values.

7) The environmental risk assessment should use the information gained during site assessment, including uncertainties, and should inform the decisions taken throughout the clean-up process.

8) The environmental risk assessment should assist to prioritise which site(s) should be cleaned up first, to decide among the various clean-up options (see below) and to set realistic targets for clean-up (see below).

9) The environmental risk assessment should be regularly reviewed and confirmed or modified during the clean-up process.

Environmental quality targets for clean-up

In some cases, the complete removal of all traces of contamination would be impractical, or would result in greater adverse environmental impact. Environmental quality targets for clean-up are the concentration of contaminant that may remain within the environment without creating unacceptable impacts on the environmental values of the site.

10) Environmental quality targets for clean-up should be determined on a site specific basis taking into account the characteristics of the site and the environmental values present.

11) From the viewpoint of biodiversity conservation, environmental quality targets should be based on the sensitivity of relevant species to the specific contaminants (such as from ecotoxicology studies).

12) Environmental quality targets are just one factor when considering the options for clean-up (see below).

Consideration of clean-up options

At the highest level the range of possible clean-up options for sites contaminated by fuel and other hazardous substances may include: do nothing (which may result in natural attenuation); containment on site to reduce dispersion; *in situ* remediation to enhance attenuation processes; removal from the site with treatment in Antarctica (clean-up *ex situ*); and removal from the Antarctic Treaty area. Within each of these options there are further choices of possible clean-up actions (see below).

13) A risk assessment should be undertaken for all clean-up options being considered, with a focus on ensuring that greater adverse environmental impact does not occur as a result of the clean-up process.

14) Options analysis should consider the environmental quality targets and risk of additional adverse impacts arising from the clean-up activity. Given the practical realities of operating in Antarctica, other relevant considerations are likely to include feasibility, available technology, practicality, safety of personnel, and cost-effectiveness.

Clean-up actions

Clean-up actions are the operational activities that happen at the site and / or elsewhere on material that has been removed from the site.

15) Wherever appropriate, plans and environmental impact assessments for new activities in Antarctica should consider the nature and scale of any clean-up activity which will be subsequently required. Actions to clean-up sites of past activities should also be subject to environmental impact assessment in accordance with the provisions of the Protocol.

16) Clean-up techniques developed for contaminated sites in other regions of the world may have some value in Antarctica but are likely to require modification to make them suitable for local conditions.

17) All clean-up options, including the 'do nothing' option, may require some commitment of resources, such as monitoring (see below) to confirm the environmental risk assessment.

18) In some cases containment on site to reduce dispersion will be identified as the best means of protecting environmental values. Techniques for containment should be designed for:

   - the types of contaminants present (the principal distinction being organic (e.g. fuel) or inorganic (e.g. metals from waste dumps); and

   - the characteristics of the environment (principally the freeze/thaw process and the highly seasonal presence of free water).

19) In situ remediation to enhance attenuation processes (e.g. enhanced biodegradation by the adding of nutrients, increasing temperature and aerating soil) can be cost-

292

effective and is likely to be less disturbing to the environment than options requiring extraction, but techniques must be appropriate for the types of contaminants and the characteristics of the environment (as above).

20) Removal from the site with treatment in Antarctica may create more disturbance at the site than in situ remediation but has the potential advantage of relocation to a site that is more easily managed such as close to a station. The receiving site should be controlled to ensure the safety of personnel and to prevent further environmental impact (e.g. clearly identifiable and known to station personnel, contained to prevent dispersal of contaminants).

21) In some cases the removal of contaminated materials from the Antarctic Treaty area may be the most appropriate option for addressing the requirements of the Environmental Protocol. As above, this may create more disturbance than in situ remediation and, in the case of ice-free sites, also has the disadvantage of removing rare soil from Antarctica. This option is also likely to be the most costly, is dependent on the availability and capacity of shipping, and may raise biosecurity or contaminated material concerns for the receiving country.

22) Monitoring and evaluation (see below) should be designed as an integral part of the clean-up process.

23) Clean-up should be considered complete only once the environmental quality targets have been met.

Monitoring and evaluation

Monitoring and evaluation are both used to characterise and record the quality of the environment but have specific and distinct roles before, during and/or after clean-up.

24) Monitoring should be undertaken to identify and provide early warning of any adverse effects of the clean-up activity that may require modifications of procedures, and to assess and verify predictions identified in the environmental impact assessment.

25) Evaluation refers to determining whether the clean-up activity has achieved the desired environmental quality targets.

26) Both monitoring and evaluation should focus on the vulnerable environmental values of the site and take into account the final use of the data.

3. Guidelines and resources to support clean-up

As the manual is developed, this section will be expanded to contain voluntary guidelines and resources to assist Parties to address their clean-up obligations under Annex III to the Protocol. Examples of desirable materials include:

- a standard approach and/or form for record keeping and reporting on clean-up activities;

- checklists and/or matrices for site assessment and environmental risk assessment;
- scientific information to inform the setting of appropriate environmental quality targets;
- techniques for preventing mobilisation of contaminants such as melt water diversion and containment barriers;
- techniques for in-situ and ex-situ remediation of sites contaminated by fuel spills or other hazardous substances;
- techniques for the clean-up of buildings or other structures at abandoned work sites;
- guidance for planning and undertaking monitoring and evaluation.

References

This list of references will be expanded to list further papers as the manual is developed.

ATCM XXXV/IP6 (Australia). 2012. Topic Summary: CEP Discussions on Clean-Up (contains links to electronic versions of papers on the subject of clean-up submitted to the Committee for Environmental Protection between 1998 and 2011)

Aronson, R.B., Thatje, S., McClintock, J.B., & Hughes, K.A. 2011. Anthropogenic impacts on marine ecosystems in Antarctica. *Annals of the New York Academy of Sciences*, 1223, 82-107.

Filler, D., Snape, I., & Barnes, D., Eds. 2008. *Bioremediation of Petroleum Hydrocarbons in Cold Regions*. Cambridge. 288 pp.

Poland, J.S., Riddle, M.J., & Zeeb, B.A. 2003. Contaminants in the Arctic and the Antarctic: a comparison of sources, impacts, and remediation options. *Polar Record*, 39(211), 369-383.

Riddle, M. 2000. Scientific studies of Antarctic life are still the essential basis for long-term conservation measures. In Davison, W., Howard-Williams, C., & Broady, P. Eds. *Antarctic Ecosystems: Models for Wider Ecological Understanding*. New Zealand Natural Sciences, Canterbury University, 497-302.

Snape, I., Riddle, M.J., Stark, S., Cole, C.M., King, C.K., Dubesque, S., & Gore, D.B. 2001. Management and Remediation of contaminated sites at Casey Station, Antarctica. *Polar Record*, 37(202), 199-214.

Stark, J.S., Snape, I., & Riddle, M.J. 2006. Abandoned Antarctic waste disposal sites: Monitoring remediation outcomes and limitations at Casey Station. *Ecological Management and Restoration*, 7(1), 21-31.

Tin, T., Fleming, Z.L., Hughes, K.A., Ainley, D.G., Convey, P., Moreno, C.A., Pfeiffer, S., Scott, J., & Snape, I. 2009. Impacts of local human activities on the Antarctic environment. *Antarctic Science*, 21, 3-33.

Site Guidelines for visitors

The Representatives,

Recalling Resolution 5 (2005), Resolution 2 (2006), Resolution 1 (2007), Resolution 2 (2008), Resolution 4 (2009), Resolution 1 (2010) and Resolution 4 (2011), which adopted lists of sites subject to Site Guidelines;

Recalling Resolution 4 (2012), which provided that any proposed amendment to existing Site Guidelines be discussed by the Committee for Environmental Protection, which should advise the Antarctic Treaty Consultative Meeting ("ATCM") accordingly, and that if such advice is endorsed by the ATCM, the Secretariat of the Antarctic Treaty (the Secretariat) should make the necessary changes to the texts of Site Guidelines on its website;

Believing that Site Guidelines enhance the provisions set out in Recommendation XVIII-1 (1994) (Guidance for those organising and conducting tourism and non-Governmental activities in the Antarctic);

Confirming that the term "visitors" does not include scientists conducting research within such sites, or individuals engaged in official governmental activities;

Noting that the Site Guidelines have been developed based on the current levels and types of visits at each specific site, and aware that the Site Guidelines would require review if there were any significant changes to the levels or types of visits to a site;

Believing that the Site Guidelines for each site must be reviewed and revised promptly in response to changes in the levels and types of visits, or in any demonstrable or likely environmental impacts;

Desiring to increase the number of Site Guidelines developed for visited sites and to keep existing Guidelines up to date;

Recommend that:

1. the list of sites subject to Site Guidelines that have been adopted by the Antarctic Treaty Consultative Meeting be extended to include a further two new sites (Orne Harbour and Orne Islands), and that the full list of sites subject to Site Guidelines be replaced by the one annexed to this Resolution;

2. the Site Guidelines for the Sites Yankee Harbour, Half Moon Island, Brown Bluff, Hannah Point, Cuverville Island, Danco Island, Neko Harbour, Pleneau Island, Petermann Island, Damoy Point, Jougla Point, Torgersen Island, Baily Head (Deception Island) and Barrientos Island-Aitcho Islands be replaced by the modified Guidelines;

3. the Secretariat of the Antarctic Treaty place the full list and the modified Guidelines, as adopted by the ATCM, on its website;

4. their Governments urge all those intending to visit such sites to ensure that they are fully conversant with, and adhere to, the advice in the relevant Site Guidelines as published by the Secretariat;

5. any proposed amendment to existing Site Guidelines be discussed by the Committee for Environmental Protection, which should advise the ATCM accordingly, and that if such advice is endorsed by the ATCM, the Secretariat should make the necessary changes to the texts of Site Guidelines on the website; and

6. the Secretariat post the text of Resolution 4 (2012) on its website in such a way that makes clear that it is no longer current.

List of Sites subject to Site Guidelines

Site Guidelines	First Adopted	Latest Version
1. Penguin Island (Lat. 62° 06' S, Long. 57° 54' W)	2005	2005
2. Barrientos Island - Aitcho Islands (Lat. 62° 24' S, Long. 59° 47' W)	2005	2013
3. Cuverville Island (Lat. 64° 41' S, Long. 62° 38' W)	2005	2013
4. Jougla Point (Lat 64° 49' S, Long 63° 30' W)	2005	2013
5. Goudier Island, Port Lockroy (Lat 64° 49' S, Long 63° 29' W)	2006	2006
6. Hannah Point (Lat. 62° 39' S, Long. 60° 37' W)	2006	2013
7. Neko Harbour (Lat. 64° 50' S, Long. 62° 33' W)	2006	2013
8. Paulet Island (Lat. 63° 35' S, Long. 55° 47' W)	2006	2006
9. Petermann Island (Lat. 65° 10' S, Long. 64° 10' W)	2006	2013
10. Pleneau Island (Lat. 65° 06' S, Long. 64° 04' W)	2006	2013
11. Turret Point (Lat. 62° 05' S, Long. 57° 55' W)	2006	2006
12. Yankee Harbour (Lat. 62° 32' S, Long. 59° 47' W)	2006	2013
13. Brown Bluff, Tabarin Peninsula (Lat. 63° 32' S, Long. 56° 55' W)	2007	2013
14. Snow Hill (Lat. 64° 22' S, Long. 56° 59' W)	2007	2007
15. Shingle Cove, Coronation Island (Lat. 60° 39' S, Long. 45° 34' W)	2008	2008

Site Guidelines	First Adopted	Latest Version
16. Devil Island, Vega Island		
(Lat. 63° 48' S, Long. 57° 16.7' W)	2008	2008
17. Whalers Bay, Deception Island, South Shetland Islands		
(Lat. 62° 59' S, Long. 60° 34' W)	2008	2011
18. Half Moon Island, South Shetland Islands		
(Lat. 60° 36' S, Long. 59° 55' W)	2008	2013
19. Baily Head, Deception Island, South Shetland Islands		
(Lat. 62° 58' S, Long. 60° 30' W)	2009	2013
20. Telefon Bay, Deception Island, South Shetland Islands		
(Lat. 62° 55' S, Long. 60° 40' W)	2009	2009
21. Cape Royds, Ross Island		
(Lat. 77° 33' 10.7" S, Long. 166° 10' 6.5" E)	2009	2009
22. Wordie House, Winter Island, Argentine Islands		
(Lat. 65° 15' S, Long. 64° 16' W)	2009	2009
23. Stonington Island, Marguerite Bay, Antarctic Peninsula		
(Lat. 68° 11' S, Long. 67° 00' W)	2009	2009
24. Horseshoe Island, Antarctic Peninsula		
(Lat. 67° 49' S, Long. 67° 18' W)	2009	2009
25. Detaille Island, Antarctic Peninsula		
(Lat. 66° 52' S, Long. 66° 48' W)	2009	2009
26. Torgersen Island, Arthur Harbour, Southwest Anvers Island		
(Lat. 64° 46' S, Long. 64° 04' W)	2010	2013
27. Danco Island, Errera Channel, Antarctic Peninsula		
(Lat. 64° 43' S, Long. 62° 36' W)	2010	2013
28. Seabee Hook, Cape Hallett, Northern Victoria Land, Ross Sea, Visitor Site A and Visitor Site B		
(Lat. 72° 19' S, Long. 170° 13' E)	2010	2010

Site Guidelines	First Adopted	Latest Version
29. Damoy Point, Wiencke Island, Antarctic Peninsula		
(Lat. 64° 49' S, Long. 63° 31' W)	2010	2013
30. Taylor Valley Visitor Zone, Southern Victoria Land		
(Lat. 77° 37.59' S, Long. 163° 03.42' E)	2011	2011
31. North-east beach of Ardley Island		
(Lat. 62° 13' S; Long. 58° 54' W)	2011	2011
32. Mawson's Huts and Cape Denison, East Antarctica		
(Lat. 67° 01' S; Long. 142 ° 40' E)	2011	2011
33. D'Hainaut Island, Mikkelsen Harbour, Trinity Island		
(Lat. 63° 54' S, Long. 60° 47' W)	2012	2012
34. Port Charcot, Booth Island		
(Lat. 65° 04'S, Long. 64 °02'W)	2012	2012
35. Pendulum Cove, Deception Island, South Shetland Islands		
(Lat. 62°56'S, Long. 60°36' W)	2012	2012
36. Orne Harbour, Southern arm of Orne Harbour, Gerlache Strait		
(Lat 64° 38'S, Long. 62° 33'W)	2013	2013
37. Orne Islands, Gerlache Strait		
(Lat. 64° 40'S, Long. 62° 40'W)	2013	2013

Improved Collaboration on Search and Rescue (SAR) in Antarctica

The Representatives,

Recalling Resolutions 6 (2008), 6 (2010), 7 (2012) and 8 (2012) regarding search and rescue in Antarctica;

Concerned about the tragic loss of life in several vessel incidents in Antarctica in recent years;

Noting the commitment of all Antarctic Treaty Parties to promoting safety with regard to activities taking place within the Antarctic Treaty area;

Mindful that anticipated increases in human activity in the Antarctic including national program operations, shipping, fishing and tourism, will add to the challenges and risks associated with Antarctic search and rescue (SAR) operations;

Expressing appreciation to the Antarctic Treaty Consultative Parties that operate Rescue Coordination Centres ("RCCs") with Antarctic responsibilities for the benefit of all persons in distress in their respective SAR regions;

Recognising the high level of coordination that already exists with respect to SAR in Antarctica among the RCCs with Antarctic responsibilities, including through the Council of Managers of National Antarctic Programs (COMNAP), and between the RCCs and the national Antarctic programs operating within their areas of responsibility;

Recalling the commitment of relevant Parties to the 1979 International Convention on Maritime Search and Rescue and the Convention on International Civil Aviation, Annex 12 – Search and Rescue, to cooperate in the execution of SAR missions and activities;

Noting the importance of discussions among experts held at the ATCM XXXVI Special Working Group on Search and Rescue; and

Desiring to increase the success and efficiency of SAR operations in the Antarctic.

Recommend that the Parties:

1. continue to collaborate actively on search and rescue in the Antarctic Treaty area;

2. commit to share best practices related to SAR in Antarctica, taking advantage of expertise developed by each of the five RCCs with Antarctic responsibilities;

3. cooperate as appropriate at the International Maritime Organization (IMO), the International Civil Aviation Organization (ICAO) and other relevant fora to promote the implementation of SAR protocols and practices that would be beneficial in the Antarctic context;

4. request that the Executive Secretary provide a copy of this Resolution and the section on the Special Working Group on Search and Rescue from the Final Report of ATCM XXXVI to the Secretaries General of the IMO and ICAO for information;

5. invite the Commission for the Conservation of Antarctic Marine Living Resources (CCAMLR) to consider appropriate means within its jurisdiction to support SAR efforts and to improve fishing vessel safety within the CCAMLR Convention Area;

6. urge their National Antarctic Programs to provide annually updated information on assets that could be used for SAR purposes to COMNAP;

7. support COMNAP to continue to foster collaborative discussions and vital sharing of information regarding SAR matters including through:

   a. holding triennial workshops on search and rescue, that include representatives of the RCCs, National Antarctic Programs, relevant experts, private operators as well as commercial emergency notification service providers, and inform future ATCMs on the results of these workshops;

   b. establishing a web portal that promotes information exchange between RCCs on shared SAR goals and best practices; and

   c. ensuring that other information on National Antarctic Programs, including assets, that could be used for SAR purposes be available to RCCs through the COMNAP website, and linked to the Electronic Information Exchange System (EIES).

8. encourage RCCs with Antarctic responsibilities to conduct SAR exercises with each other, National Antarctic Programs, IAATO, and other relevant entities to continually improve SAR cooperation and response.

International cooperation in cultural projects about Antarctica

The Representatives,

Convinced that international cooperation is one of the fundamental principles of the Antarctic Treaty system;

Recognising the merit of promoting knowledge about Antarctica through art projects;

Recalling Resolution 2 (1996), promoting scientific, aesthetic and wildlife values in Antarctica, through inspiration of young people and contributions by writers, artists and musicians;

Recommend that:

Parties be encouraged to promote the dissemination of knowledge about Antarctica through the development of art projects about Antarctica on the basis of international cooperation, to reflect, in particular, scientific activity and the importance of the preservation of the Antarctic environment.

Biological Prospecting in Antarctica

The Representatives,

Recalling Resolution 7 (2005) on Biological Prospecting in Antarctica and Resolution 9 (2009) on Collection and Use of Antarctic Biological Material;

Convinced of the benefits for the progress of humankind of scientific research in the Antarctic Treaty area;

Reaffirming in this regard Article III(1)(c) of the Antarctic Treaty, which provides that, to the greatest extent feasible and practicable, scientific observations and results from Antarctica shall be exchanged and made freely available;

Noting that biological prospecting continues to occur in the Antarctic Treaty area;

Noting the lack of a working definition of biological prospecting in the Antarctic context;

Noting also ongoing discussions in other international fora on biological prospecting and genetic resources;

Noting also the need for further research and analysis to be undertaken related to the status and trends of biological prospecting in the Antarctic Treaty area and the wish that results be presented at future Antarctic Treaty Consultative Meetings:

Reaffirm that the Antarctic Treaty System is the appropriate framework for managing the collection of biological material in the Antarctic Treaty area and for considering its use;

Recommend that their governments report, as appropriate, on biological prospecting carried out under their respective legal regimes, with a view to facilitating a better understanding and assessment of these types of activities; and

Encourage their governments to examine ways to improve information exchange in this regard and to consider whether to adapt the Electronic Information Exchange System for this purpose.

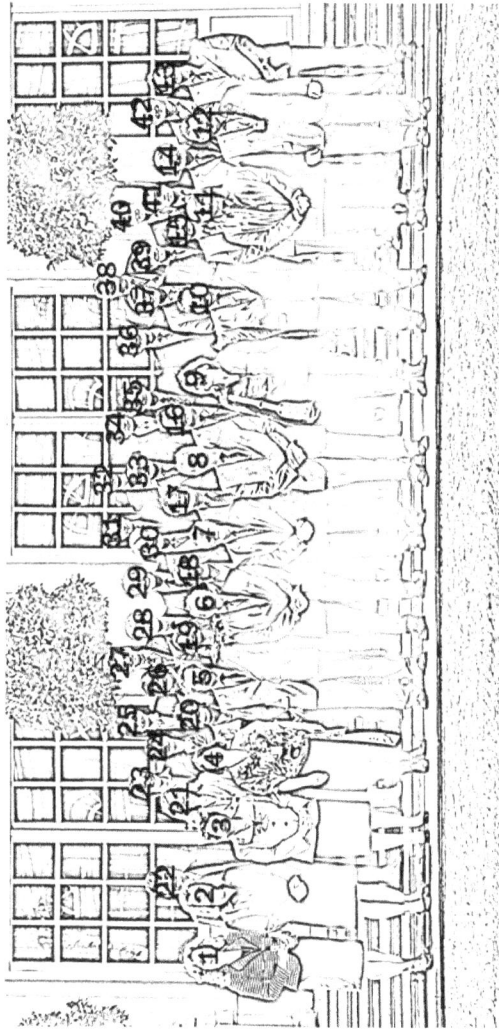

1. Hana Kovacova, Slovak Republic
2. Liisa Valjento, Finland
3. María Elvira Velasquez, Peru
4. Jillian Dempster, New Zealand
5. Camilo Sanhueza, Chile
6. Michel Rocard, France
7. Richard Rowe, Australia
8. Marc Otte, Belgium
9. Helena Ödmark, Sweden
10. Fausto López Crozet, Argentina
11. Andrzej Misztal, Poland
12. José Olmedo Morán, Ecuador
13. Siro Beltrametti, Switzerland
14. Vladimír Galuška, Czech Republic

15. Kamuran Sadar, Canada
16. Evan T. Bloom, USA
17. Atsushi Suginaka, Japan
18. Abu Samah Azizan, Malaysia
19. Martha McConnell, IUCN
20. Maria Stefania Tomaselli, Italy
21. Else Berit Eikeland, Norway
22. Dmitry Gonchar, Russian Federation
23. Jane Rumble, United Kingdom
24. BLANK
25. Kim Crosbie, IAATO
26. Michelle Rogan-Finnemore, COMNAP
27. Mike Sparrow, SCAR
28. Ihar Rahozin, Belarus

29. James Barnes, ASOC
30. Juan Luis Muñoz de Laborde Bardin, Spain
31. Sönke Lorenz, Germany
32. René J.M.Lefeber, Netherlands
33. Sivaramakrishnan Rajan, India
34. Branimir Zaimov, Bulgaria
35. Roland Moreau, Belgium
36. Patrick Van Klaveren, Monaco
37. Manfred Reinke, ATS
38. Luc Marsia, Belgium
39. Fábio Vaz Pitaluga, Brazil
40. Álvaro González Otero, Uruguay
41. Wensheng Qu, China
42. Mehmet Ali Türkel, Turkey